...they told me, that I shouldn't tell anyone... I should say that I was brought in to make coffee... Yes. When I was asked where I had gone, I was to say that I had gone to make coffee for their army.

PHOTOGRAPHS BY
CORNELIA SUHAN

SILENT WITNESS

Bosnia and Herzegovina and the war—
women who survived look back.

GOST

LIVE ON
THINK ON

VERENA
BRUCHHAGEN

Imagine you are on vacation visiting a spa, you are looking forward to the holiday you have for, for a long time, you are in need of relaxation, you settle down in your 'all inclusive' vacation suite hoping for the amenities and services advertised for tourists. You get comfortable, and feel at peace...until you discover what had happened about three decades earlier at this place: mass rapes and sexual violence as part of the warfare tactics during the Yugoslavian War happened right here.

You suddenly become part of the history of this place. Presumably, however, only very few people are really interested in history. This materialised history of the 'Stone Witnesses' only speaks when we pay attention to it. For such an interest, we need our determined, conscious attention to be able to turn to it.

How do we react to this information? Are we outraged? Do we leave it at that? 'Oh really? Interesting!' 'No hard feelings!' 'It's all gonna be fine...' Or do we want to know more about it, some more concrete details and context? Does the feeling you suddenly find yourself having, encourage you not to turn away immediately, but to give room to knowledge and understanding? What does this lead to in the respective subjective reading? What do we react to primarily, perhaps superficially? And—what can follow the moral outrage? When having a look at the book and reading it, is it possible to follow this awareness of a terrible chapter of violence against women up with a factual and sober interest in the subject and to develop empathy with those affected and their perspectives?

Cornelia Suhan presents a photo-documentary work on the 'effects and consequences of sexual violence against women' in the former Yugoslavia from 1992 to the present day. The book is a representative inventory that focuses on buildings, buildings in which war crimes—specifically rapes of women of all ethnic groups living in Bosnia and Herzegovina—were committed. The photos let private houses and various public buildings speak as 'silent witnesses' of these events. They show that this 'war strategy' was organised by no means accidentally, they point to the perfidious use of a civilian infrastructure and the self-evident usage of public resources, i.e. resources assigned to the common good (!) for the perpetration of this form of sexualised violence.

The buildings stand for the silencing of the unspeakable cruelty that they could bear witness to if only they spoke. In line with the assigned factual information and the selected interview excerpts from the women concerned, they enable a combination of factual presentation, information, evidence, communication of perspectives and approaches to subjective realities and meaning for the public awareness. This documentation allows us—indirectly—to perceive what happened then...and still has an effect today. It opens a field of truth, reality, subjectivity and objectivity with a view to responsibility and those responsible, to understanding and processing. But above all, it narrows in on the idea of how the preserving of trauma cannot be made the task of women alone, but how society, the public, can be asked to expose themselves to the procedure and process of remembering. In 1993 Alexandra Stiglmayer wrote: 'By deliberately not uncovering the crimes, there is no need to act. The second method of avoiding compulsion to act is to conceal the context. With consistent perseverance, the UN puts all warring parties on an equal footing and, in its reports on the human rights situation, tries to make all sides equally responsible for the war crimes...'

How astonished I was, when in mid-December, when UNHCR spokeswoman Sylvana Foa suddenly told me that the UN refugee agency was 'getting constant reports on rapes from Bosnian refugees,' that rape was 'widespread' and that it was 'really a shocking thing!' Behind this mysterious change was the public pressure that had arisen from the press reports. (1993: 53/ 54) In addition to highlighting the terrible events and experiences, the photographer points out to a critical culture of remembrance. We know that not coming to terms with it can have negative effects for generations after the events of war and violent crime. It is all the more important to develop cross generational possibilities and perspectives of individual, social and societal coping and to put them up for discussion.

The consequences of traumatisation and the forgetting that often results from this are related to the need for remembrance and public commemoration. Speaking in a therapeutic setting ensures a trusting and intimate sense of security in order to be able to approach the unspeakable and thus perhaps make survival more certain. But not speaking on a societal-public level becomes a blockade that is counterproductive for all people, for the whole community, even more—it supports a far-reaching taboo and trivialisation of what is happening in society. The buildings and places represented in the photographs are an occasion for a process of remembrance and commemoration. They speak to us in a different way than the women (can) do themselves. They—these places, these houses—as 'talking objects' impose on us images that are difficult to bear and that shake up our usual perception. They enable insights into (experience) spaces that we 'normally' isolate well in everyday life and manage with shame, silence or concealment. If the event is witnessed and brought up, we challenge its tabooing. Keeping quiet is no longer the seemingly alternative way to deal with what is happening.

All these women who were victimised but were not able to speak about their rape seem almost invisible in public. A lack of response from family, the public and society, leads to a silencing as witnesses. The 'stonewall witnesses' can continue to be seen as a true sign of the violence experienced. The are shown as factual and symbolic places. The diverse information collected on what happened in the buildings, on their use and utility, etc. point to the temporary context of bringing together houses—women—rapes on the background of warlike annihilation politics. Space is given here for the factual recognition and confirmation of these real places in their function and management in the events of war. This also gives the women with their real experiences of suffering, an affirmation.

Houses are also symbolic objects. We relate to them, we are and feel connected to them. They envelop us, give us protection and stability. They shape impressions and experiences, they can narrow and widen, create and manifest positive or negative images and feelings. They become inner spaces (cf. Hirsch 2010). More importantly, houses are visible matter, while rape escapes visibility beyond the act of violent assault. So what is there to talk about? For example, we talk about the function of the buildings as 'innocent scary' placeholders for the suppressed, as tabooed bodies in space, onto which the crime against the physical bodies is only projected as a taboo that cannot be named?

The photos in this volume open up a paradoxical simultaneity of making visible and concealing—on the one hand, the factual existence and visibility of the objects/houses that 'testify' to the violent crime committed against women, and on the other hand, the invisibility of the rapes. A double speaking/silencing of these objects challenges us when we look at them: they conceal and disguise and yet, when we look closer, they again demand space for imagining the crimes. Behind (often new) façades, old images with horrific scenarios emerge. Representation and reflection of the violence, the crimes, the rapes, the violent acts are in conflict here. Reflection works its way through the representative façade and is exhausting. The photos lead us to what should be forgotten but cannot be forgotten.

The 'normal' connection, the connection of body and space, on which we base our experiences from childhood, is violently disconnected here. The violent crime turns the (everyday) places into objects of the cruel experience of dehumanising actions. Women—as formulated by Susan Brownmiller (1994)—are expected to 'experience the use of their bodies as an extracurricular battlefield' and are torn from their intimate context, also and especially the collective access/attack on the body in the context of mass rape snatches the victims from everyday normality. War unabashedly reaches for the civil, private, intimate sphere: extended hostile takeover.

By using the random acts of rape as building blocks of an intended strategy of annihilation, the danger of being exposed in a completely uncontrolled manner intensifies, because expected shelters become places of de-regulation and dehumanisation. Moral and human norms and values become invalid. Rules that actually provide security in everyday life and enable trust and reliability become ineffective in this functional context. Previously valid agreements dealing with normality or underlying norms and values are suddenly cancelled, delimited, invalid. Those affected can no longer escape to shelters. There are no protective walls, no safe demarcations, because the boundaries between public and private, social and intimate, humane and morally corrupt spaces are violently crossed. Neighbourhoods suddenly no longer offer security, adjacent buildings become danger zones...Places of social and private infrastructure are mined, 'toxically charged' and are poisoned as living spaces far into the future.

Unlike Susan Brownmiller, Maria B Olujic (1998) assumes that these strategies of body politics do not only come into effect during a war but are already established in times of peace. The individual body, which is experienced as a place of everyday violence and aggression in the sense of patriarchal dominance already before the outbreak of warlike conflicts, transforms into a form of strategic body politics that is used in a highly symbolic and manipulative manner. These acts appear arbitrarily warlike, but are part of a strategic and systematic exercise of violence and destruction. This in turn requires targeted logistics, management, localisation, networking—without which the symbolic and intended effectiveness cannot be generated and organised.

Harald Welzer (2021) discusses another aspect in his book about perpetrators, regarding the mass murder trial in Yugoslavia: 'The brutality of the Resolution War has...to do with the unclear boundaries between the groups; the extreme violence, in turn, plays the role of clearly marking boundaries. In addition, the claimed 'defence identity' of warriors on all fronts of this bewildering war is based on a concept of civil defence designed against attack from the outside and turned inward at the moment of state collapse.' (p. 236) He goes on to describe how an existing administrative structure unfolds under these new social signs and how the potential it already contains becomes a productive force of extreme violence.

Here, Hannah Arendt's debatable thesis on the relation between power and violence, formulated as early as 1969 could be used: '...we know, or should know, that every decrease in power is an open invitation to violence, if only because those who hold power and feel it slipping from their hands, be they the government or be they the governed, have always found it difficult to resist the temptation to substitute violence for it.' (1970: 87)

In the discussion of different feminist analyses of warfare, the sexism approach versus the genocide approach, Pascale R Bos describes the weaknesses of these approaches: 'By focussing exclusively on rape and female injury, in many feminist analyses, women are not only victims who have been badly hit, but victims in general. This interpretation leaves no room for a more complex understanding of women's agency in war.' (Bos 2008:30) Especially during the war in Yugoslavia, according to Bos, there was a strong victimisation of women. As war victims see both positions relevant: '...the original concerns that feminists raised about this are...no longer discussed, for example: How exactly are the rapes defined as genocidal? Do we accept the underlying assumption that rape by a member of a different ethnic or racial group is more serious than intra-ethnic rape, or that rape between certain ethnic groups is worse than between others?... And does the definition of genocidal suffering depend on the intention of the rapist or on the interpretation of the victim?' (Bos 2008: 117)

In addition to these diverse and multi-layered approaches, looking at the houses and buildings as the place of action also makes it clear, how, in the context of the mass rapes, the division between public and private that was so laboriously created with patriarchal gender ideology, is thwarted and undermined. The neighbour next door rapes women in their private living quarters. Neither the patriarchal constructed protection of the (strong) man against the (weak and vulnerable) woman nor the shelter of the private sphere offer security and salvation. This shows the fragile, dysfunctional functionality of patriarchal (thought) systems.

What can this book do to not allow the issues to rest, but to pick them up again, to open up the space of perception again? Who wants to expose themselves to which images, which imaginations?

The places/spaces compiled here are numerous: whether school, sports hall, hospital, industrial building, police headquarters, fire brigade, administration building, garage, apartment building, hotel and spa, agricultural facility, mill, factory, canteen or bus station, army headquarters, prison, museum or mosque...The buildings are visible, but not what happened in them. Renovations can be observed outside—from the outside. But who lives, learns, works in these houses today, who knows anything about them...what has been published and communicated? Many women and their daughters, their sons, their families live again or continue to live in these places. How can the old experiences be endured? How can new, healing experiences arise here? And how does the (village, living) community deal with the knowledge of these places?

From the documented individual cases, a network of specific and yet generalisable places emerge, which bear witness to how rapes have taken place across the entire national territory. A map shows how inescapably women were exposed to the attacks. Not a house, a hill, a place, a monument is made accessible in this photodocumentary project of remembrance, but an entire infrastructure. This network, which initially appears random, is brought into context through the documentation and brought out of the fragmentation. The specific locations of the physical and sexual assaults become visible in their overall strategic networking. The houses can be read not only as places of subjectively experienced horror, but also as respective parts of the systematic policy of annihilation.

The effort of remembering is always turned into an individual achievement, which is now responsible for psychosocially processing the fragmented memory as part of individual traumatisation.

Against this backdrop, however, the privatisation and individualisation of memory is a mockery, because remembering is made into a laborious individual achievement split from public discourse and public consciousness.

Women are expected to come to terms with the crime more than those responsible are willing to do in order to give space to the collective and society-wide remembrance and commemoration of the crimes. Rather, it is to be feared that commemoration will continue to be functionalised politically and ideologically to this day. With this documentation, possibilities and forms of coping with crimes in dealing with remembrance and commemoration are to be discussed. How extremely difficult this is, when shown alongside the narratives of a specific masculinity that still prevail in public today. To this day, an orientation towards heroism can be observed, which is characterised by an aggressive, often nationalistic machismo. The war not only aroused heroic forces, but also allowed, even demanded, individuals to evade any applicable legal basis with their acts of violence in order to practice the scope and framework for a collectively (not legally, not humanely) legitimised exercise of violence (the regressive process of giving up individual responsibility in the context of groups would certainly be worth discussing here). To this day, (male) heroes are celebrated in the aftermath of war crimes. In this way, acts of violence committed individually continue to be embedded as heroic performances in collective cultures of remembrance. How should the women as victims of war rape fit in here with their work of remembrance?

Memories are to be psychosocially processed in the context of individual traumatisation. (In the process, more reappraisal is demanded of women than those responsible are willing to provide). But without giving space to the collective and public coming-to-terms-with, remembering and commemorating the crimes, it is to be feared that commemoration will be politically and ideologically functionalised.

So how can events like those in Bosnia, in ex-Yugoslavia, be remembered appropriately without—as Suhan notes—always just letting the affected women be heard, letting them 'use' their painful stories again and again... and so to reduce the memory to traumatising experiences as the sum of individual negative experiences. How can access to the processing of the reprehensible events be found that allow oneself to be included in the processing and coping instead of diving away?

As affected and non-affected, as viewers, we need to develop forward-looking perspectives of witnessing. It takes the integrative strength and the will to counteract the fading of memories, or rather the inability to remember, psychologically, socially and culturally.

The production of images has developed rapidly in our society, but the learned handling of images does not develop exponentially. What does photography enable us to do as a method, as a methodical approach to a documentary work? Which reflections open up here when we see the (old) buildings with their old or new façades in their current use? And asked photographically: what is in the foreground or in the background, for whom? Who sees what and how clearly?

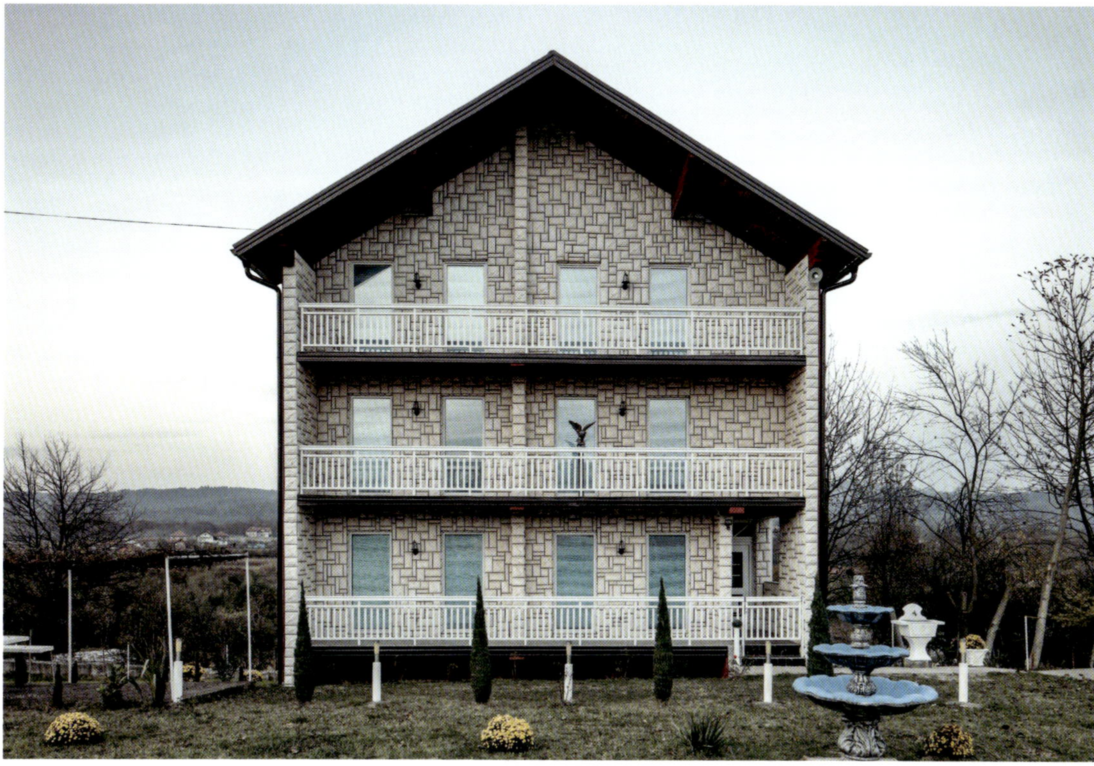

Osmaci
Caparde

The Caparde camp existed from June to July 1992. During the deportation of the Bosniak population from Podrinje and Posavina, crimes such as murder and rape were committed in this area. This area, under the control of the Bosnian Serb Army. In Caparde there were more than twenty-five victims who were violently kidnapped and raped and sexually abused in abandoned houses like this one. M, who was raped by a soldier in the Caparde detention centre, said: 'He pointed his gun at me and ordered me to undress. I cried and refused. Then he hit me hard and pushed me onto a couch in that room, stripped me and raped me.' M, who was only eighteen years old at the time, also saw other women being taken away during their stay and suspected at the time that they were also raped.[1]

44°23'49.9"N 18°58'12.2"E

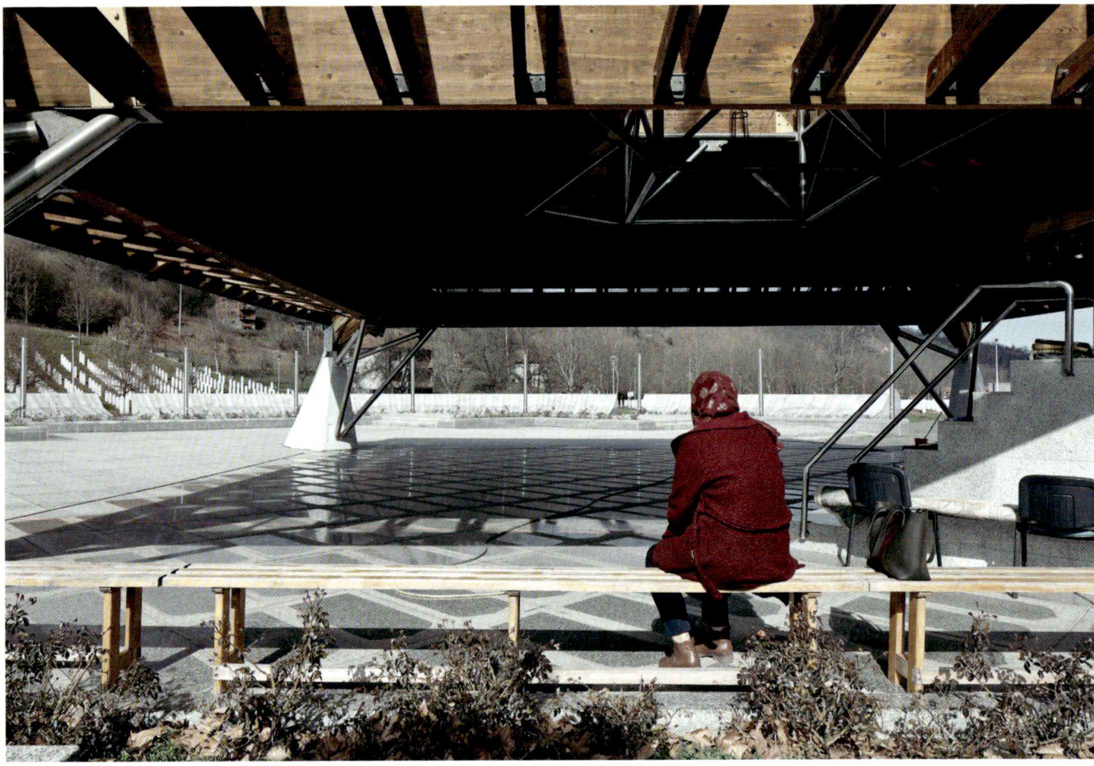

SARAH FROM SPIONICA

'Arkan's army came. Chetniks were already in the villages nearby and in 1993 they also came to my village, when we had to flee to Srebrenica. My son was two years old. They set all these villages on fire and destroyed everything, only Srebrenica was a free zone, all the people from the surrounding villages fled there. We were locked up there, we couldn't get out, only convoys got out.

I stayed there with my husband and gave birth to my daughter in May 1995, she was only forty days old when we had to flee Srebrenica.

We were living in the attic of a house when shells fell and Srebenica was taken. While planes were bombing the town, men and women separated, the men fled into the forest and the women with the children ran to Potočari.

I never saw my husband or other male family members again.

A cousin of my husband's helped me. On the way to Potočari we saw many dead people, people without arms and legs, people shooting from the mountains with guns. We arrived in Potočari in the afternoon, we sat in the grass in front of a factory. One of the military men set a horse on fire, lit its tail with a lighter, the horse was tied, it couldn't run away and burnt to death.

At 2 or 3am, when we were sleeping in the battery factory, soldiers came in and suddenly people started screaming. The women said they had come to kill us. I just held my children and stayed like that until morning.

In the morning I went with other women to the river to fetch water. I left my children with a woman at the factory and when I got to the hill, there was a cornfield and behind it I saw many hanged people in a field. There were also many dead in the river (a tributary of the Drina). That was a big shock, I dropped the canister and ran away, telling everyone not to go there because there was a big massacre.

When I got back to the factory, someone said that Ratko Mladic had come and brought bread. He asked where our men were and where our army was, and if we answered his questions, he would let us all go and no one would be harmed. Mladic threw bread into the crowd and we fought over it because we were so hungry. We had nothing. It was hot. There were many flies because of all the dead bodies, it was terrible. In other tents there were many girls, about fifteen years old, but after that night they disappeared without a trace, they said they died there. That was the night Mladic brought bread.

I didn't have a watch, we didn't know the time, we orientated ourselves by the sun. When the sun rose, we knew it was morning.

Then one of the Chetniks came into the factory and said, you, you and you come out, and we thought that they were taking people to Tuzla, and someone also said to me, 'you' and pointed with his finger, 'you woman with two children.'

Then I went out, there were two Dutch soldiers, and I will never forget their faces because they are lighter skinned and their eyebrows are different.

The night before, the Dutch had celebrated with Chetniks that Srebrenica had fallen, they sat together and drank. The Dutch also gave them uniforms, some Chetniks wore Dutch uniforms... Whether they had to do that, give the uniforms, I don't know.

The soldiers, the Serbian Army, the Chetniks were like animals, like on drugs or drunk. They didn't care if someone was hungry or in pain. They just wanted to kill as many people as possible. They only left older men alive, even boys, they killed them later. Men also disguised themselves as women to survive.

They called me to give me milk for the baby because my daughter hadn't had milk for three days, I hadn't eaten anything and there were other women with babies and I thought they will give me milk.

They took me to a tent behind the factory and told me to wait there until they brought me the milk. I waited a whole day in the tent, with the children, it was hot and stuffy. In the evening, someone came and unzipped the tent, and I got up because I thought I would get something now. But then a hand pushed me to the ground, I fell, I was weak, I hadn't eaten for three days, the children were crying, but I couldn't do anything.

In the morning, my son's crying woke me up, he shouted 'Mum, Mum, get up!' I wanted to get up but had no strength, my son pulled my trousers to make me get up, the baby was lying on a jacket.

Then I saw that my blouse was torn, the dark blue trousers were also torn and full of blood. There was so much blood under me as if an ox had been slaughtered.

I went out of the tent and fainted again, I don't remember anything, I then woke up in an ambulance. My mother-in-law and her husband took care of the children.

I spent one night in the ambulance in Kladanj, then they took me to Tuzla.

The children came with my mother-in-law in the ambulance, and I recognised the children's voices from their crying.

In Dubraj there was a tent settlement. The people who came from Potočari were housed there in the first months (after the fall of Srebrenica). We were then taken by bus to schools in Tuzla. There we got help, food and medical care, it was ok.

I was able to get help! I have a pension today—my daughter also gets a pension as a victim of war crimes because her father was murdered. She has a future!

My childhood wasn't so nice, I wasn't happy in marriage either, but the children should have it better, I didn't have the support when I was young.

Fortunately, I and my children survived everything. It wasn't natural, they killed little boys with knives. That was quite horrible. What would my life be like without the children?

If I should give a punishment for my rape, it should break this man's dignity and pride, so that he comes down to my level. It is not good to forget everything, but I have put it aside and with the children growing up I have started a new chapter in life.

They know what happened, they were also in the tent, my son was five years old.

Now I am happy to get up in the morning every day.'

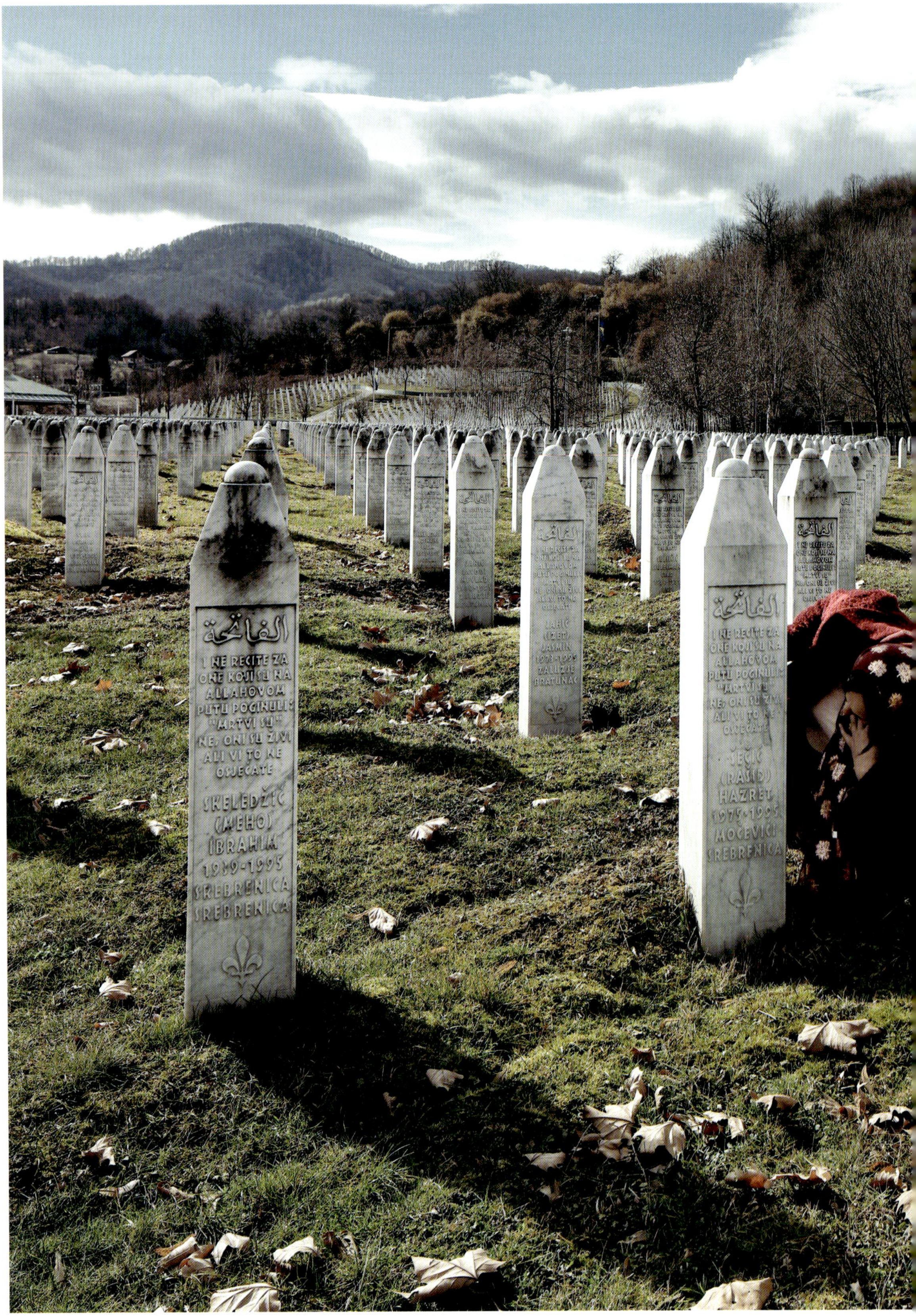
الفاتحة
I NE RECITE ZA
ONE KOJI SU NA
ALLAHOVOM
PUTU POGINULI:
"MRTVI SU"
NE, ONI SU ŽIVI
ALI VI TO NE
OSJEĆATE
SKELEDŽIĆ
(MEHO)
IBRAHIM
SREBRENICA
SREBRENICA

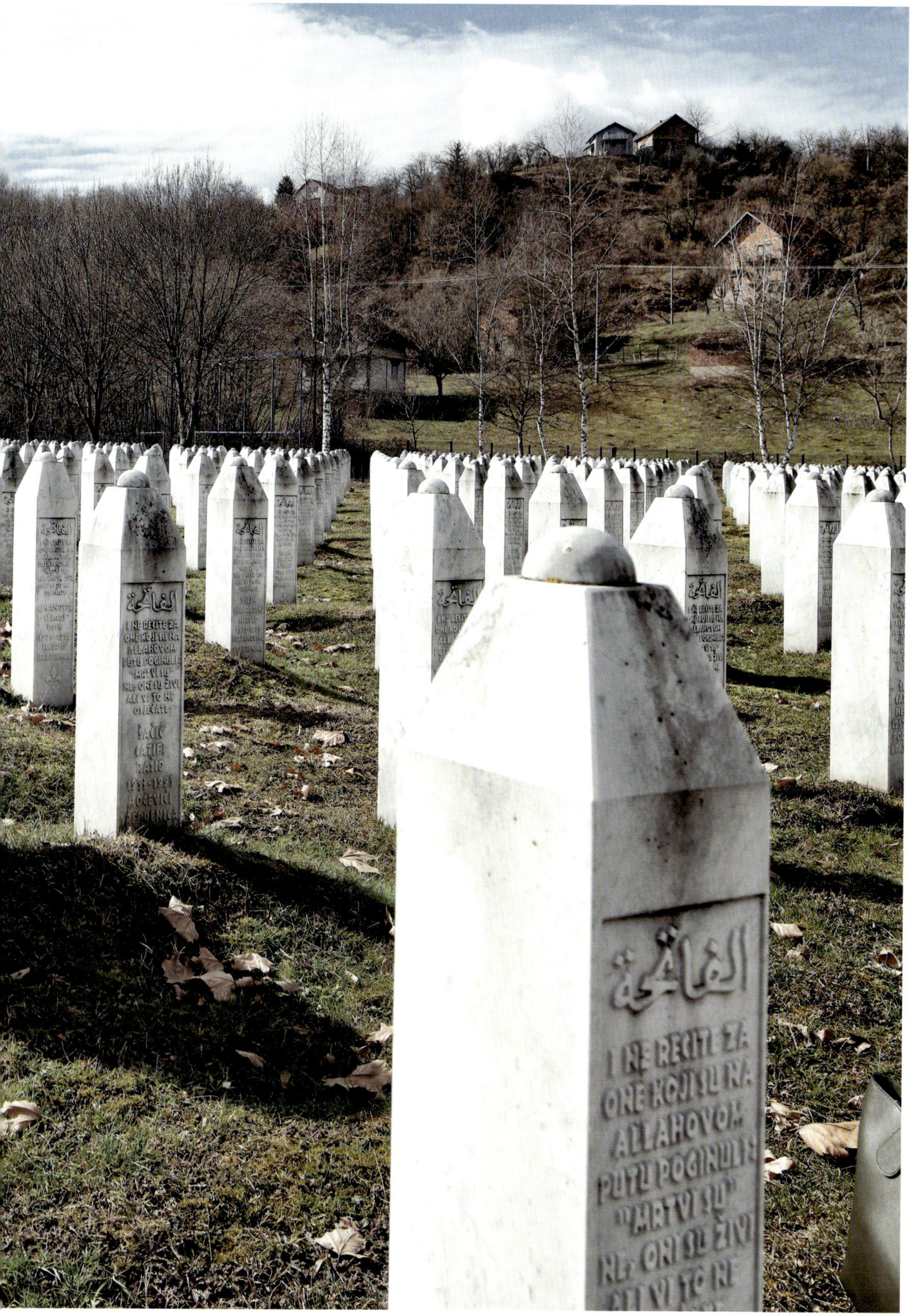
الفاتحة
I NE RECITE ZA
ONE KOJI SU NA
ALLAHOVOM
PUTU POGINULI:
"MRTVI SU"
NE, ONI SU ŽIVI

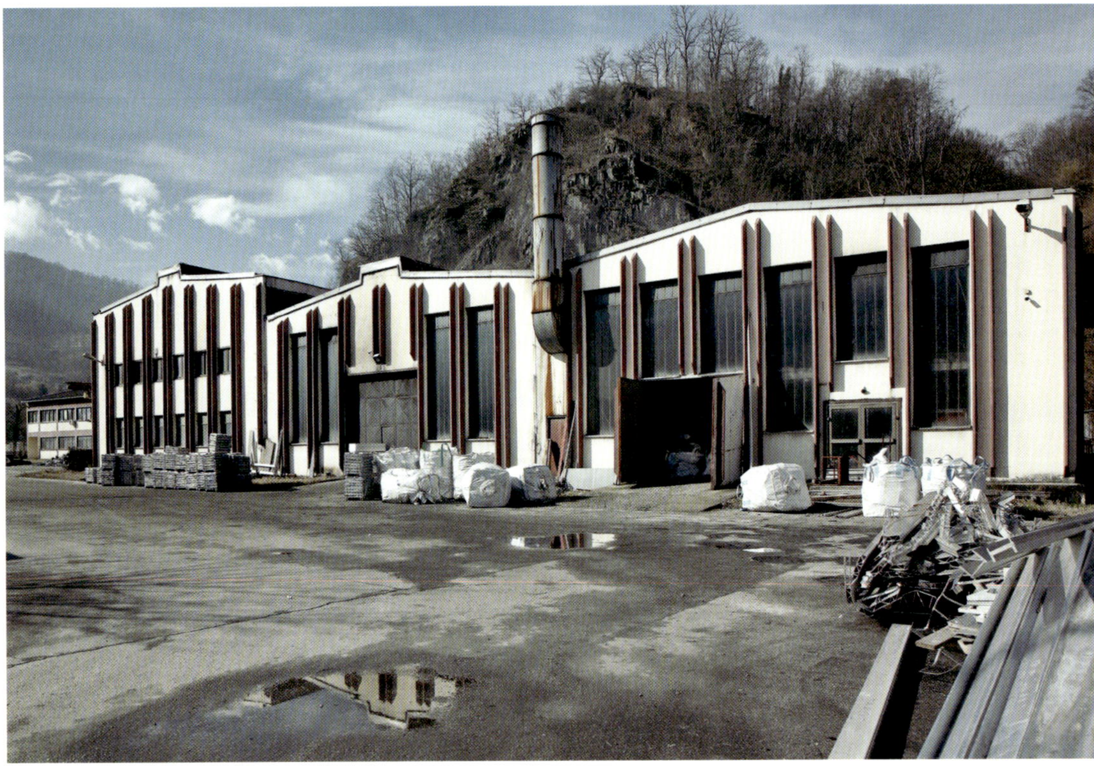

Left
Potočari
Metalworking Factory

Sarah (not her real name) lost her brother who was murdered when she was twenty years old, her father who was murdered when she was forty-four years old and her husband who was murdered when she was twenty-eight years old. In July 1995 Sarah was here with her two children, the son three years old and the daughter two months old. She was waiting in a tent next to the factory building in the sweltering heat. She had been promised food would be brought for her children. Her son was with her, he was crying, then one by one they came into the tent: four men, two Serbian soldiers from the Drinakorps, two speaking other languages...only years later she was able to talk about it.

44°9'4"N 19°17'53"E

Overleaf
Potočari
Metalworking Factory

The conclusion of this war was heralded by a genocide that could be watched on TV—Srebrenica in July 1995, about 25,000 people were in the UN protection zone, women were taken out of the group and raped, men were questioned and tortured. On 11 July, the protection zone fell to the Serb-Bosnian military unit Drinakorps. Mostly women and children were expelled and transported to Tuzla in buses. Over the next few days, more than 8,000 Muslim Bosnians were murdered by Serb-Bosnian soldiers and buried in mass graves.

44°9'4"N 19°17'53"E

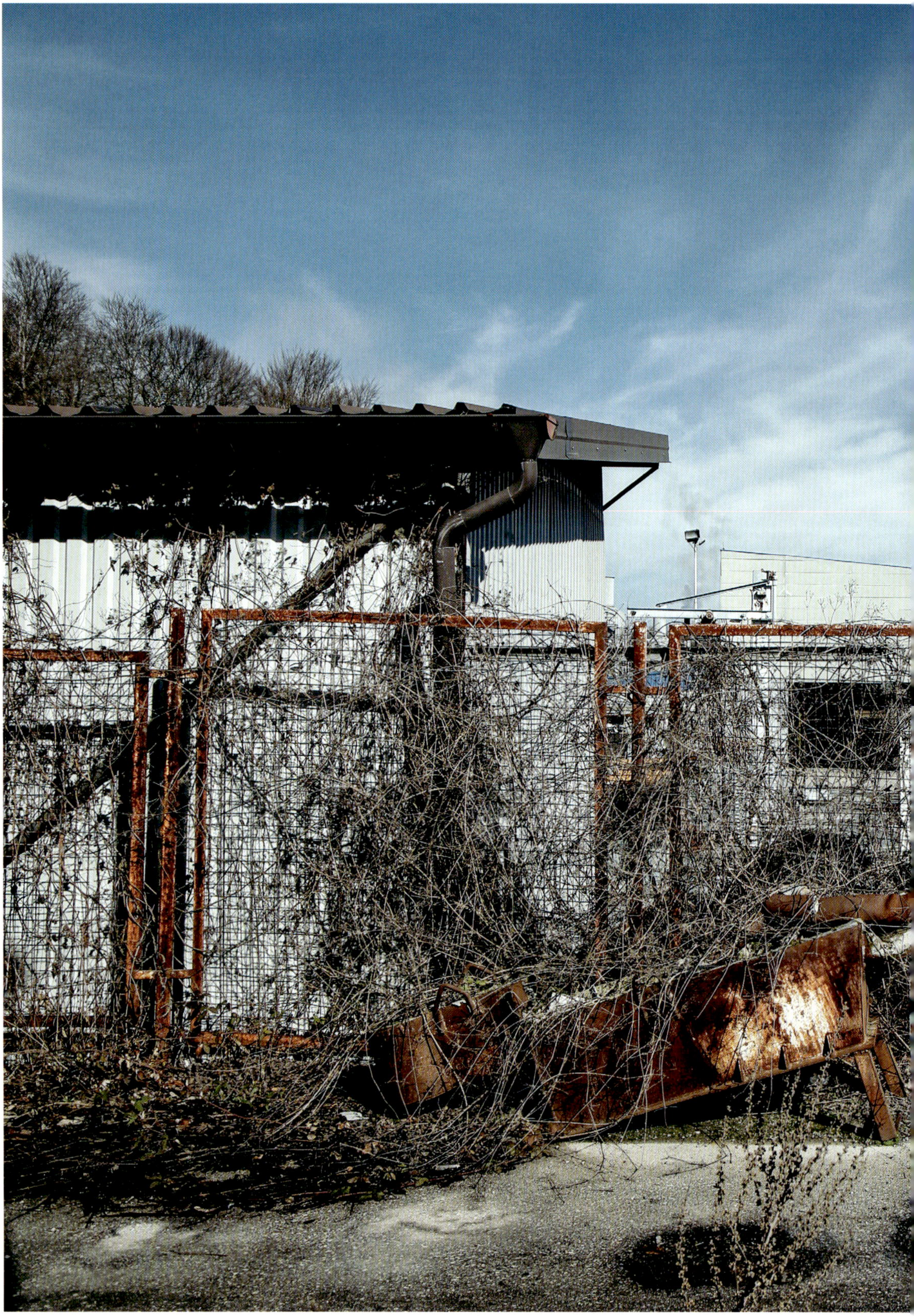

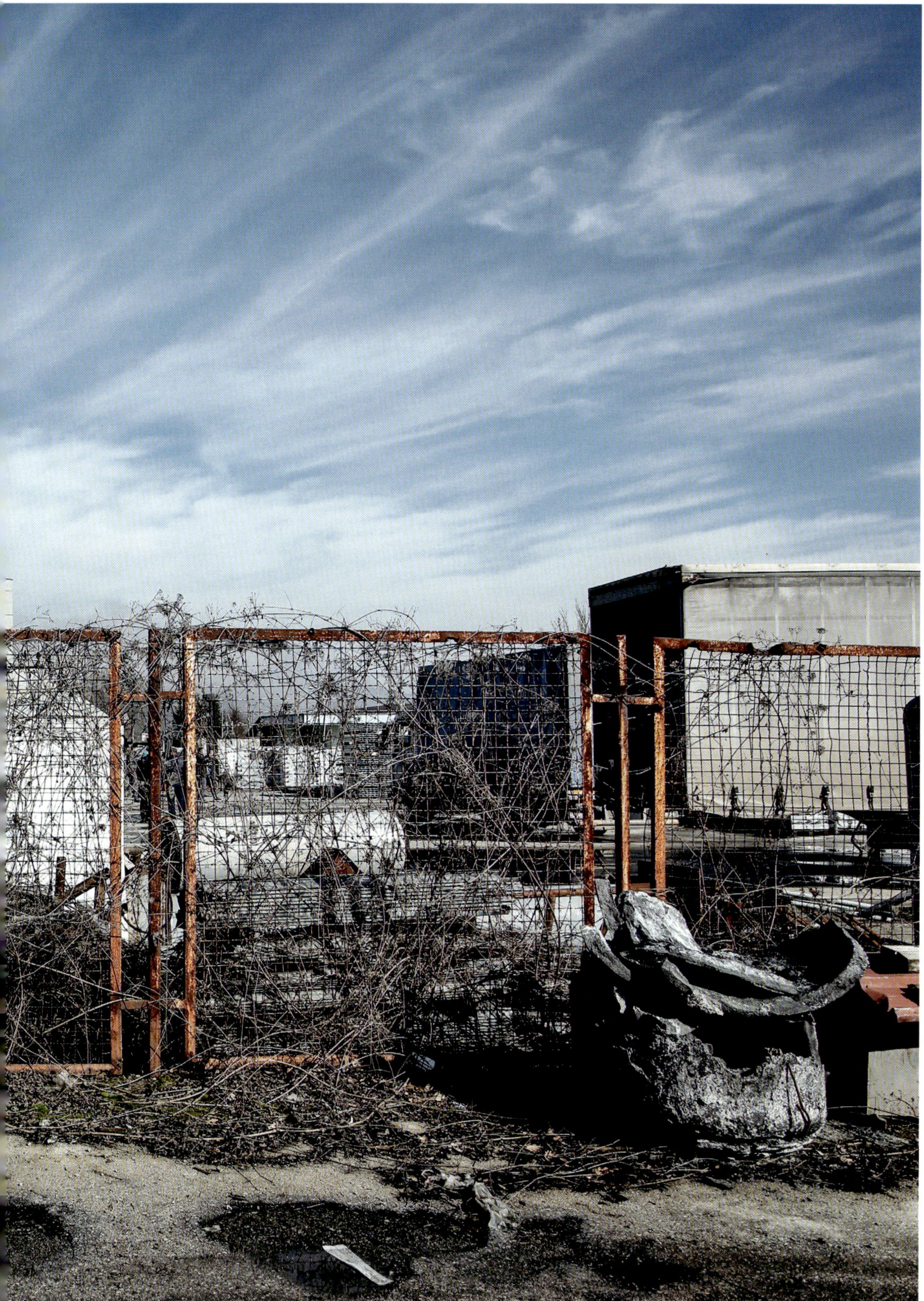

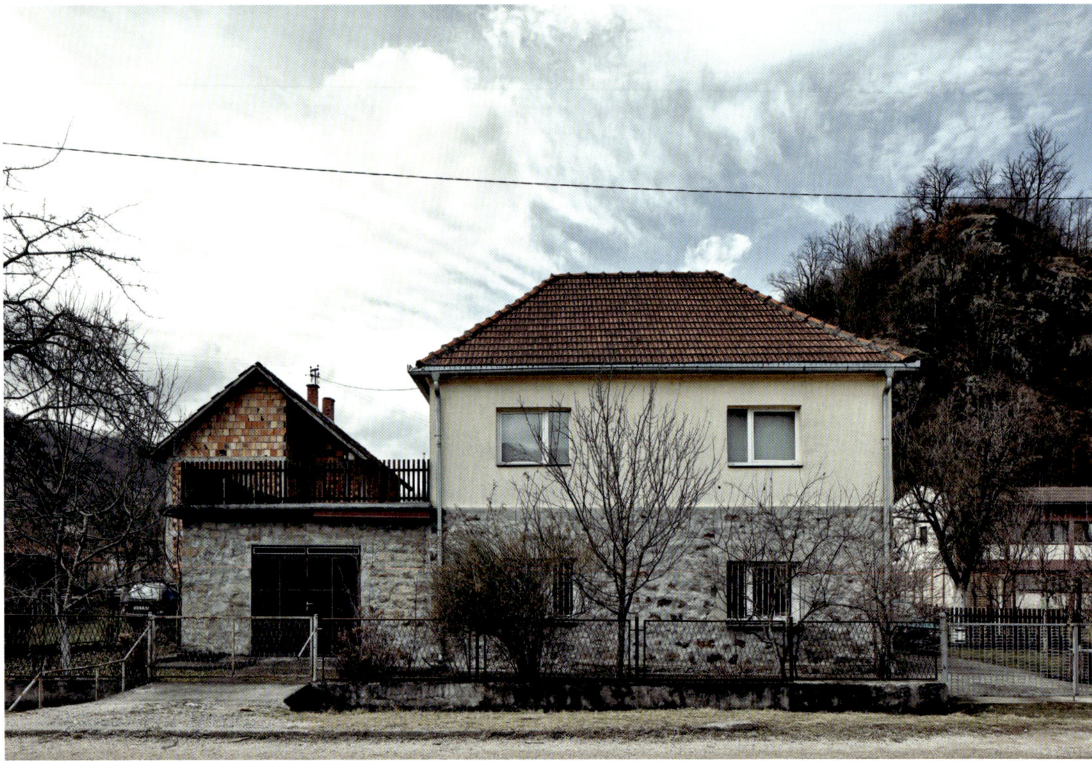

Potočari
Residential Building

'From 1993 to 1995 I was exposed to acts of war together with my family. I had many traumatic experiences. In 1993 my sister died and I witnessed her death. I got married in besieged Srebrenica. In 1994 I gave birth to a son. In 1995, with the fall of Srebrenica, my father was shot by Chetniks, and I was with my mother, son, brother and sister in 'Potočari' camp—Potočari factory, where I suffered psychological, physical and sexual abuse by a person that I knew. In the evening around 6pm a Serbian soldier came, he had a mask on his face, I didn't recognise him, he took my child from my arms and threw him on the ground. My son was eleven months old at the time. He took me to the first house next to the factory, a Bosniak house that was empty. He ordered me to undress and raped me. He kept the mask on his face and when it was all over he took the mask off and said to say hello to my brother and he did it because of him, because he was in the Bosnia and Herzegovina army. He was my brother's friend, they went to school together.'[2]

44°08'59"N 19°17'51.0"E

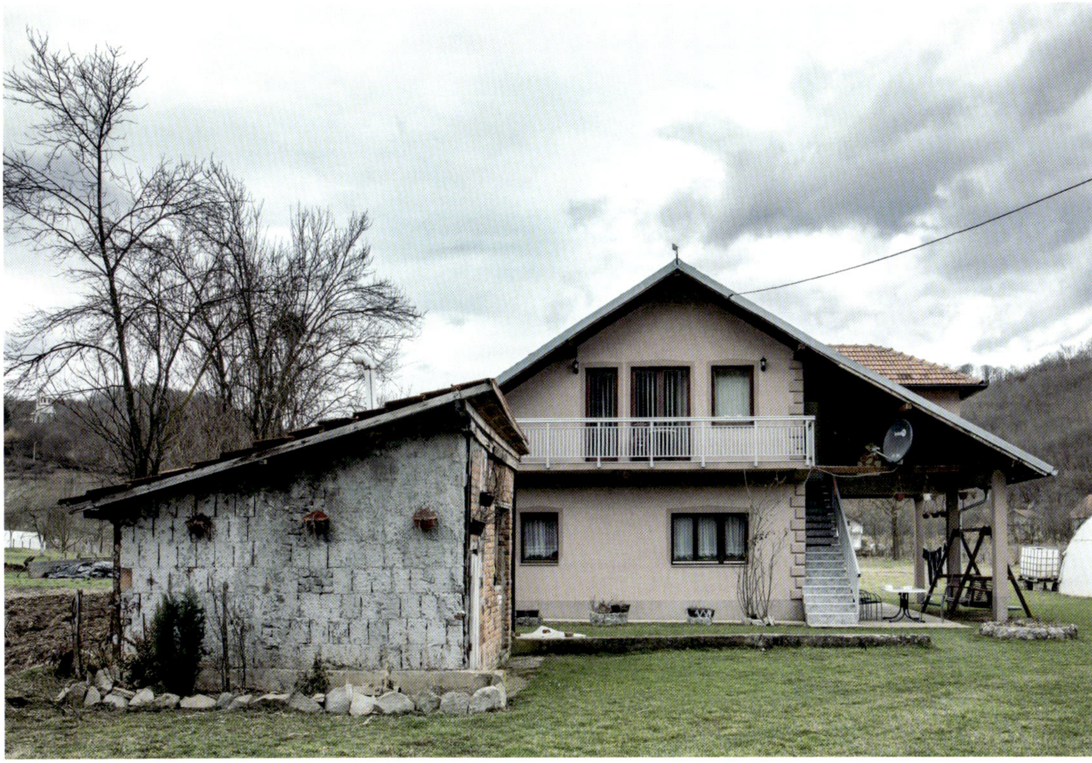

Potočari
Private House

Witness Snaga Žene She has rebuilt her house three times. During the war she was raped in her home by soldiers from Serb Bosnian units. Nobody could drive them away. She stayed.[3]

44°09'52"N 19°18'27.0"E

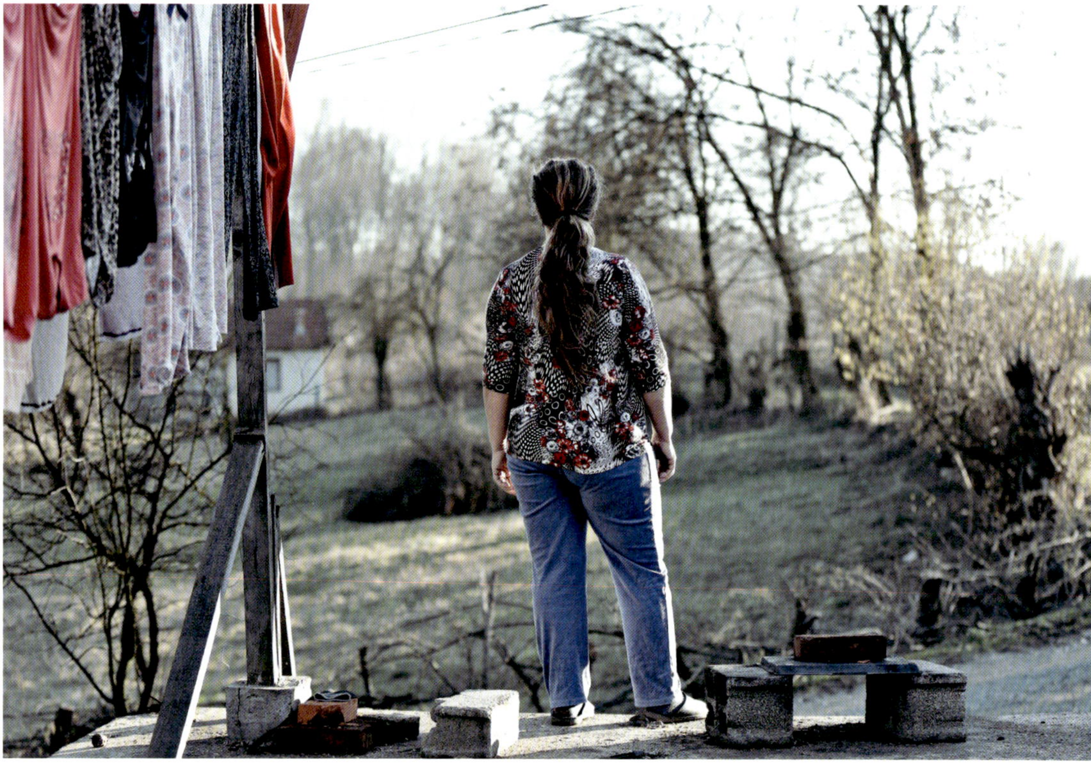

EMINA FROM MRAMOR

'When the war started in May 1992, I fled my husband's family home with my daughter, my twin sister, my other sister, my mother-in-law and my sister's mother-in-law. We hid in the basement of a house, but Serbian soldiers found us and took us to Kitovnica, where we spent two hours. From there they transported us to Karakaj to the 'Standard' camp near Zvornik. We were interned for ten days in a building belonging to Vezionica Embroidery. During those days, I was raped more than three times by people I didn't know. In addition to the rape, I witnessed torture and mistreatment of others. My sister and I were forced to throw dismembered human body parts into the Drina River. After ten days, Serbian soldiers took us to the Vidikovac field, the demarcation line at the time. From there I walked to Tuzla.'

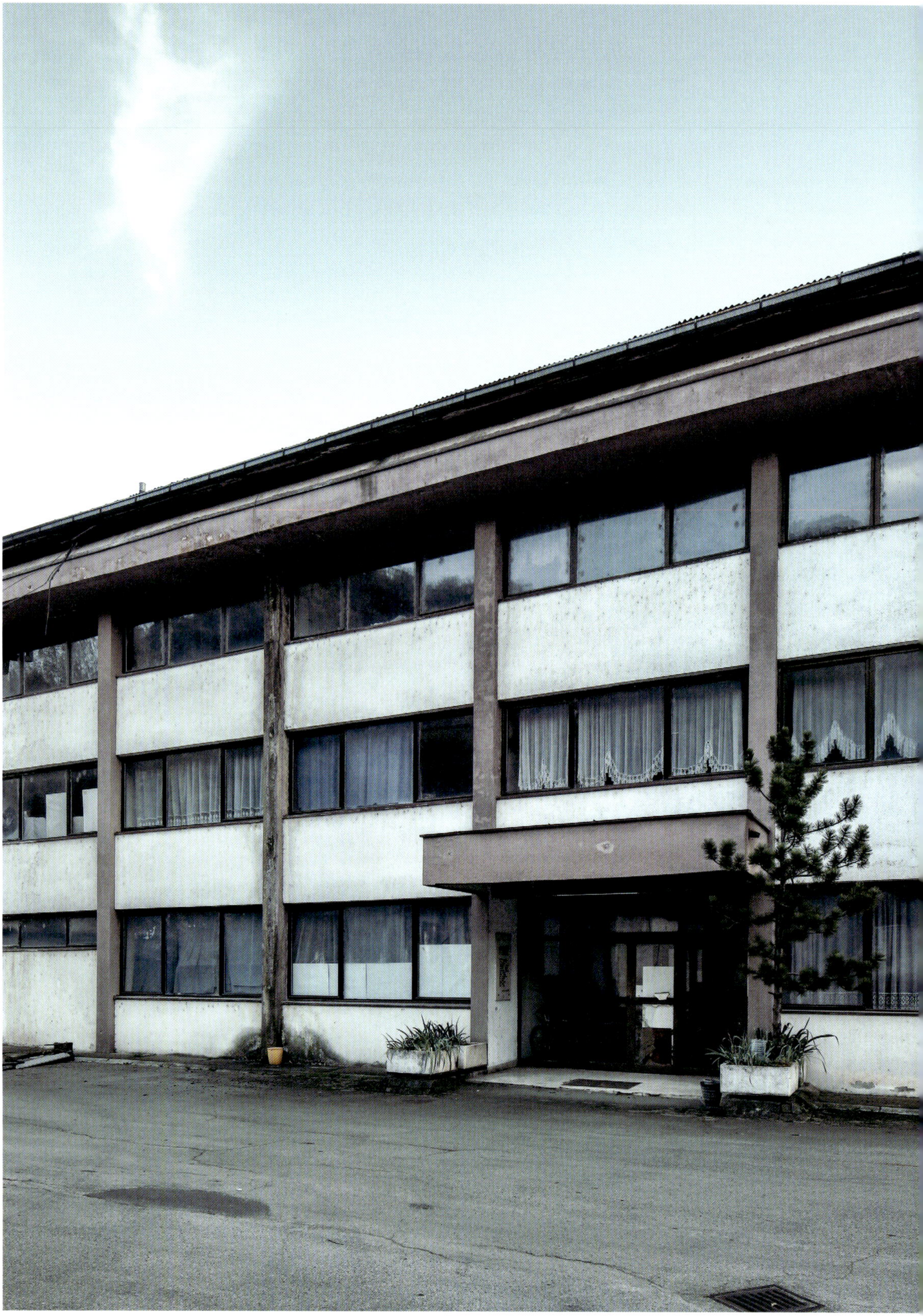

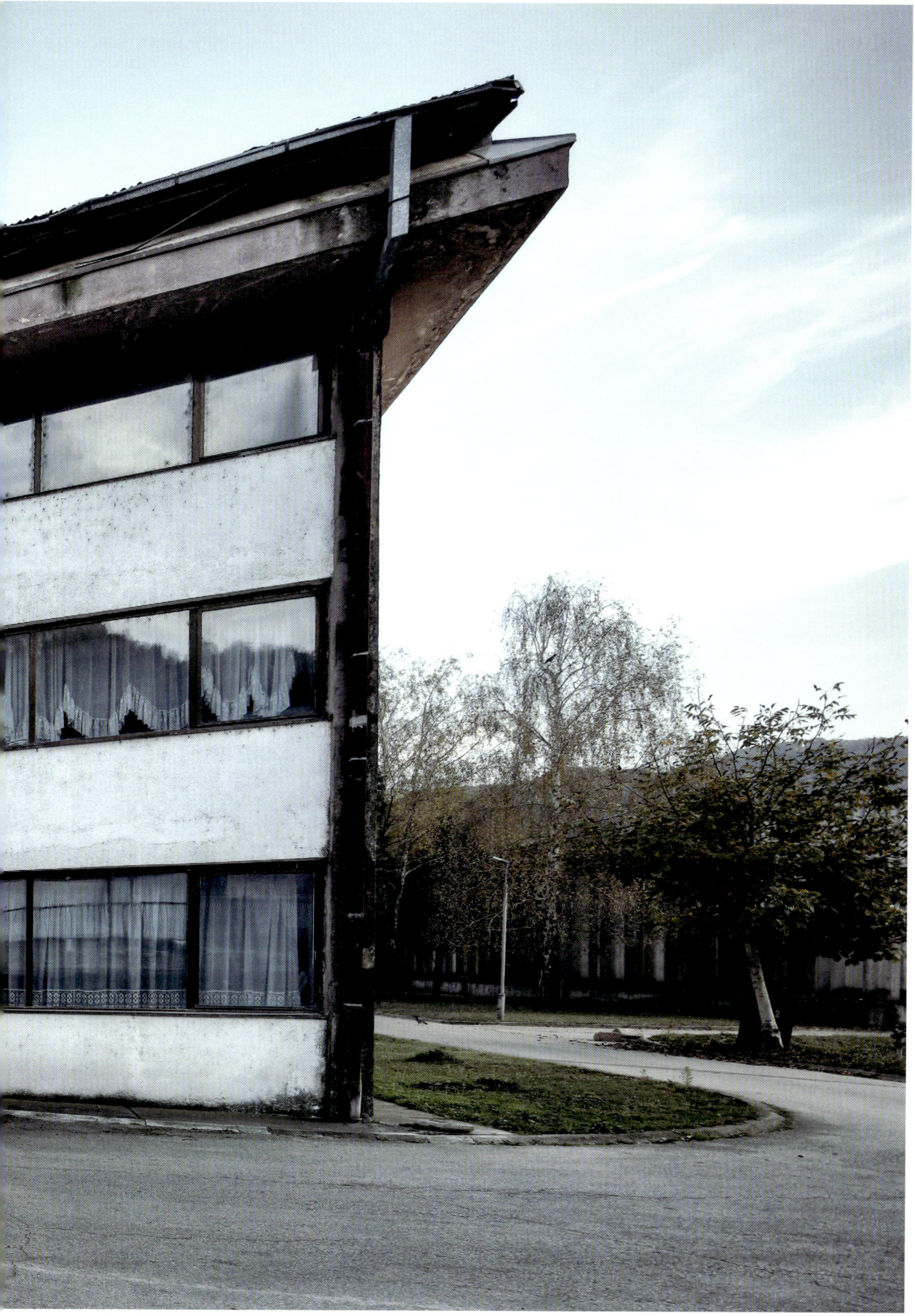

Previous spread
Zvornik - Karakaj
Embroidery Factory 'Vezionica'

The detention centre, where the Muslim population from the region was held, existed from April to June 1992. It was controlled by the Bosnian Serb Army. According to ED's testimony, when the war began in May 1992, she fled her husband's family home with her daughter, twin sister, mother-in-law and her sister's mother-in-law. They hid in the basement of a house, but were found by Serbian soldiers and taken to the 'Vezionica' embroidery factory in Karakaj. They stayed there for ten days. In those ten days she was raped more than three times by strangers.

In addition to the rape, she witnessed torture and illtreatment of other women and men. She and her sister were forced to dispose of dismembered body parts of the people who had been killed there. After ten days in Vezionica, Serbian soldiers dropped them off at a field (a demarcation line between the war fronts) in Vidikovac. From there they went on to Tuzla. They stayed in Tulza for a short time in the collective centre Mejdan (Tuzla Sports Centre). After that, ED went to Croatia and met her husband again in Zagreb, where he worked as a construction worker. She lived with him and her daughter in a hut husband had used as a field hand for years. After a year they decided to leave Croatia. They received residence in Germany (Ulm) as war refugees. In 1996 they returned to Bosnia and Herzegovina.[4]

44°24'45"N 19°7'38.0"E

Opposite
RS Vlasenica
Private House

According to witness M, in the summer of 1992, Muslim women were raped in this private house in Vlasenica.[5]

44°10'54.0"N 18°56'14.0"E

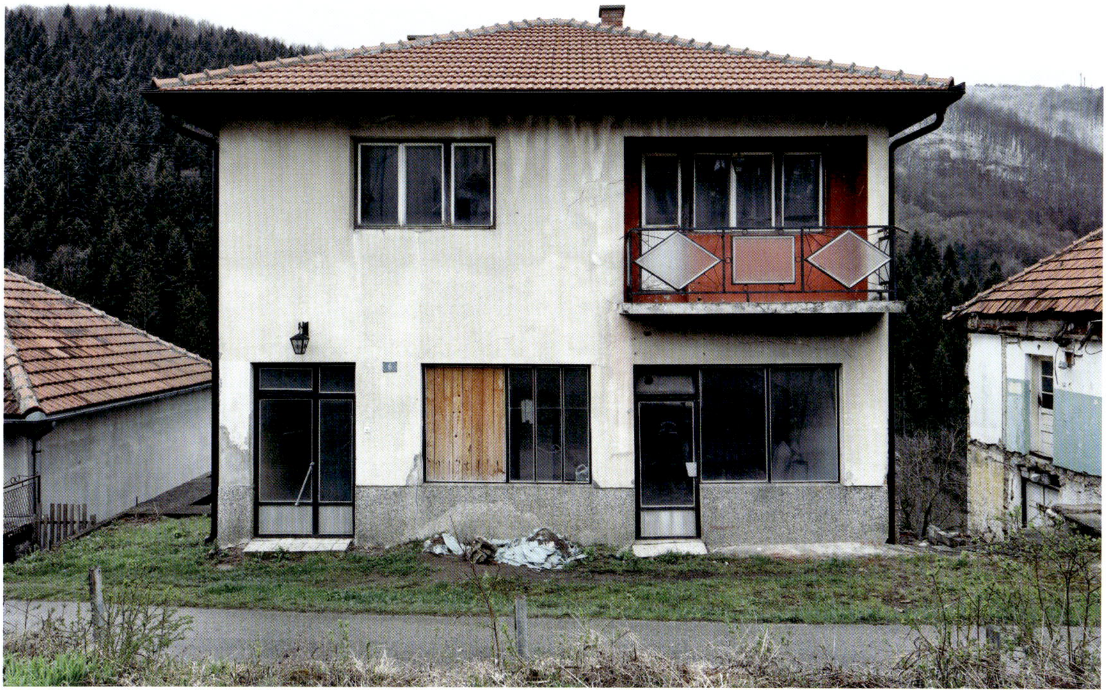

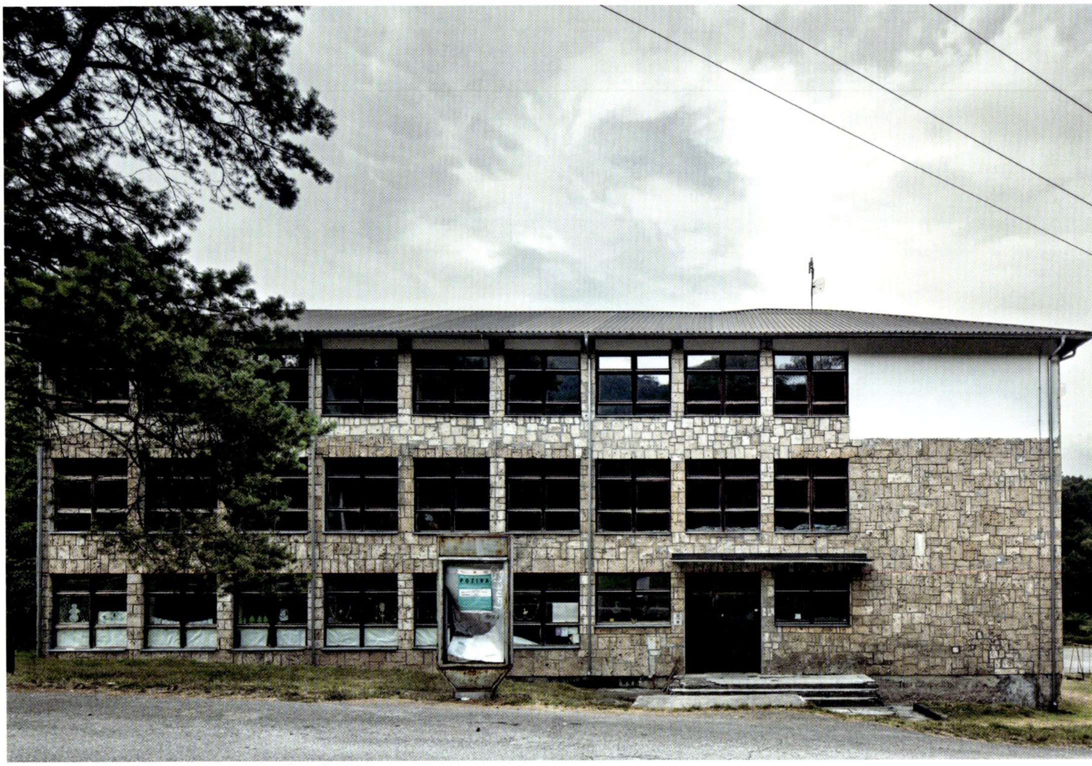
POZIVA

Left

Vlasenica

Village Cerska, Elementary School

Many civilians were housed in the school. Until March 1993 the area was controlled by Bosnian units. In March 1993 Chetniks occupied the village and the school came under their command. A witness gave her testimony: 'Two Serbian soldiers wearing camouflage uniforms and capmasks with openings on the eyes and mouth and armed with long rifles came. Since I had two of my children, Muhammad and Medina, with me, I tried to hide behind everyone else. The Chetniks cursed and asked me what I was waiting for. They tore off my clothes, threw me to the ground, and both raped me. They did it before my two young children. After that I took my kids and went to Konjevic Polje where I managed to join other people and we went to Srebrenica. When I got there, I continued to the village of Soce to the old house of Mehmed. I stayed there for the time being.'[6]

44°15'12"N 19°3'5.0"E

Overleaf

Kamenica

Private House

In her private home, the witness was raped by a neighbour and other men. 'Suddenly I found myself in my own house in front of three Chetniks. I knew one of the three. It was my neighbour Velimir. I tried to run away. 'Oh good pussy, do you know her?' The larger Chetnik sends Velimir to guard the house and orders me to sit on the bed. He sat down next to me and put his hand under my tracksuit, on my chest. I'm shaking with fear. I call on Velimir for help. The Chetnik says, 'It's Velimir's turn now.' He hits me and ties a scarf over my mouth so I don't scream. He throws me naked on the ground. He ties one hand to my bed and the other to the table and he begins to rape me. When the rape is over, he sees that we are both bleeding. Only then does he realise that I'm menstruating. He starts hitting me on the body, face, but also with a knife. The scars are still visible today. Then the two pick me up off the floor. He runs his genitals over my face, my mouth, my chest, shoves it into my mouth, really deep. Since I don't know how to do it right, they beat me up. It disgusts me, I vomit and I get hit harder because of it. I beg him to untie me, but it went on for a long time. Suddenly I hear the sound of a car that I didn't see. They get dressed and leave. I was left alone When I was sure they had gone far enough, I ran away.'

44°19'47.4"N 19°3'8.4"E

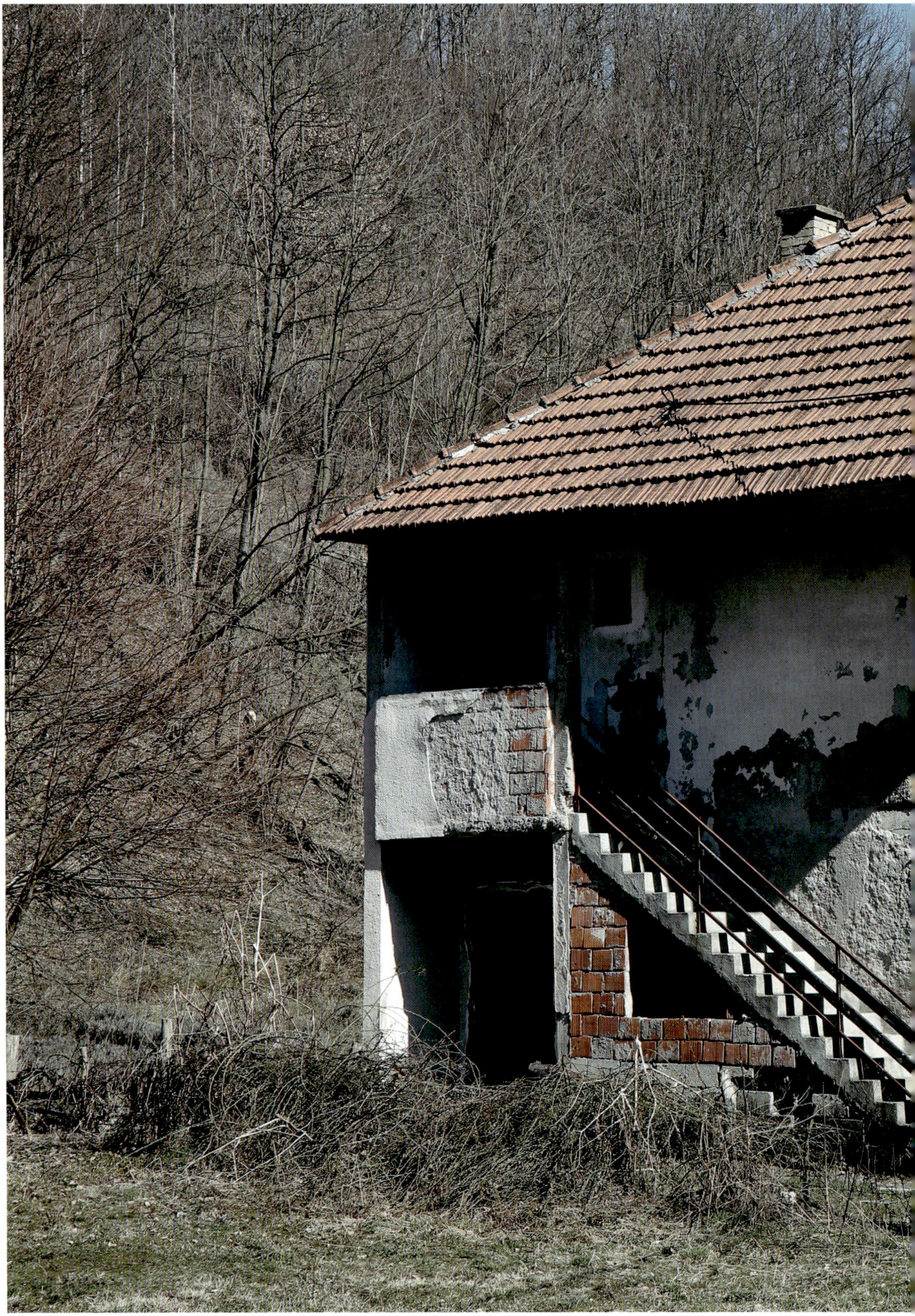

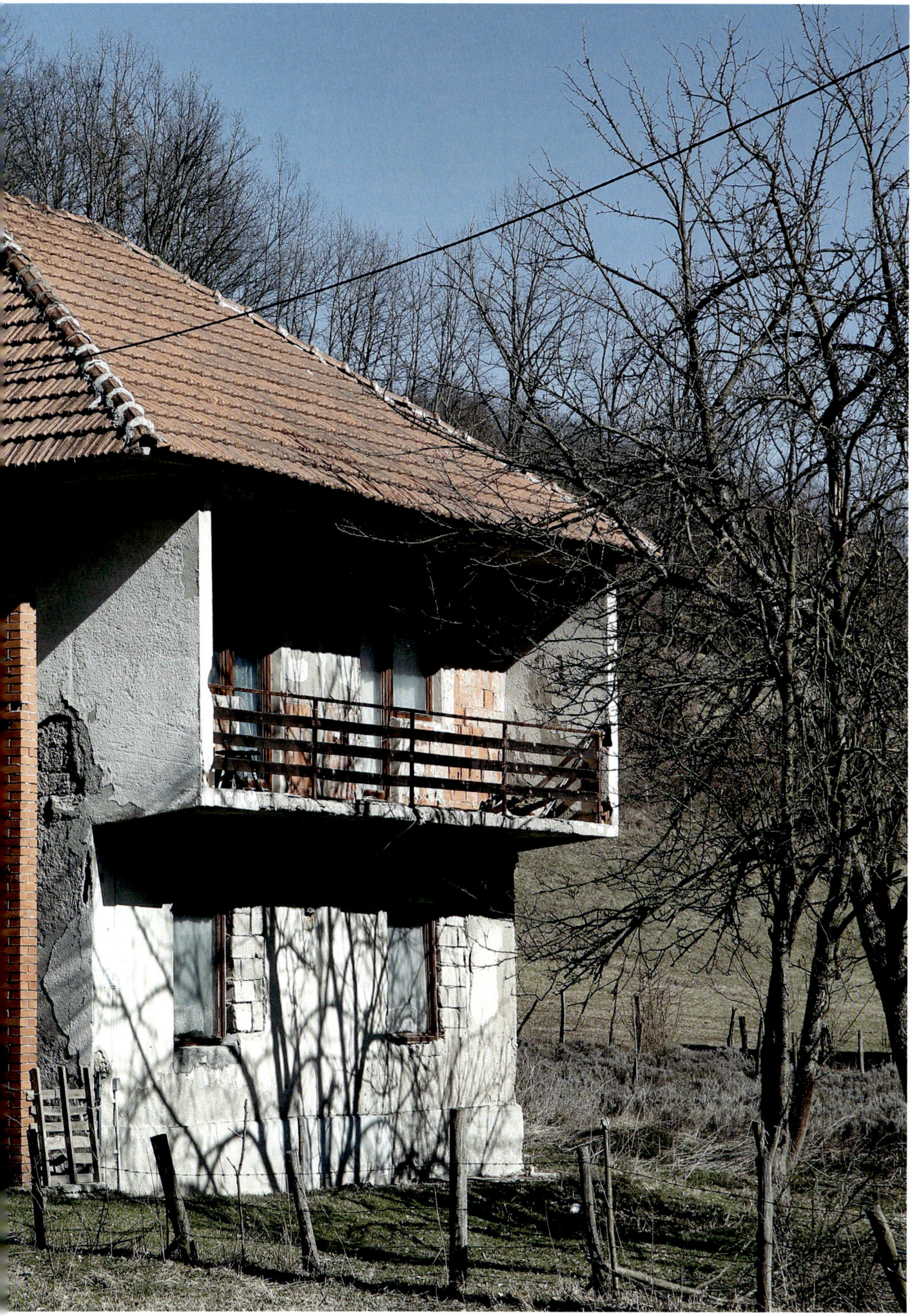

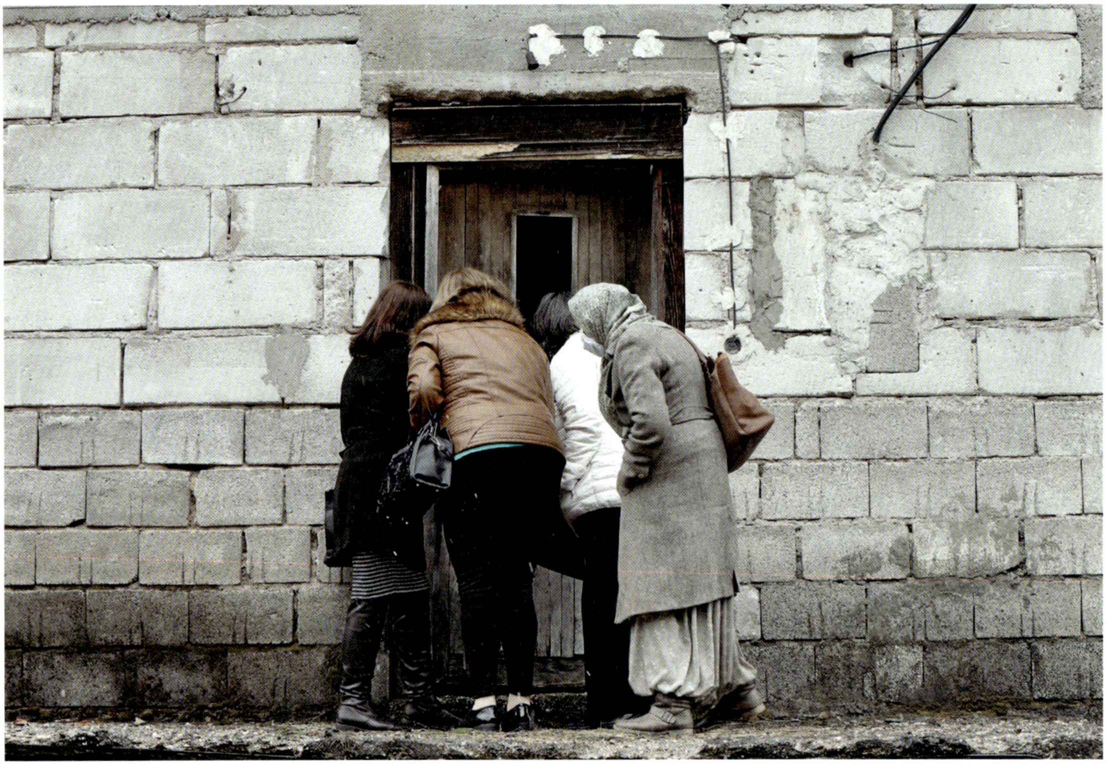

FIKRETA FROM TUZLA

'I came to Pijuk...to get food...Rasim Limi and Merima Sandžić...they went to Džemat, I walked alone through Kućište, barefoot, on my toes looking over my shoulder, making sure that no leaf could be heard. I was so careful that my heart beat a hundred times faster because I was afraid, of walking alone through the forest.

When I got near my house, I went out onto the road. On the other side I found my father and we hid there in his hut. He asked me where my mother was, I said she had stayed in Cerska. My mother and I had gone there together and only met again later. We were separated in Susica, and for three years no one knew anything about anyone. Fear and terror. Later my mother received the news that I had been killed, someone came and said that they had slaughtered me.

In Cerska we had nothing to eat. I had come home to pack something and the others had gone to Džemat—we all wanted to return the next day to bring food. Father said that no one would come, everyone was hiding in the forest.

Then we went to our house, he said we would prepare food, slaughter a sheep. We will load it on the horse and go to Pijuk to get more food, flour, etc. He started to prepare everything with his uncle. They slaughtered a sheep, packed it up, that's when the shooting started. When I looked up at the hills, there was an army. There was nowhere else to go. We were surrounded...and then they caught us all. I was captured too. They told me to go and call everyone, father, uncle, I should call them by name. They captured aunts, people, children, women from our neighbourhood... they told me to come down, and I went to my house, the house was on fire, it was on fire. I called my father... There was a brook and a hornbeam, I saw him running down and I ran after him...yes. And from below he was fired upon, cutting him in half, so that only one leg was still attached to the hornbeam...when I saw that, I screamed and called him 'father'...I fell, I fell on him. At that moment I didn't know what had happened, nothing...I just felt someone pulling my hair. And I see a man as if through a fog, I can't see his face. I don't see his face, he was all masked, I only see his eyes, the gun is in his hands, they're in his hands. They are in gloves; his fingers are naked, black gloves. He tells me to leave, he shouts, he curses 'you Balija (a slang name used as an insult for Muslims from Bosnia), motherfuckers', he shouts, 'We're going to kill you all!'

I was so lost, at that moment I didn't know what was happening, I...when I saw my father, I fell, I lost consciousness. They shouted at me: 'Do you now know where Hasib Kolarevic where he hid the gun?' I said I didn't know. They shouted, 'You're going with us to Hasib's house!' and we entered the barn...he told me to climb into the attic, he followed me and held the gun. Downstairs there was a calf in the barn and he shouted at me: 'You see this calf, I'm going to slaughter you here like this calf, if you do not tell us where Hasib Kolarevic hides his rifle!' 'I don't know,' I repeated. And when we went outside, one of our men tried to sneak into the forest to escape. He spotted him and fired a shot.

Far above, I see again the aunts who were captured all sitting on the hill...I came to this hill, the rifles were lined up, the Serbs were sitting down to rest, and I, still a child at the time...I looked at those rifles and I said to myself, 'I'm going to take this rifle...and I will kill them all.' ...I didn't care what was going to happen to me, it was was so hard for me when I saw my father, I was so tired of everything.

I wanted to take a rifle, grab a rifle. Mother said later that if I would have done it I wouldn't have survived either. But it was as if me, 'don't do it'... We went to Ivan's house, I was barefoot, I had nothing to wear, I was scared. I saw Mile Rebic, my neighbour, with a gun. He was standing there and asked me, 'Where are you going?' I said I was going to Ivan's house. 'Go in there, to Ramo's house, find something to wear.' When I got there someone had locked a dog in the closet, I got scared like a little kid. I opened the wardrobe, the dog whimpered, I was scared. I'm dying, I thought, I was shaking all over. I came out and went to Ivan's house, women, children, screams, everything, everything was burnt, it seemed to me that there was not even a cat left, they captured and killed everything, even dogs in front of the houses, just everything.

We were sitting in Ivan's house. Children were screaming, crying, some people came, Zoran from Piskavica, Vojin, came and took my aunt to test a sniper, he told her to go fifteen metres forward... Her children were small, they started crying. Someone told him to let her go and 'Don't shoot her, you see that the children are crying, we can cope with them in another way.' When the aunt returns, she says, facing him, 'We were neighbours until yesterday and today you kill us.'

Then they took us to Sušica, there were so many people there, you couldn't throw matches, it was so crowded. Then Dragan Nikolic came, he said to me, 'Why are you crying?' I told him, 'You killed my father.' He told me: 'We will kill you all.' I cried, I sobbed as he hit me on the back with the butt of his rifle. And I kept silent. What was I supposed to do? The one I saw most often was Dragan Nikolic. He was everything in there, he gave orders, he told who should do what and where. One time Dragan Nikolic came in and shouted at me, Zikret and Meho Sinanovic to go to Sušica to rob Muslim houses. He said, 'Gold, money... whatever you find, You bring it here.' And we went from house to house, everything was turned upside down. We searched and couldn't find anything. I said even if I wouldn't take it with me, I'm not going to take anything with me, I'll just walk around. I said to Zikret, 'What do you think, let's escape from here.' 'We have nowhere to flee to. We are surrounded.' Yes, that was all. 'Let's go back,' he said, 'whatever God wills, it will be.'

And we came back with nothing. 'Did you find anything?' 'Nothing.' They examined us: 'Raise your hands, unbutton this, unbutton that,' he searched down to our underwear to see if we had hidden any money, anything hidden in our trousers. 'Open your mouth,' they were looking there for gold.

Yes...we watched them kill and I saw Galib Muslic when they killed him and others.

He was beaten. I said the man had a healthy heart that he could take so many blows, and in the end he ended up on the Pelemiš, to be torn apart by horses. One leg was tied by a horse with a rope and the other by another horse, he was torn apart by horses, alive.

We spent twenty-two days there, watching all kinds of murders, kidnappings, rapes and killings, we had nothing to eat, we lay on the concrete...

I will never get the image out of my head of Chetniks taking me from the camp to that house. And when we got there, I went inside, I went up the stairs. The Chetnik said: 'Go in there.' He told me to undress. I was standing there with tears running down my face. I had no more words, I was not allowed to say anything. I was shaking. He tore everything from me, he raped me, he told me... He told me: 'Listen to me, the other man is coming too.' I passed out. I don't remember what happened. The other man came in and he told me to do it to him. It's hard for me to tell this story.

He ordered me to do it, I had to do it. It was a matter of...death or life, I didn't know what to do with myself. I was in...in their hands.

When I was brought back, I was lost. I entered the camp, I saw no one, it went dark before my eyes. I fainted again, I felt sick, nauseous, I can't explain it to you, my body was shaking. My whole body was shaking. I couldn't stop my hands from trembling, my hands were trembling with fear. I came there, I couldn't tell my mother (at that time also in Sušica) couldn't say anything immediately. She saw that I was not well, she saw that I was going mad. I sat down next to her, I asked her for her Turkish salvar (traditional loose trousers) and told her what happened.

I told her not to talk about it because they told me, that I shouldn't tell anyone and if anyone asks me what happened I should say that I was brought in to make coffee... Yes. When I was asked where I had gone, I was to say that I had gone to make coffee for their army.

And then they took me out the second time...

Again, I couldn't tell my mother straight away what had happened. She saw that I'd lost my way, that I'd lost my train of thought. She asked what was wrong and I whispered to her to be quiet, not to talk, and that they had raped me.

And she started crying and I told her to shut up, not to cry, someone would notice. Someone would come in, and she would have to tell them what she was crying about, and then what would they do—worse. I still have nightmares, mostly I dream of running through the woods, that's my eternal dream: to run, to hear the sounds, the cries of women, of children...the screams of the women, the children...that's what I remember most, and running in the woods. And everything else...when I sleep at night, it's as if I'm falling from the sky...from above. And they chase me, they run after me, I run, I run, I can't get away, and I start screaming in my sleep. That stays with you for the rest of your life. You can't erase that...the things of Pijuk will never leave my mind. It is engraved, I was then fifteen years old.

I saw what I saw. That was it, scare and horror.'

Opposite
Vlasenica - Sušica
Private House

After more than twenty years, in April 2021, employees of the NGO Snaga Žene from Tuzla accompanied witness F. Together they visited the place where F was raped in 1992. 'I grew up with two brothers and one sister in a family house in Vlasenica. In May 1992, I fled my village...with my mother, my younger brother and my sister. During the escape we were captured and taken to the Sušica camp, where we spent ten days. After leaving the Sušica camp, went to Cerska, where we were housed housed on the school grounds and spend ten days there. On the tenth day of my stay in Cerska, I went to my house with the army of Bosnia and Herzegovina to pick up groceries for the family and to visit my father who was staying at the house. Upon arrival I was recaptured and my father was killed on my doorstep. After the capture, I was again taken to the Sušica camp, where I stayed for twenty-one days. During my stay in the Sušica camp in June 1992, I was raped twice, physically and mentally abused, and starved by soldiers.[7] I witnessed physical abuse of other prisoners. After twenty-one days in Sušica I was taken to Pšelemiš—the demarcation line—from where I went to Kladanj in the Bosnian Federation. In Kladanj I stayed twenty days in the kindergarten school, then in Živinice in a school where I stayed fifteen days. Then I went to Tuzla to private accommodation. In the time between my second capture in Sušica and my arrival in Tuzla, I did not know what happened to my mother, brother and sister. In 1995 I found them again and lived with them in a rented house in Tuzla's Piskavica district.'

44°10'21"N 18°56'40.0"E

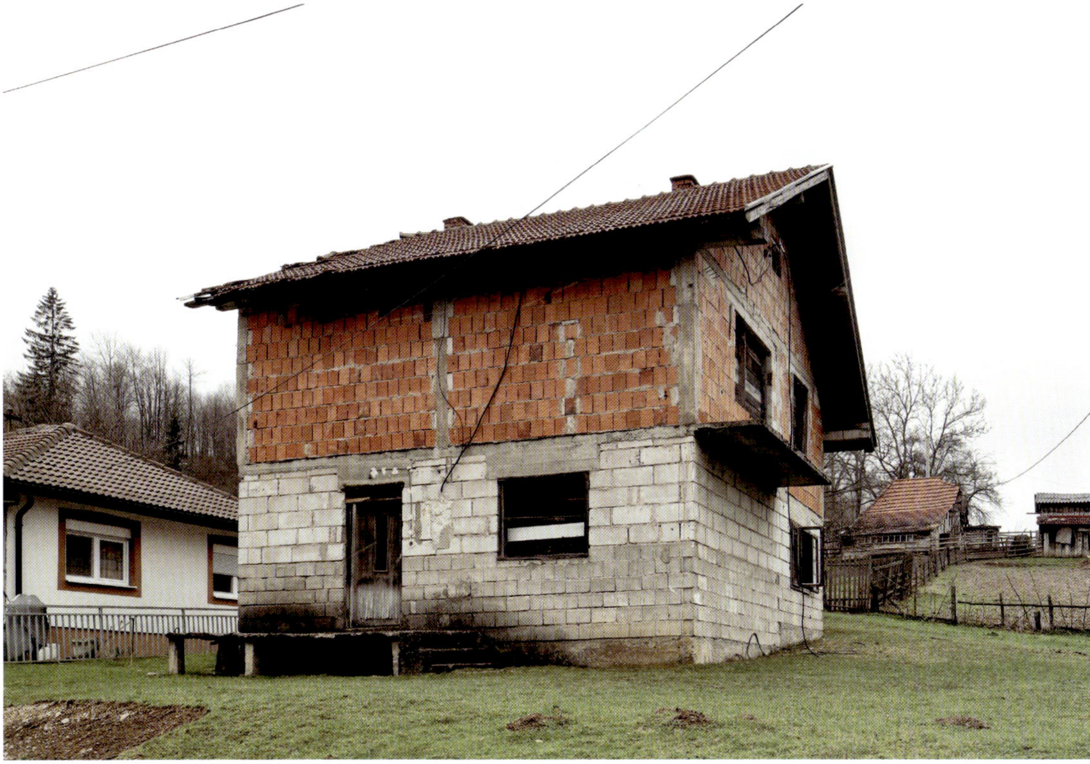

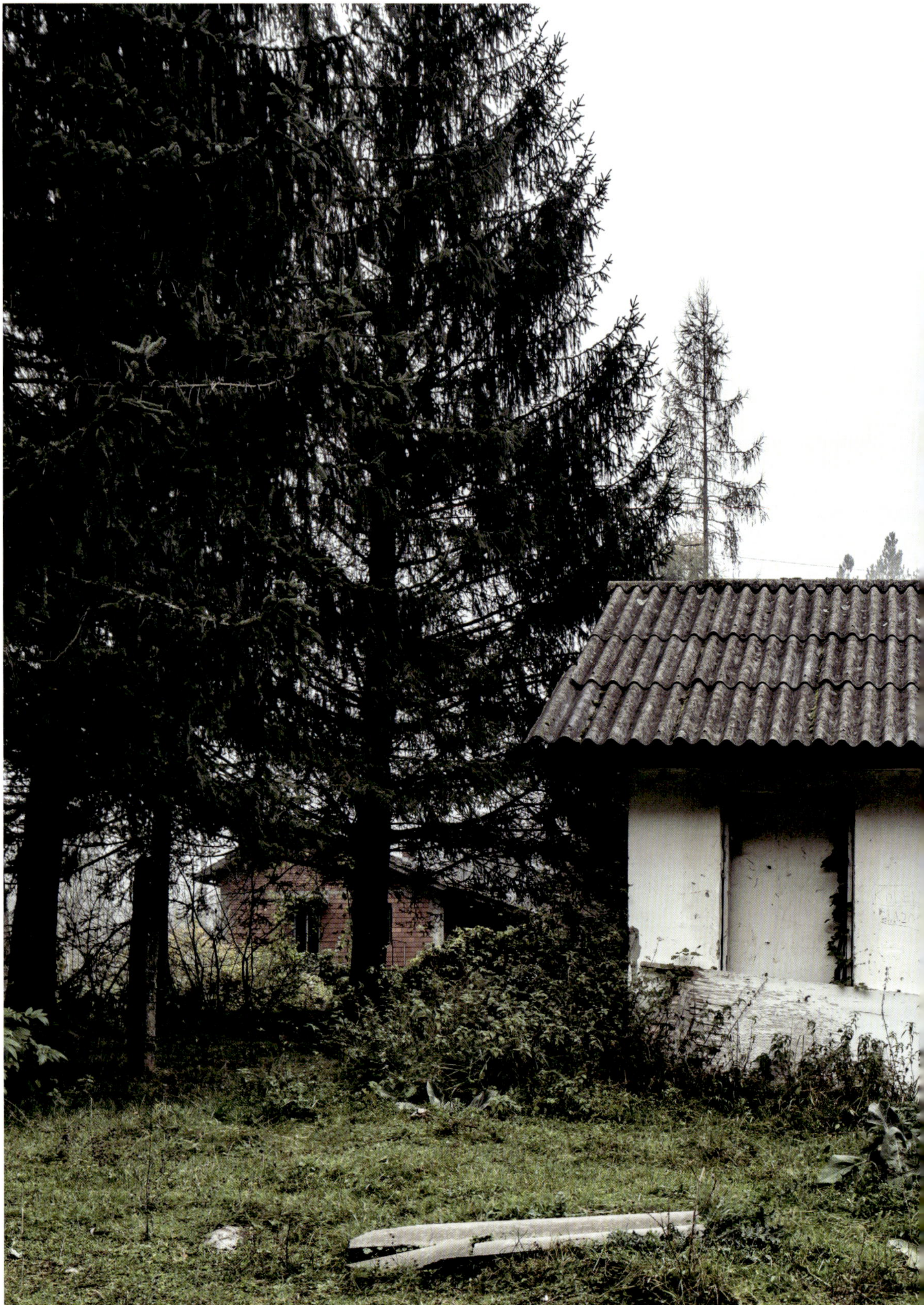

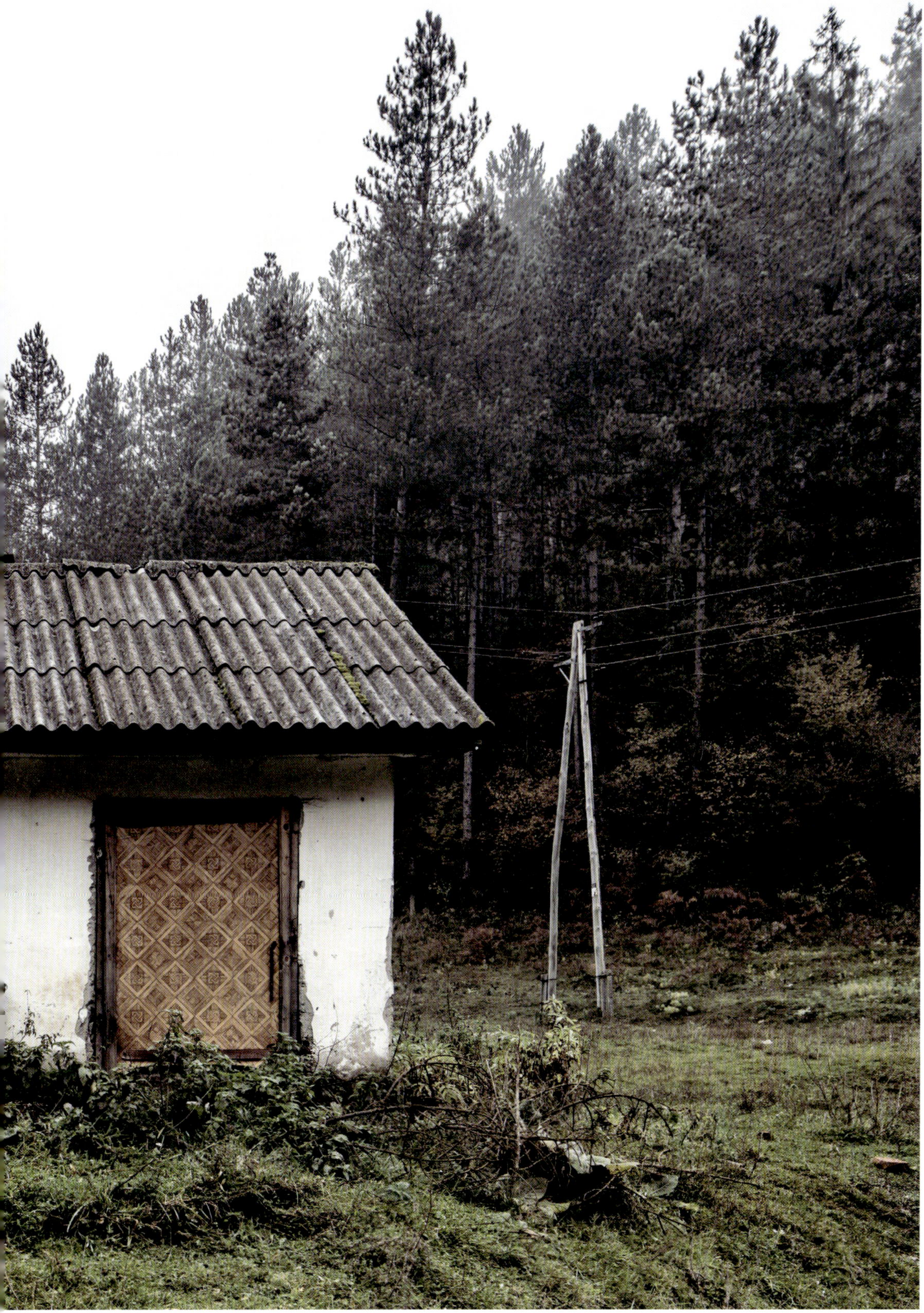

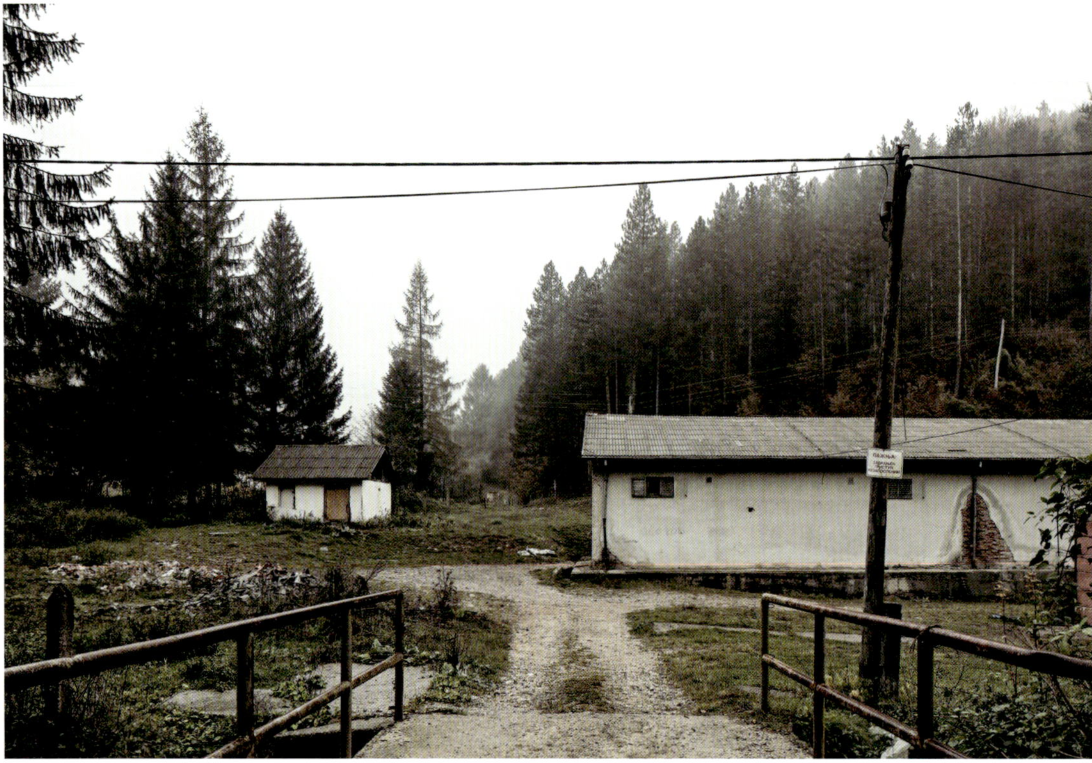
ПАЖЊА!

Previous spread and left
Vlasenica
Sušica Detention Camp

The Sušica camp was established on 31 May 1992 by order of the commander of Brigade Bircanska, Army of the Republic of Srpska (VRS) and operated until October 1992. During this time, 8,000 Muslim civilians passed through the camp, of which around 3,000 people left the camp dead. Detainees of both sexes and all ages passed through the Sušica camp. It was later converted into a prison and functioned as such until the end of the war. From early June to late September 1992, female prisoners in the Sušica camp were subjected to sexual assaults by camp guards, special forces, local soldiers, and other men. Women were abused in different places: in the guard house, in the houses around the camp, in the Panorama Hotel, in a military headquarters and in places where they were taken for forced labour. On the one hand, Dragan Nikolic personally selected female prisoners to be raped. He repeatedly gave other men access to female inmates. He allowed women prisoners, including girls and older women, to be subjected to degrading sexual threats and assaults in the presence of others and encouraged these forms of war crimes. In the first half of June 1992 at around 11pm, Goran Viškovic took Witness 8 from the Sušica camp. He took her to a guardhouse next to the hangar where several of the camp's guards were standing. He said, 'Shall we do it as we know it?' He then handcuffed her, first hitting her hand and foot, and after one of the Serbian soldiers pushed her onto the iron bed and held her hands, he stripped her of her clothes, raped her, and then drove a police baton into her genitals.' Testimony of an elderly witness before the war crimes tribunal in The Hague: 'We women were terribly ashamed,' reported the only witness, a sixty-three-year-old woman. She appeared calm and collected until she described how the Bosnian Serbs selected a group of around twenty-five young women. 'Some were still children, just fourteen years old. There was also a pregnant woman and a mother who was separated from her three-year-old child. It was so awful. We will show the Muslims what our seed is!' she said the soldiers shouted.[8]

44°10'21.8"N 18°56'41.7"E

Overleaf
Vlasenica - Sušica
Private House

Private house right next to the buildings of the prison camp in Sušica. Neighbours pointed to the house and said that women from the camp were also being raped here.[9]

44°10'21"N 18°56'40.0"E

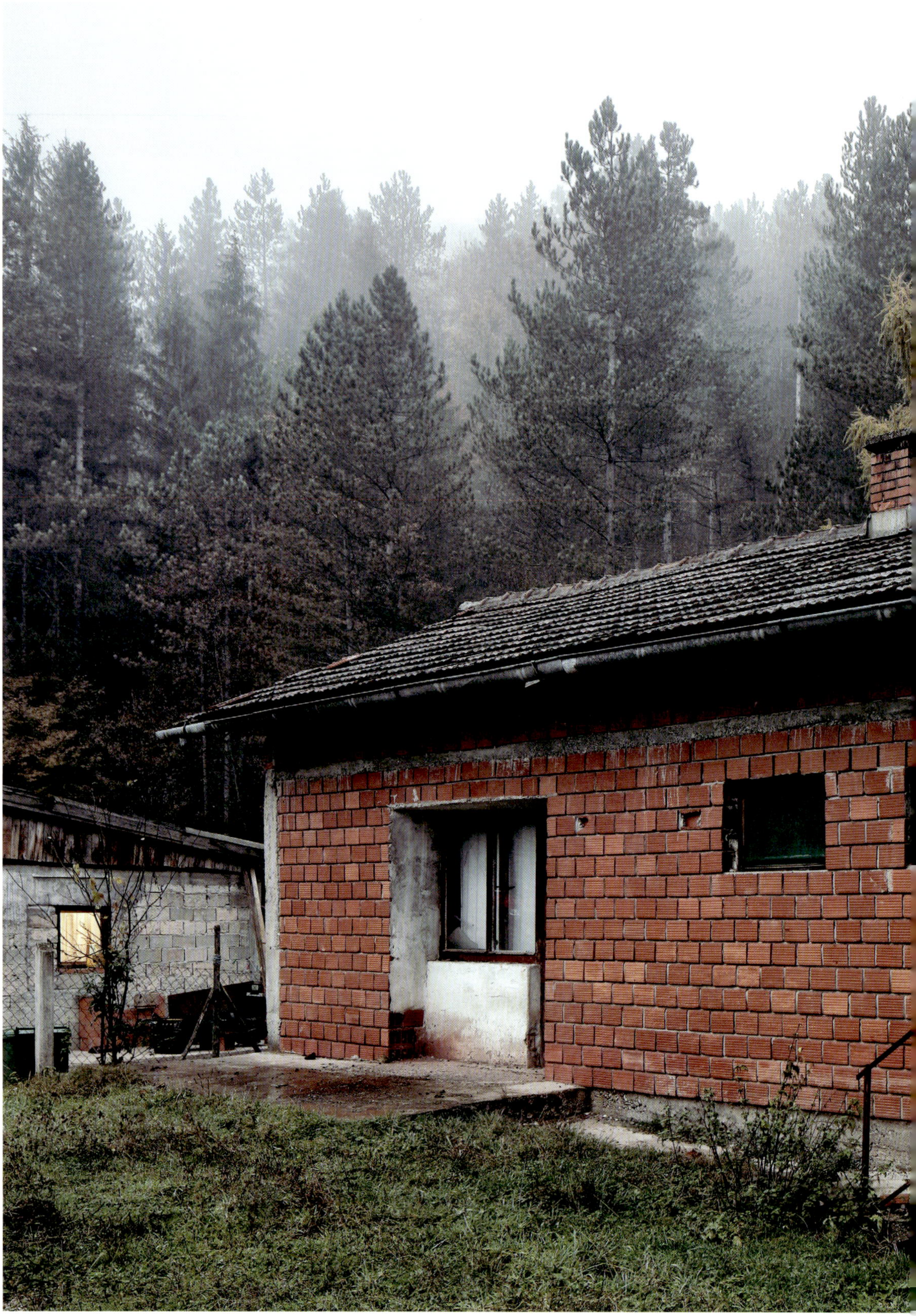

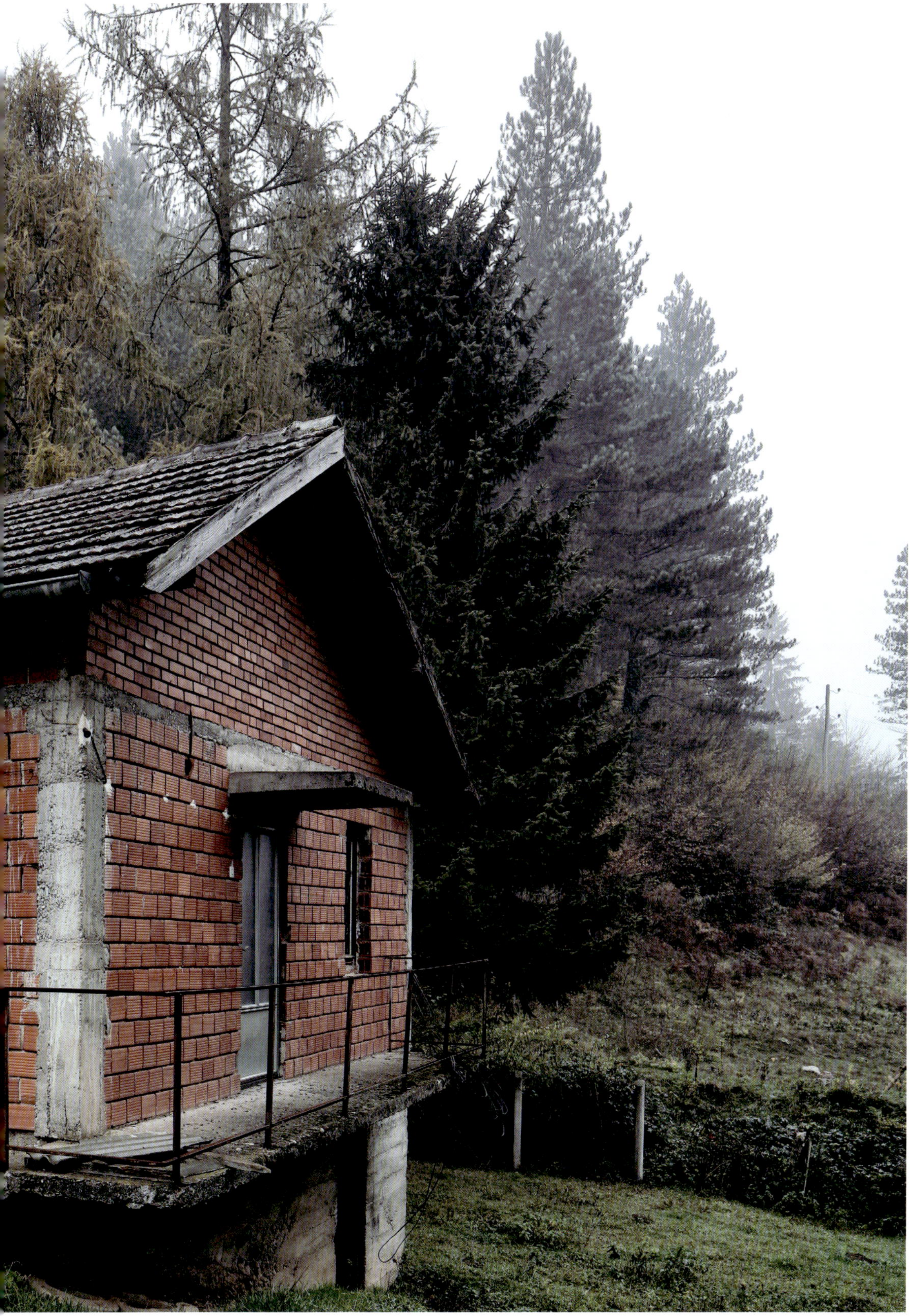

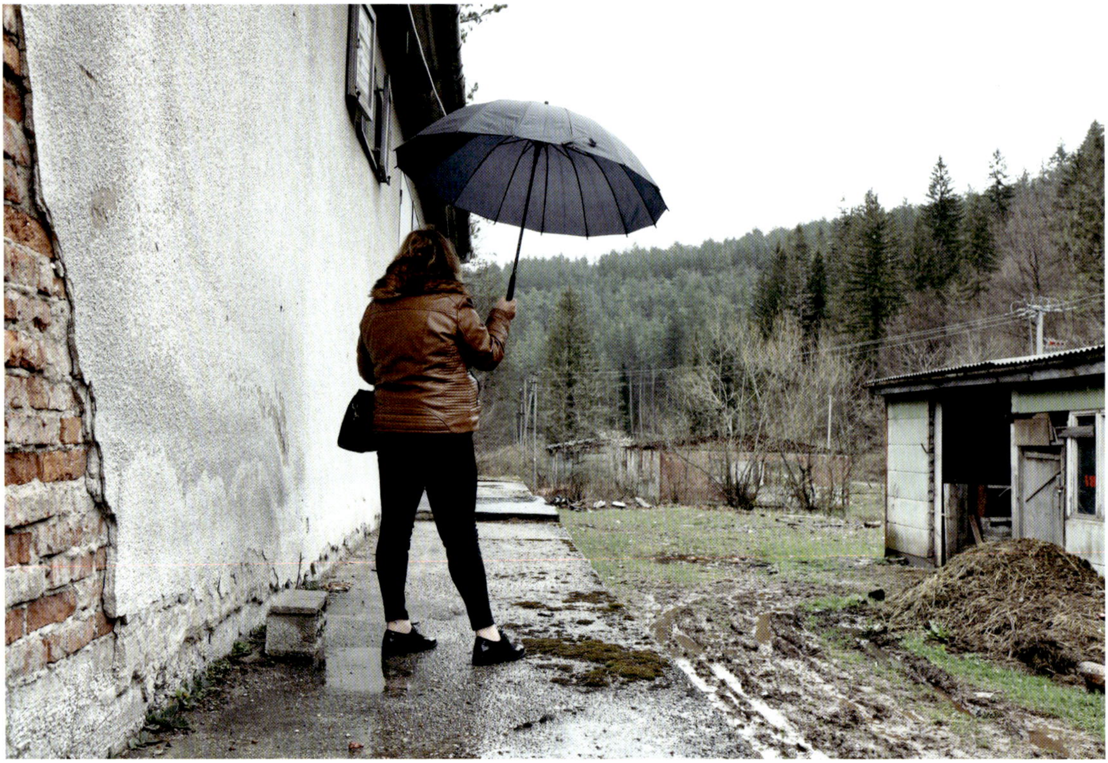

MUŠKA FROM TUZLA

'At the end of April 1992, my Serb neighbours stormed the village of Pijuci and murdered fifty of us Muslims. Then it started, they drove through the streets by car and said through the megaphone: 'Surrender! You are surrounded.' And so we really surrendered.

Then they captured us and drove us towards the Sušica camp.

In the process I saw my aunt Ajša's son, Hus, and two grandchildren being murdered. When I arrived in front of the camp, I saw Nail Sajdzija, one of the most famous men in the bazaar, who was also murdered. He is engraved in my memory, his eyes were red and his stomach was bloated. He stayed in my memory the most, often I even dreamt of him.

As evening fell, a Chetnik walked through the camp carrying a machine gun on his left shoulder with a large bayonet on it. I was with my mother, who had died in the meantime, and my sister Jules.

Shortly afterwards, an unknown Chetnik pointed his finger at me just like that. I went outside without knowing what they wanted from me. When I was in front of the camp, a car was parked there to take me to be raped. Dragan 'Jenki' asked these Chetniks what they wanted from me. 'Leave them to me.'

They returned to the camp and took other girls with them, younger—twelve to fifteen years old. They took the young girls out, put them in a white car and drove them towards Muslim houses to rape them.

Afterwards three Chetniks from the porter's lodge approached me and Dragan 'Jenki' asked one of them to 'lead me.' They took me on the pavement behind the camp and there he was, the man who raped me...first he started kissing me on the neck. He was wearing a Chetnik suit. He had these gloves, like Fikra said, his fingers were only half visible, and he had a machine gun with a bayonet on his shoulder. So...he started kissing me on the neck, I resisted, then he hit me hard once, hit me another time, thank God I fainted, and came to my senses later. I was strong, by the way... He just pulled me to him and took off my trousers and raped me there. And when I was forced to cry a lot, he said to me, 'If you tell anyone, if you shout around the camp what I have done to you, I will slaughter you immediately in the same minute.' I entered the camp, he brought me back. I cried, the women just shrugged their shoulders, and thought, 'what did they do to her, she cried so much.' The women whispered, they are not allowed to speak... The night he raped me, of course I was awake all night, you're on the concrete, you don't sleep and you can't sleep. I cried the whole night.

The next day, when morning came, they drove us out again. I saw my colleagues there who had worked with me. They were all dressed in Chetnik suits. So I asked my neighbour Nedeljko Golijan, 'Nedeljko, who is that man there?' The one standing opposite me was my rapist. And I asked Nedeljko who that man was. It was Ljuban from Piskavica. I was not allowed to ask his surname, but I found out that I had been raped by a certain Ljuban from Piskavica.

That's how it ended, I was in the camp for seven days and seven nights. Every night they took girls from twelve to fifteen years old. Women and girls, and in the morning some returned, some did not return for three days.

Many people were slaughtered outside the camp, many of those who were beat were also shot. You hear men being taken out of the camp in the evening, if no man returned to the camp in the morning, it meant they had killed them.

In front of the camp there is a reception where they get drunk, Dragan 'Jenki' Nikolic was in the porter's lodge. They roasted lambs on a spit, turned around, got drunk, made a massacre, when we went there I spoke to a work colleague: 'Biba died, she died, unfortunately she is no longer with us.' Her two sons were slaughtered in front of her—Enes and Beka and then Biba was forced to wash Dragan Nikolic's feet and drink this water, they made coffee for her from it and so...

I suffered in the camp for seven days. They only brought us a slice of bread once, you can see the sky through it, and a cup of tea. After seven days the bus arrived, thank Allah, and I was lucky enough to be exchanged in the first group. We got on the buses and went to Luka towards Kladanj. In Luka we were thrown off the buses.

From there we went through the forest because barricades were erected on the road. The barricades were erected on the road, the trees were uprooted, it was not possible to walk on the road. We walk through the forest, they shoot at us, someone falls dead, someone fights, we continue, no one has time to turn around.

And so I moved to Kladanj, we came to the school, we were taken to the school with parquet floors, there were no mattresses. They gave us some horse blankets and so on. From there I went first with Irfanka Pašicka to Tuzla to the health centre to see Melika Kreytmeier, the doctor. I had to be examined by Melika the gynaecologist because I was afraid of being pregnant and what did I know... And that's how my story ended. I still carry trauma today...I can't be cured unfortunately. That, in a nutshell, is my story.

We are survivors, I would never want it to happen to anyone again, and it should be heard, talked about, written about and passed on to the younger generation so that it doesn't happen to anyone again.'

Opposite
Osmaci
Caparde

44°23'49.9"N 18°58'12.2"E

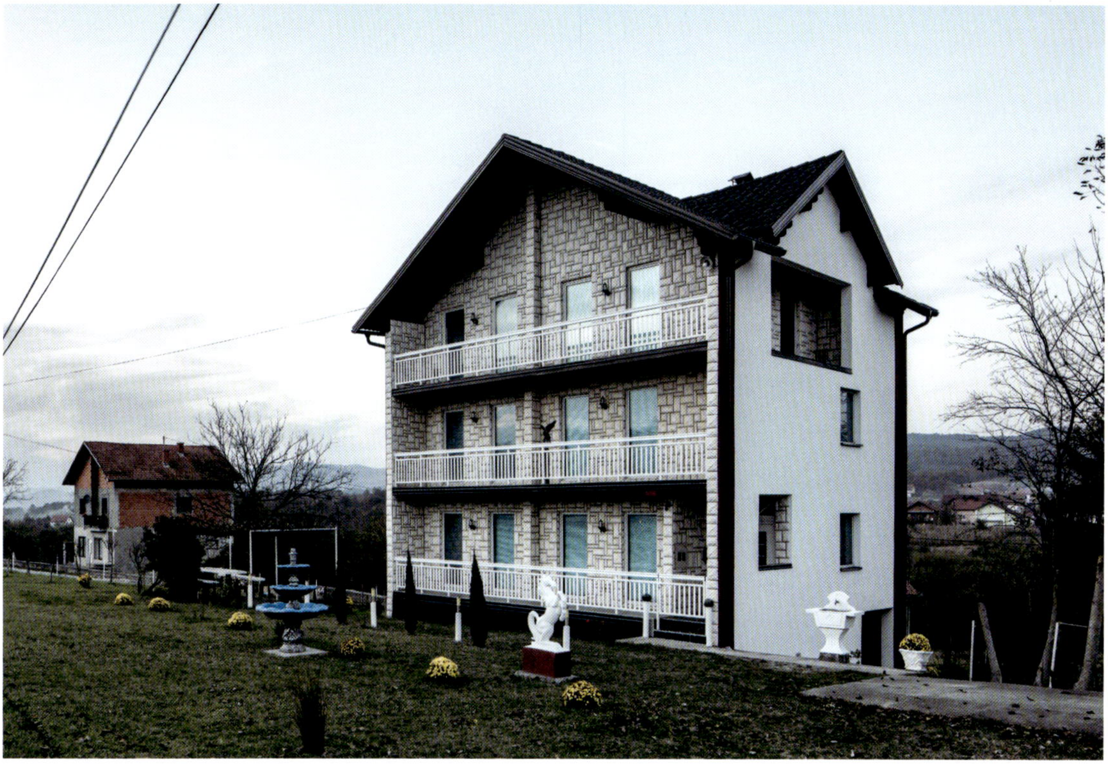

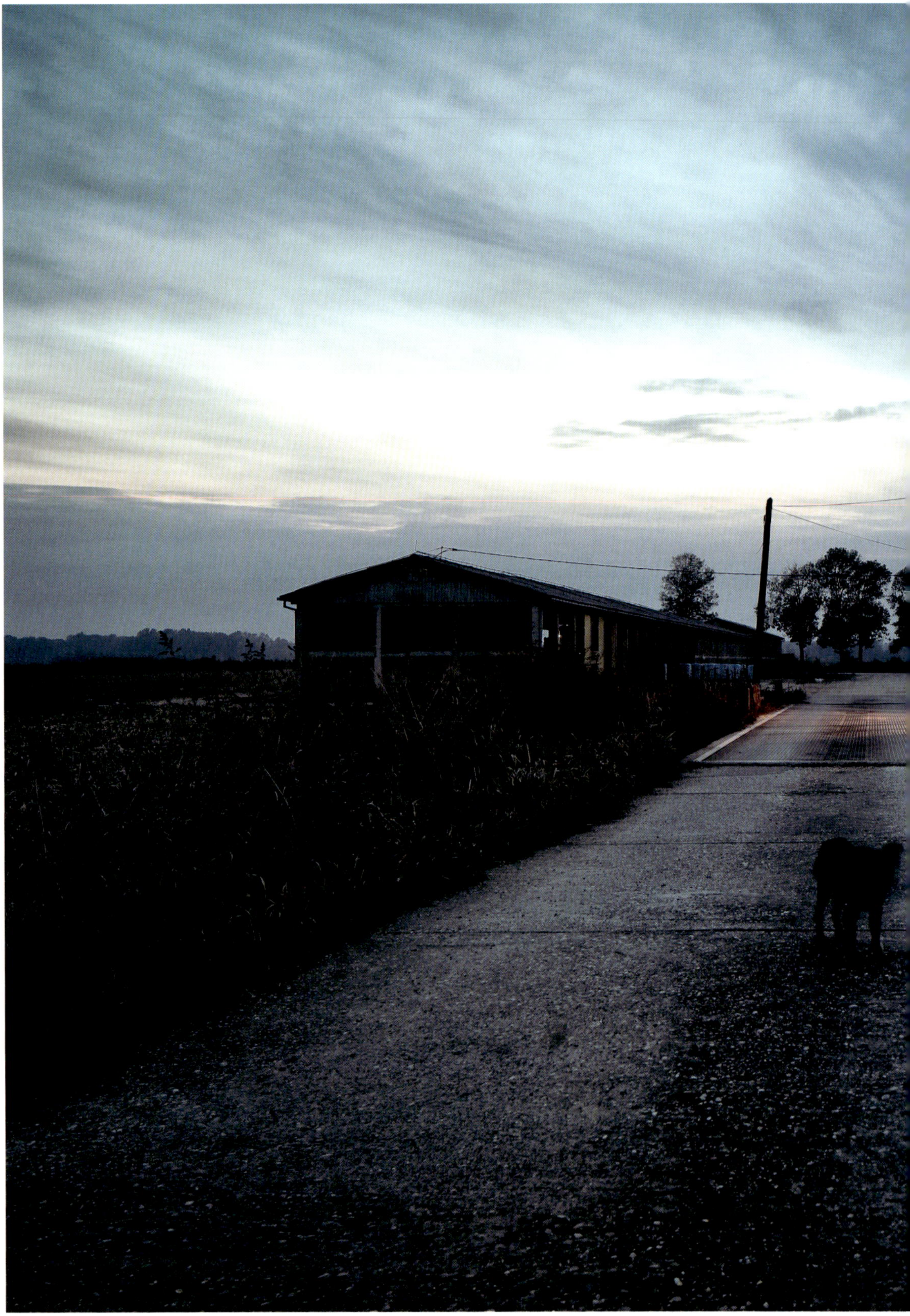

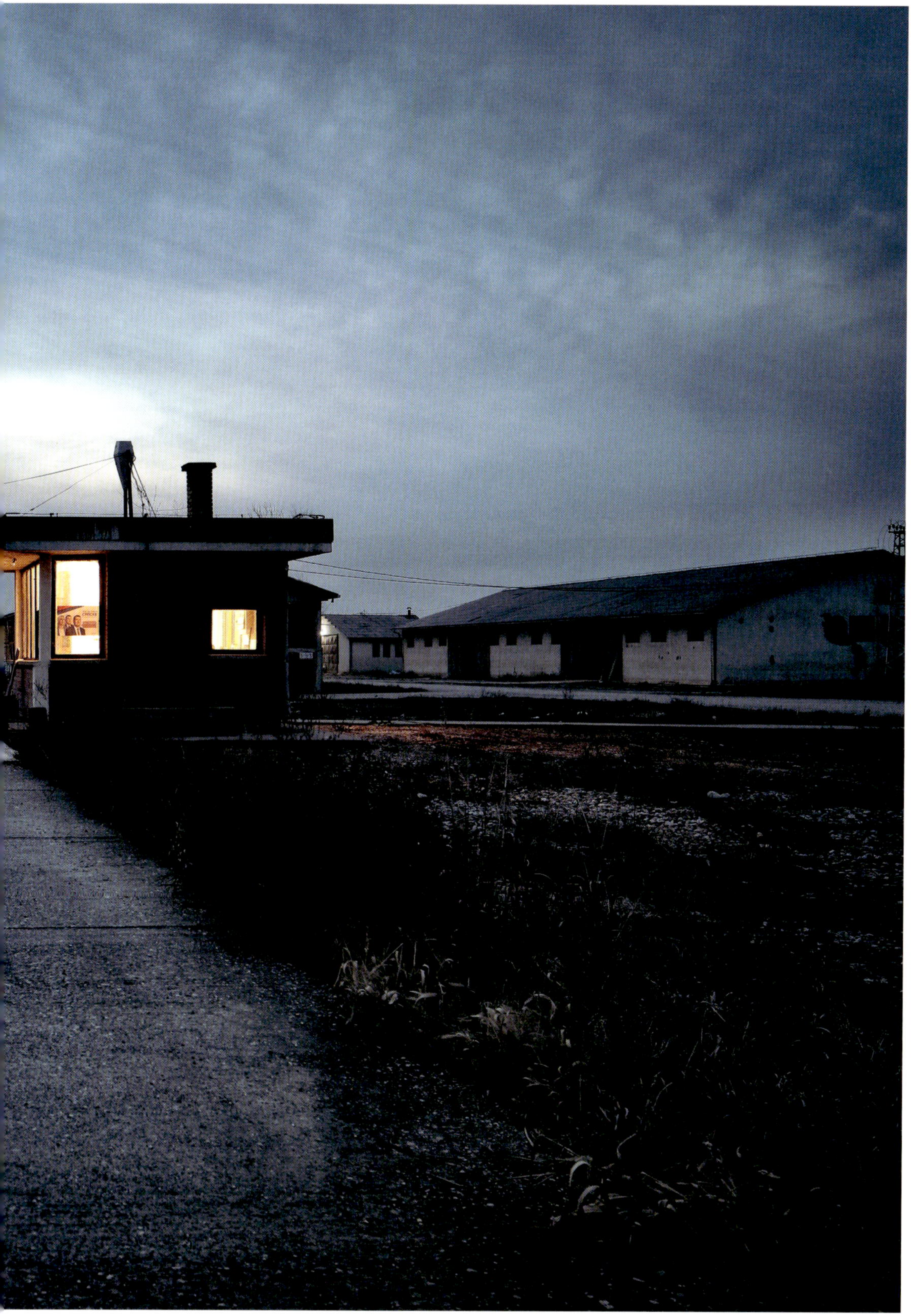

Previous spread
Bijeljina
Agricultural Property 'Semberija' (detention camp during the war)

The Batkovic camp was established by the Yugoslav People's Army (JNA) on 1 April 1992 and closed at the end of January 1996. It was one of the largest camps in Bosnia and Herzegovina. More than 4,000 prisoners from all over the country were held at the premises of the agricultural cooperative in the village of Batković twelve kilometres from Bijeljina. Men, women and children were interned. The conditions in the camp were extremely difficult. Hygienic and medical care as well as food and drink were completely inadequate. Visits were not allowed. The camp was registered by the International Red Cross, but this did not improve living conditions. In addition to severe psychophysical torture and forced labour, women and girls were raped on a daily basis. Women were forced to do agricultural work as slaves on the estates of Serbian peasants. NN from Cerska, a Bosniak, reports that she was deported to Batkovic from another camp after two months of imprisonment. In her statement she describes her experience: 'They took me into the room where there were about 100 girls between the ages of thirteen and twenty-five. Along with all these girls, I survived all sorts of humiliations there...' The Serbs took them to various farms for at least nine hours a day to do heavy farm work, often forcing them to strip off all their clothes and continue digging naked. From the testimony of a Bosniak from the Batkovic camp, one can only guess what situation the women were exposed to. 'Girls and young women were taken almost every night. About every third or fourth night they came to pick me up. They took us to a separate, empty room. There were always a few people, mostly new ones, so I couldn't remember everyone. They were Chetniks from Serbia and from Zvornik and Bijeljina. The worst were Ilija Prodanovic, Jovan Lazic and Ratko Simic. I remembered them because all the women and girls remembered them for their bloodthirsty cruelty and hatred towards us Bosniaks. Every time I experienced it, it was like going to the hanging. The rapes continued throughout my imprisonment in the Batkovici camp.'[10]

44°51'13.0"N 19°11'47.0"E

Opposite
Tuzla
County Prison (military remand centre during the war)

In the former Yugoslavia, this prison in Tuzla was a civil prison, which also functioned in this capacity during the war. Located in the middle of the city, it was under the control of the RBiH Army's military police.[11] According to the Interior Ministry of the Republic of Srpska, 197 Serbs of different sexes and ages were imprisoned in this facility.[12]

A man from SV from near Vareš was thirty-six years old when he was raped in captivity by members of the RBiH army. The girl, SR, from Vlasenica was repeatedly raped not only by guards in the military and district prisons, but also by Bosnian prisoners. SR was registered by the International Committee of the Red Cross. Witness SR testified to the RS investigating authorities: 'At the time I was in prison, the prison warden was a certain Fikret. There were other women in prison with me who were also abused. I know this because we mentioned it to each other. They took us around midnight at night, ostensibly for an informative talk, and held us for about thirty minutes, long enough to abuse us, mostly under threat of killing us.

They threatened to kill us even if we told anyone about the beating and abuse. I remember that among the women who were raped was a mother with a sixteen-year-old daughter. One evening they took her daughter away first, and the mother started to cry for her, and a little later the guards came to pick up the mother and take her away. Both were abused that night.' The prison authorities arranged abortions for women who became pregnant after being raped. As a result, some of the women lost the opportunity to become pregnant again.[13]

44°32'07.4"N, 18°40'56.8"E

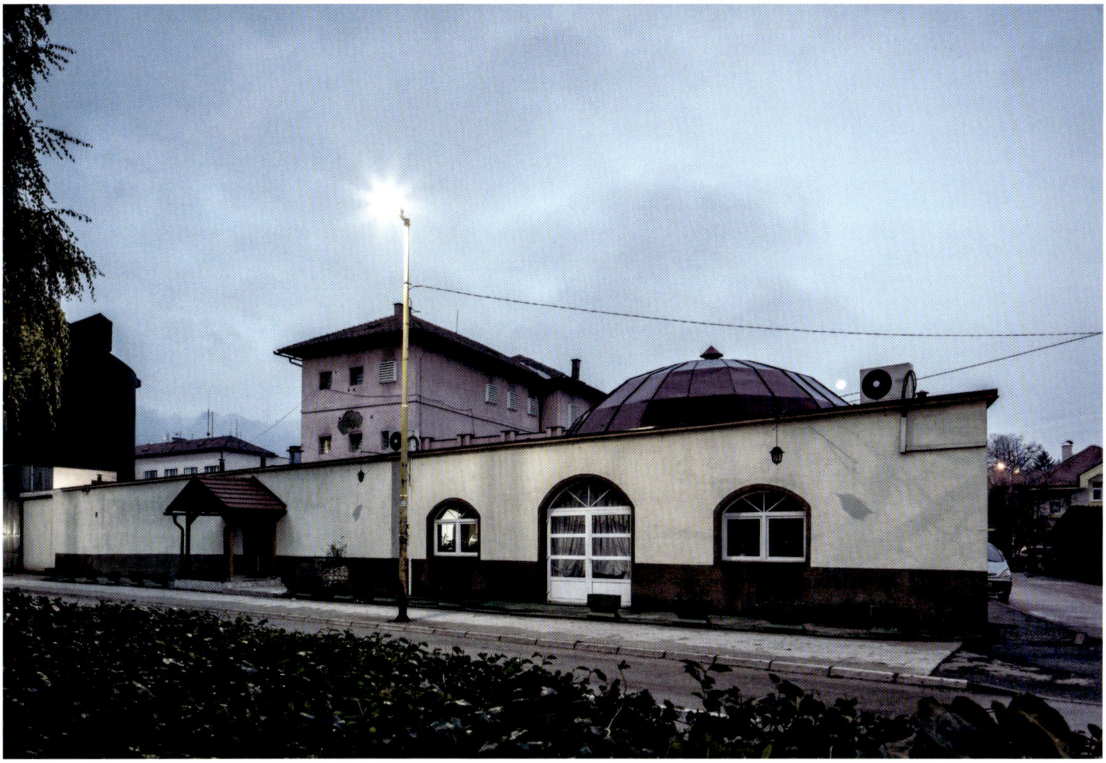

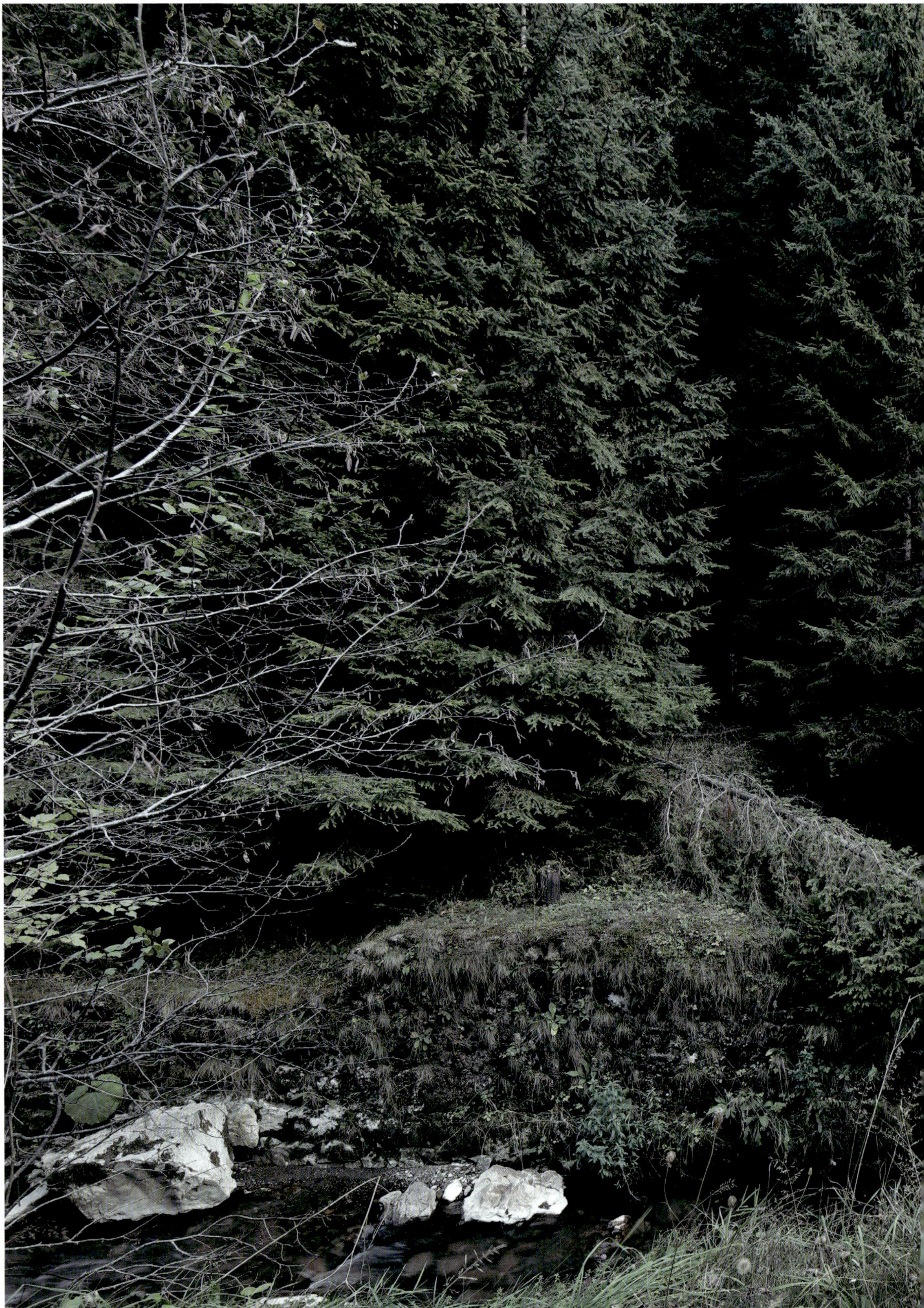

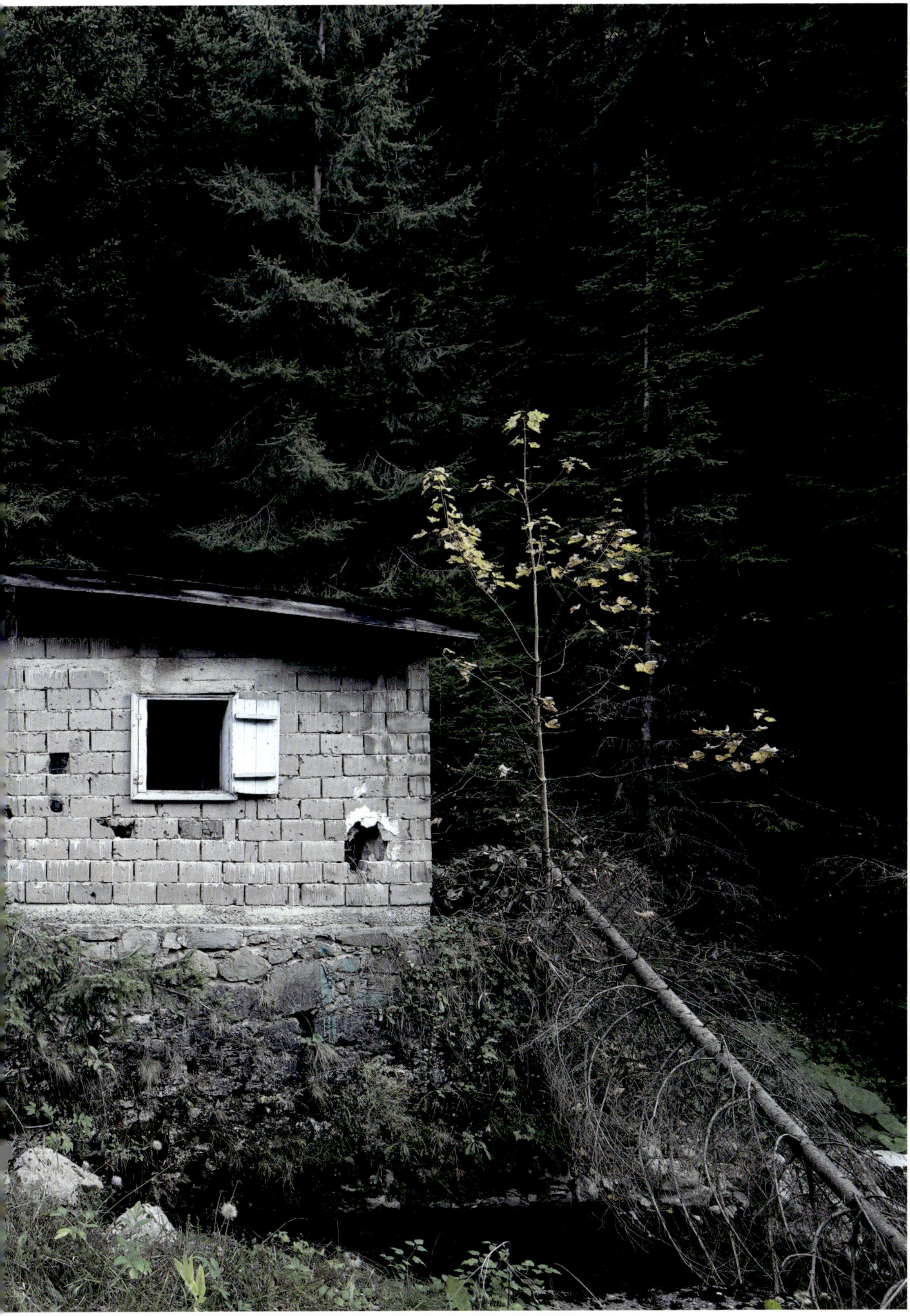

Previous spread
Vareš
Stone House Below the Main Road

In November 1993, Croatian civilians fled Vareš as federal cooperation broke up and war between Bosnian Croat units and Bosniak units began The Second and Third Bosnian Army Corps took over the town of Vareš. Most Croatians had left the city within twenty-four hours, about 750 of them stayed on site. An unprecedented raid by Bosnian Army units began. Many were transported to Breza, Zenica and Tuzla. General chaos reigned. Very few police officers remained in Vareš. They could not keep order in the city and prevent the looting. The witness Ž[14] recalled: 'In that riot, Bosnian Army soldiers discovered that my mother and I had stayed and that we were Croats. We were pressured for fifteen days mainly because the soldiers were looking for food. We gave what we had. Then they tried to evict us from the house so the army could move in. I got a decision about the obligation to work as an engineer and started to work. At around 5pm on 25 November 1993, four soldiers came to our door as police officers. Two of them stayed with my mother and abused her. They stripped her down to the waist and demanded money. They put a gun and a knife on her neck. The other two took me to a stone hut 300 meters from the house and raped me. They let me go because a police car and an UNPROFOR car were passing on the high main road, so they got scared and let me go but threatened not to tell anyone what happened to me. They beat me, but I informed the police anyway. They came to the house, rescued my mother and took me to the hospital for an examination. The perpetrators were caught, arrested and confronted. They were tried and sentenced directly in the war. The perpetrators were Second Corps soldiers from Tuzla, members of the BiH army. I know two of them were serving their sentences.'

44°10'30.0"N 18°20'12.0"E

Opposite
Đulići
Shed on the road next to the mosque in Đulići

44°27'17.2"N 19°04'00.1"E

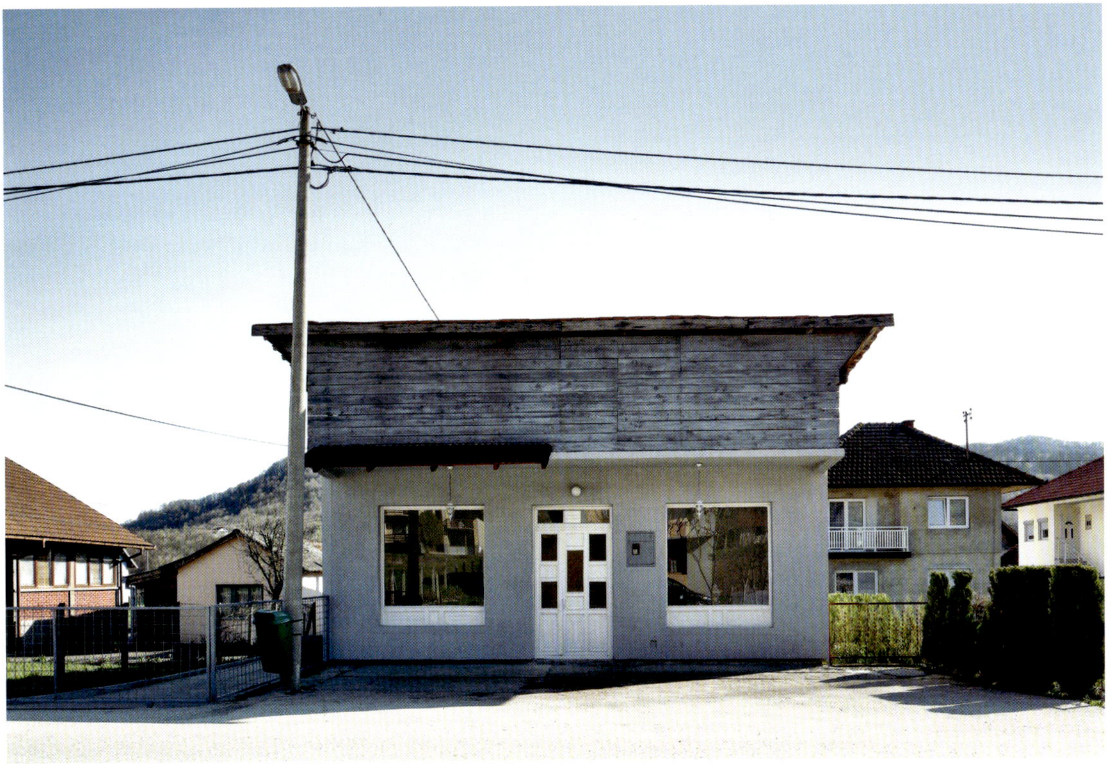

Overleaf
Đulići
Mosque

The mosque in Đulici was used as a warehouse from 15 June 1992 to 12 July 1992. According to testimonies of women concerned, there were rapes in this mosque as well as in a neighbouring shed. The Imam was not sure how many people were being held in the mosque, but it was mostly women, elderly men and children who were being held, tortured, abused and raped here. The mosque—he reported in April 2021—was destroyed. 'One of those affected said that they took women from the mosque to the neighbouring houses, where they were raped...and this happened every night.'

On 7 July 1992, a client of the women's organisation, Snaga Žene was raped in the mosque in full view of everyone. She reported that it was the worst thing she had experienced. She became pregnant after the rape, but was able to have an abortion after coming to Tuzla.[15]

44°27'17.2"N 19°04'00.1"E

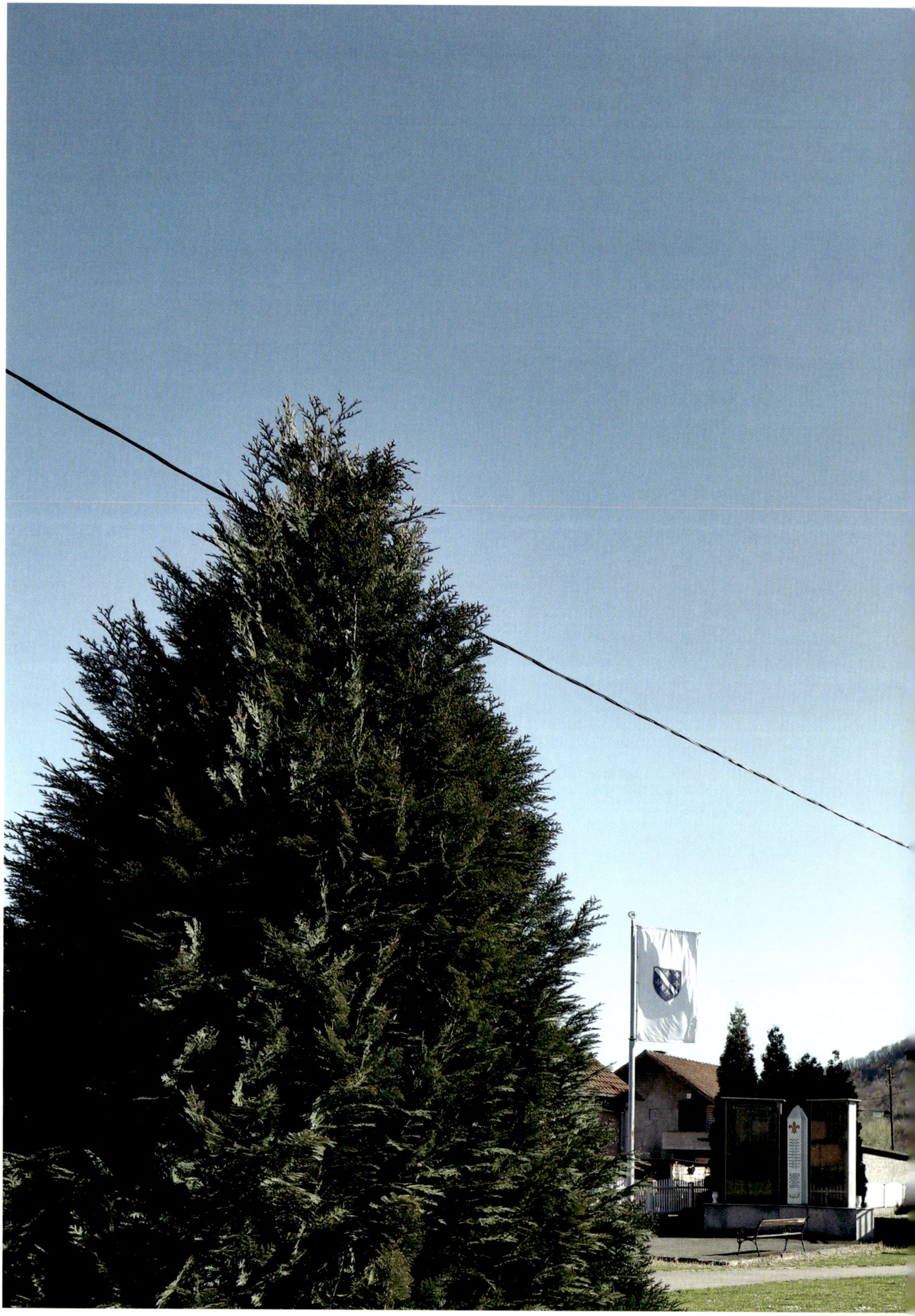

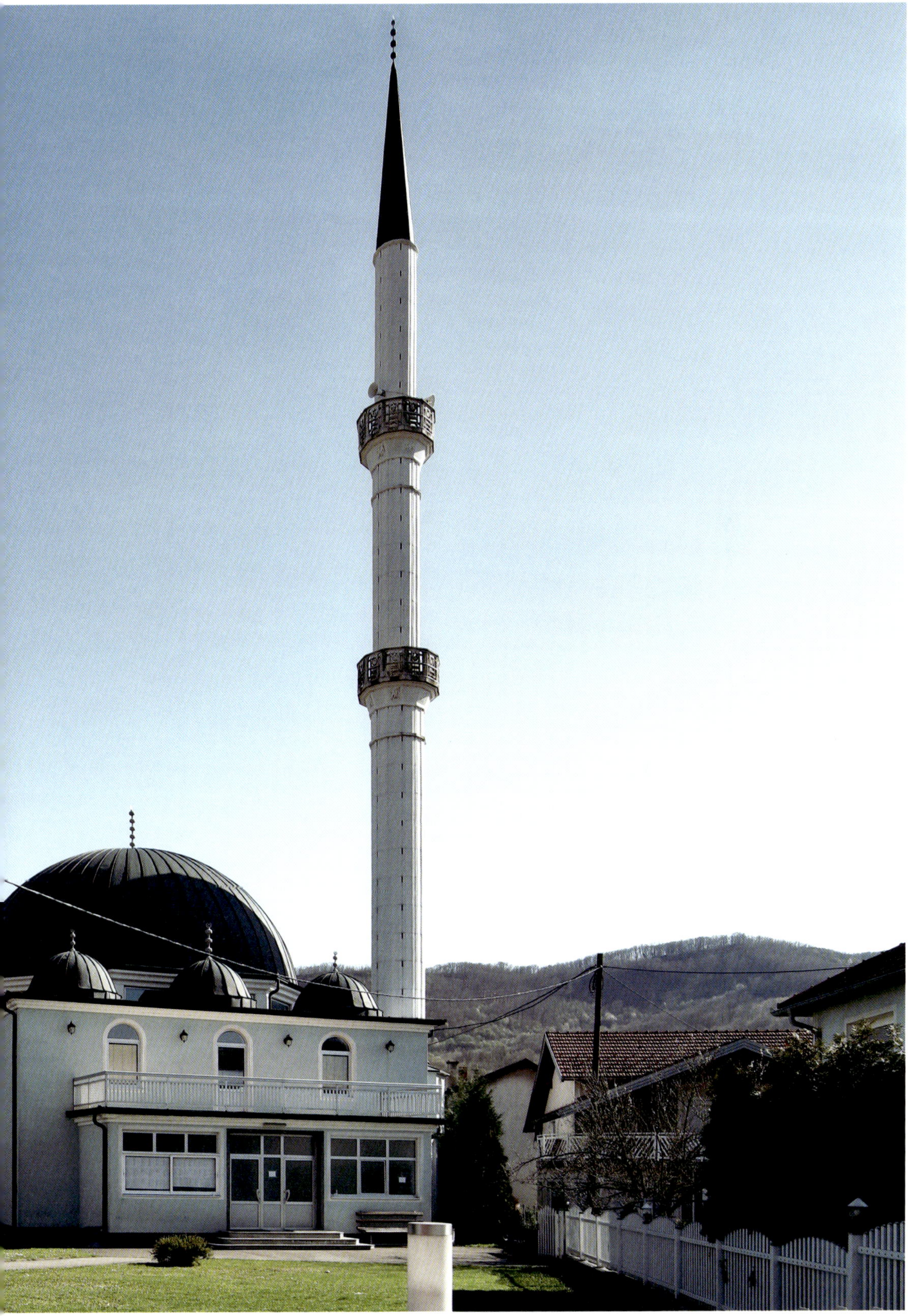

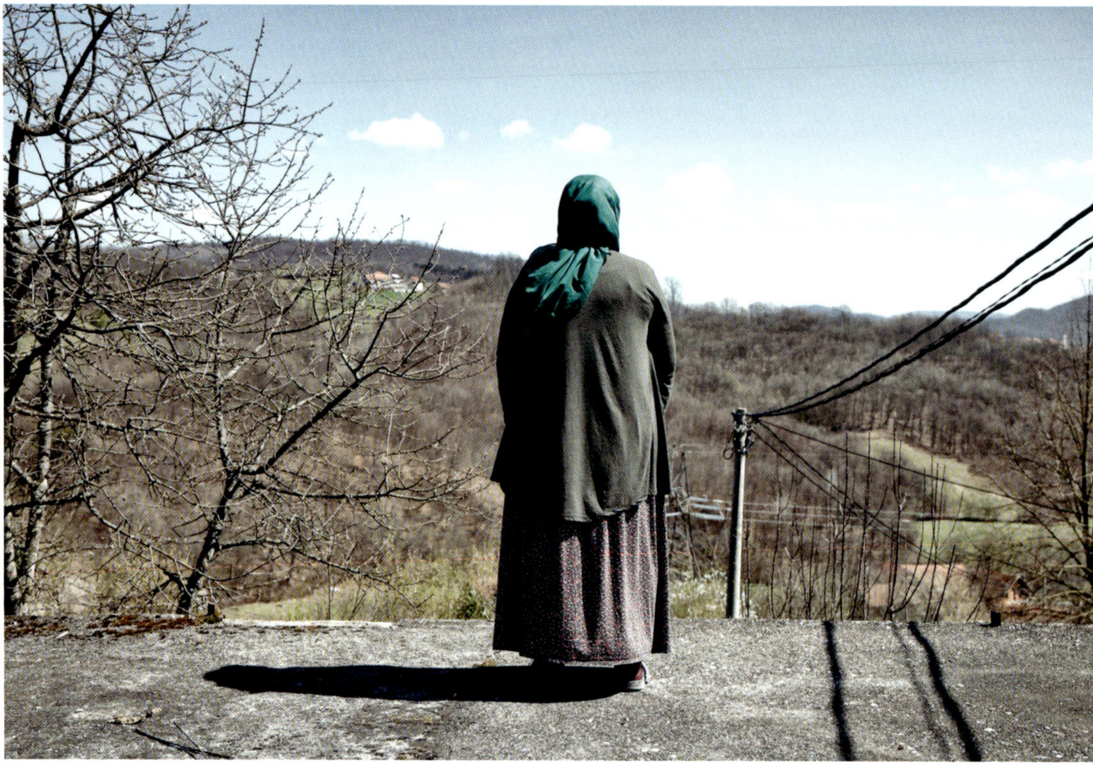

ŠERIFA FROM TUZLA

'At the end of April 1992, my village Liplje, Zvornik municipality, was occupied by the Serbian Army. They came in the morning and called over a megaphone for the surrender of men fit for military service. Those who were militarily able fled and did not return home. We women and children were enslaved and locked up in my house and other houses in the village. And then all hell broke loose. Every day Serbian soldiers came and took girls and women out and raped them. The women came back dishevelled and crying, some unconscious.

In the middle of May 1992, the soldiers ordered us to leave with them and took us to another house in Liplje. There we met ten to fifteen Serbian soldiers we did not know. They took our jewellery and money and started beating me. They set fire to a plastic bucket and dripped melted plastic on my hands. My mother-in-law watched, begging them not to touch me because we had already given them everything. The men stripped us naked and herded us out for all to see. They took me to SM's house where I was raped by several Chetniks. On my naked body they wrote 'Serbian whore' in blue ink.

I was raped so many times that day that I lost consciousness. After the rapes, they poured cold water on me until I regained consciousness, and so they took me back to my house. In the same way, they brought other women back to the house. The next day, the same men came again and took me to the same house as the day before. In this house I found an elderly man, KS, who was seventy-six years old. All his clothes were torn off him, he was beaten, everything was bloody. The man who was beaten in this way was forced to rape me by Brzi and Tihi, two men from a Serbian special unit. KS cannot do that, he says I could be his granddaughter. Then Brzi orders them to cut off the old man's ear in front of me. They started beating me and continued beating KS. They cut off his nose and other parts of his body with a knife. KS died on the spot.

We survived this hell every day. We never knew when they would come or what to expect. They raped us, beat us, tortured us, forced us to do all their other work, sewing uniforms, washing, etc. They put an inscription on my house: 'Great Serbia', and they told me that it is no longer my house.

On 2 June 1992, units of the Bosnian Army came to our village of Liplje and we were liberated.'

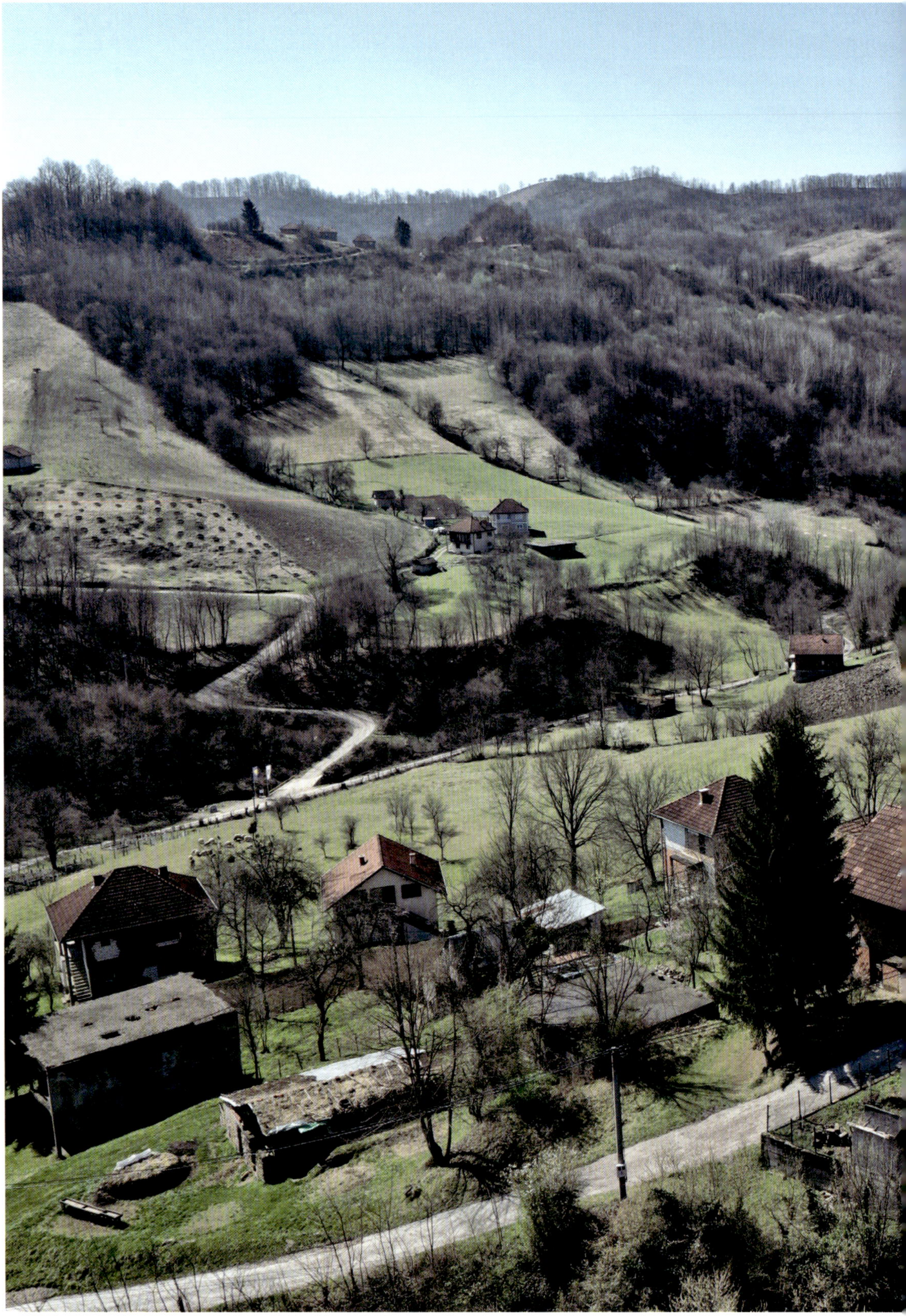

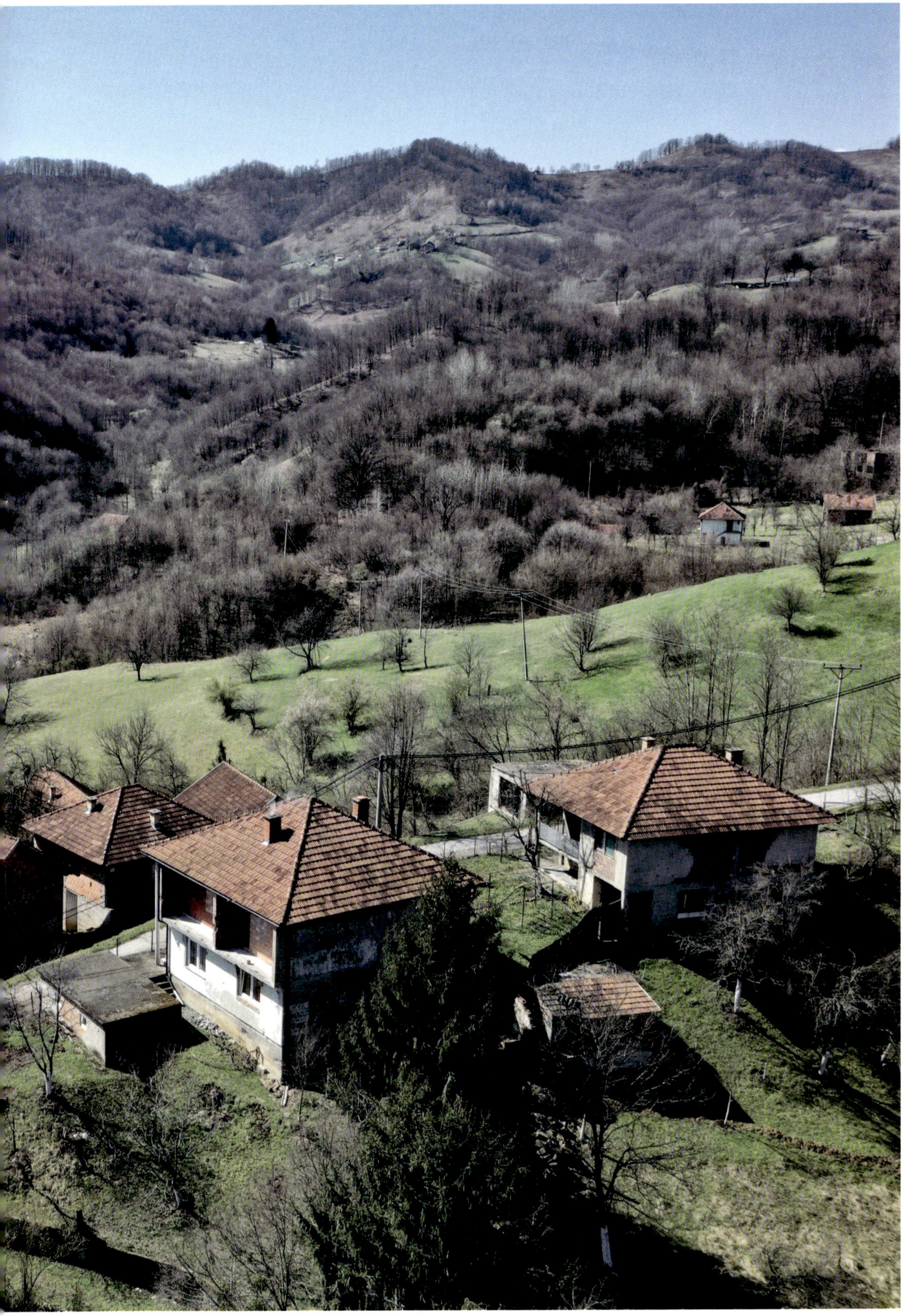

Previous spread
Zvornik - Liplje
Village

The Liplje camp was a concentration camp operated between 25 May 1992 and 2 June 1992 by Serbs in the village Liplje near Zvornik. It was set up for Bosniak men, women and children, in an effort to ethnically cleanse the area of all non-Serb residents.[16]

In Liplje, a school and two private houses nearby were turned into one of the most notorious detention camps in the Zvornik municipality, where, according to testimonies from survivors, around 460 people were imprisoned.[17]

Women, children and whole families were brought to Liplje. Adult men were then separated from women and children. There were boys under the age of thirteen with adult men. They slept on school desks, on floors and in hallways. The men were taken out of the classrooms, beaten, cruelly tortured and many of them were raped. A woman, witness NN, says that her stepfather was raped in front of her and his daughters. It was a regular, frequent and mass occurrence. Chetnik rapists did not differentiate between women, children and men. They raped and sexually abused when and whom they wanted.[18]

'When they captured us, they transferred us to a house in Liplje. We were in that house for four to five days, during that time we were raped and beaten every day. They beat me to unconsciousness. From there they took us to a school in Liplje. Women were placed in another classroom. There I found women from the village of Marcici, which is located near the village of Snagovo. I have to point out that me and the other women were raped and beaten in the classroom...it was literally gang rape. They lined up one by one on us as they pleased.'[19]

Until today, no one has been held accountable for the killings, the torture and rape of men and women in this camp. The Liplje concentration camp was liberated after one week of occupation by Bosnian Army units; it is known for being the only camp with Bosniak victims liberated during the war.[20]

44°21'32"N,19°3'59"E

Opposite
Zvornik - Liplje
Private House

44°21'32"N 19°3'59"E

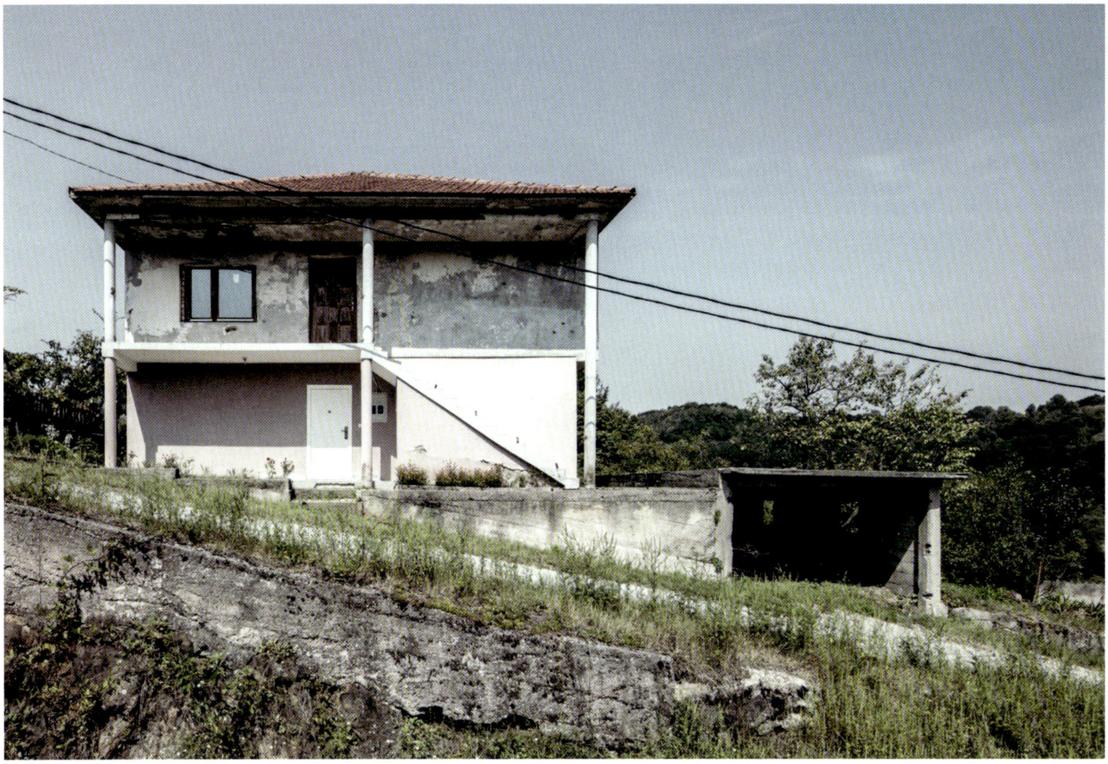

Overleaf
Zvornik - Liplje
School

44°21'32.6"N 19°04'12.0"E

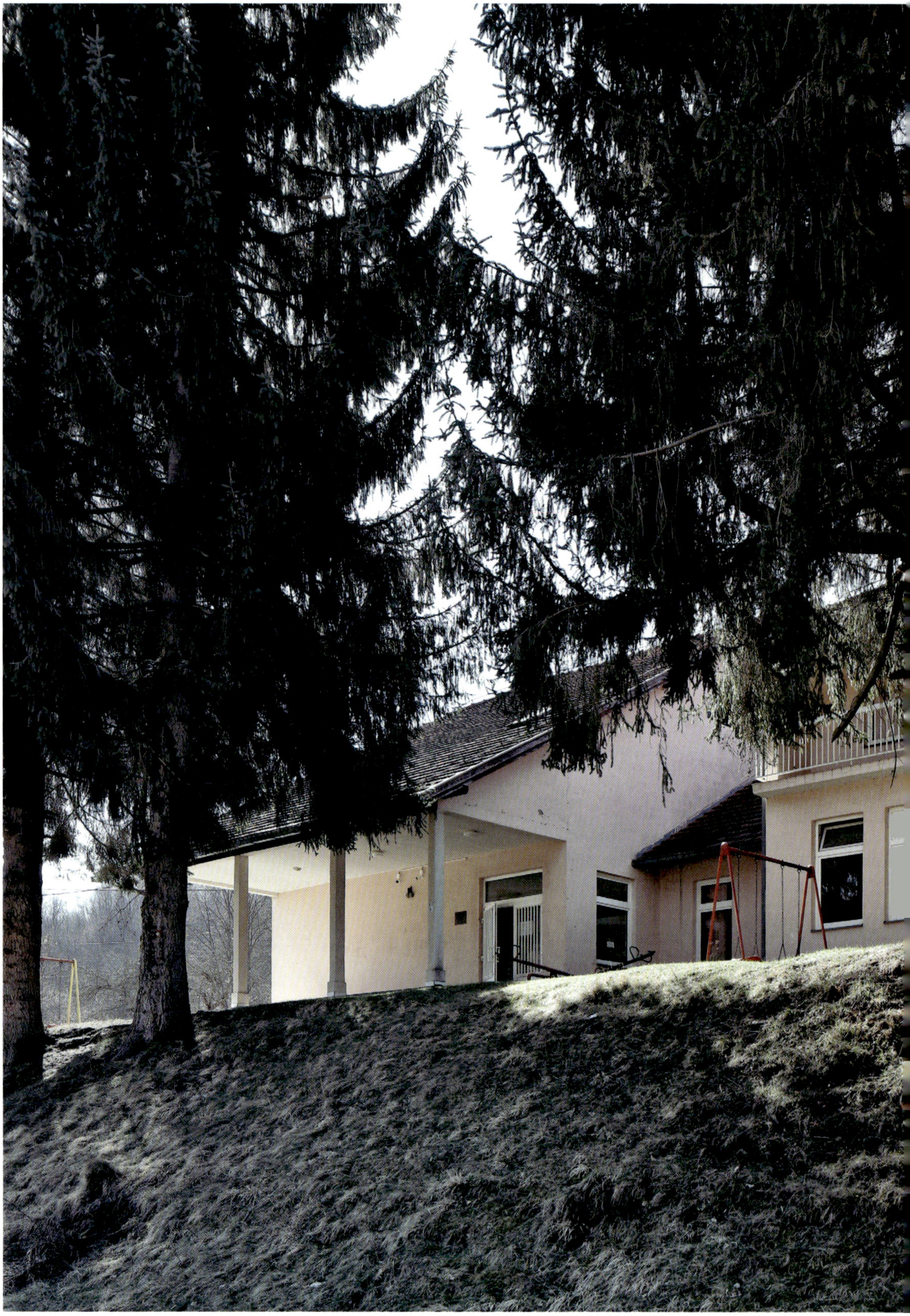

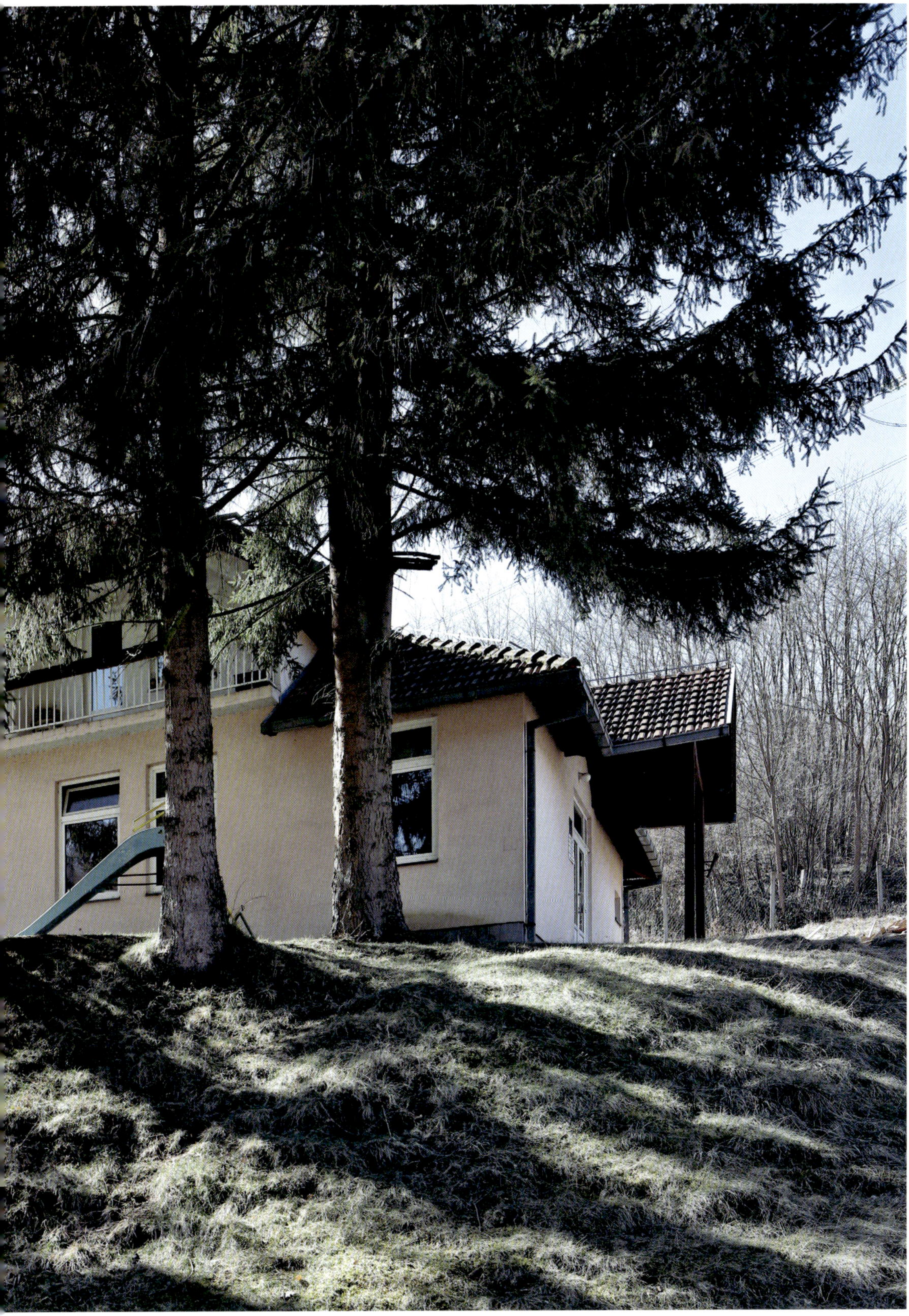

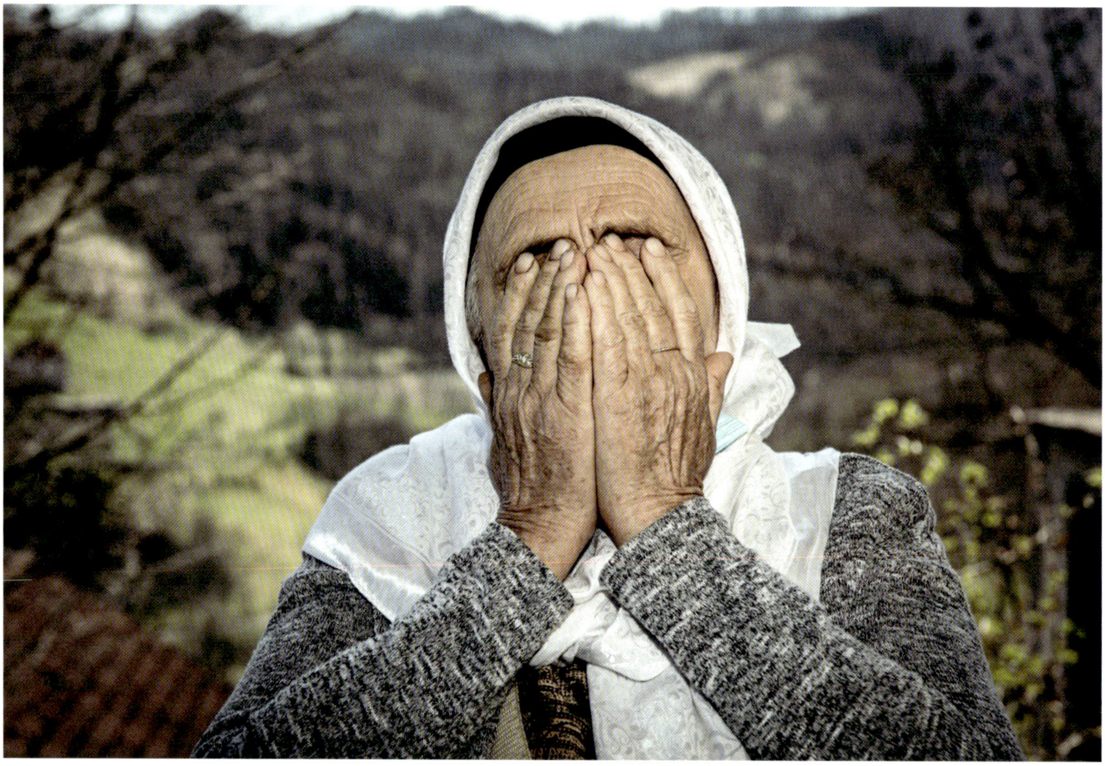

SADETA FROM TUZLA

'Serbian soldiers captured us on 22 May 1992 and then all hell broke loose.

We women and children were enslaved and locked up in the house of SS, my neighbour. This is the house directly below mine. There was a kitchen in my house, we had to cook for the soldiers there. They came every day, took the girls and women and raped them. The women came back dishevelled and crying. My three daughters were with me. The youngest was not touched, but they took the two older ones and raped them.

My oldest daughter managed to escape from the Liplje camp. They started looking for her, but they did not find her. They harassed me, beat me, raped me and demanded that I tell them everything I knew about my daughter's escape. I didn't even know how she had escaped and could tell our Bosnian soldiers what happened to us.

We were liberated on 2 June 1992 when the army came to Liplje.'

Opposite and overleaf
Sarajevo - Kemala Kapetanovica
Shopping Mall

A Muslim resident from Grbavica was forcibly taken from her apartment by Bosnian Serb units to this garage under the Kemala Kapetanovica shopping mall, a shopping centre in Sarajevo. There she was held captive for over two months and repeatedly raped. This happened in a period from May to June 1992.

43°51'01.9"N 18°23'30.4"E

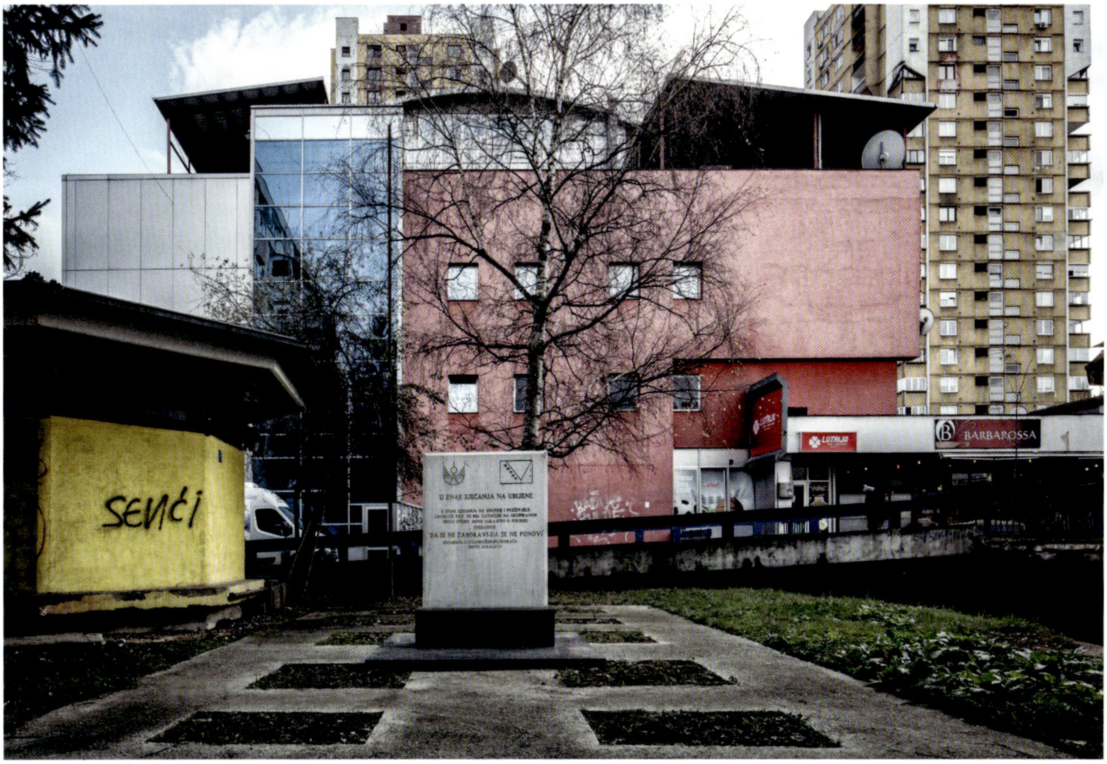

SENĆI
U ZNAK SJEĆANJA NA UBIJENE
DA SE NE ZABORAVI-DA SE NE PONOVI
LUTRIJA
BARBAROSSA

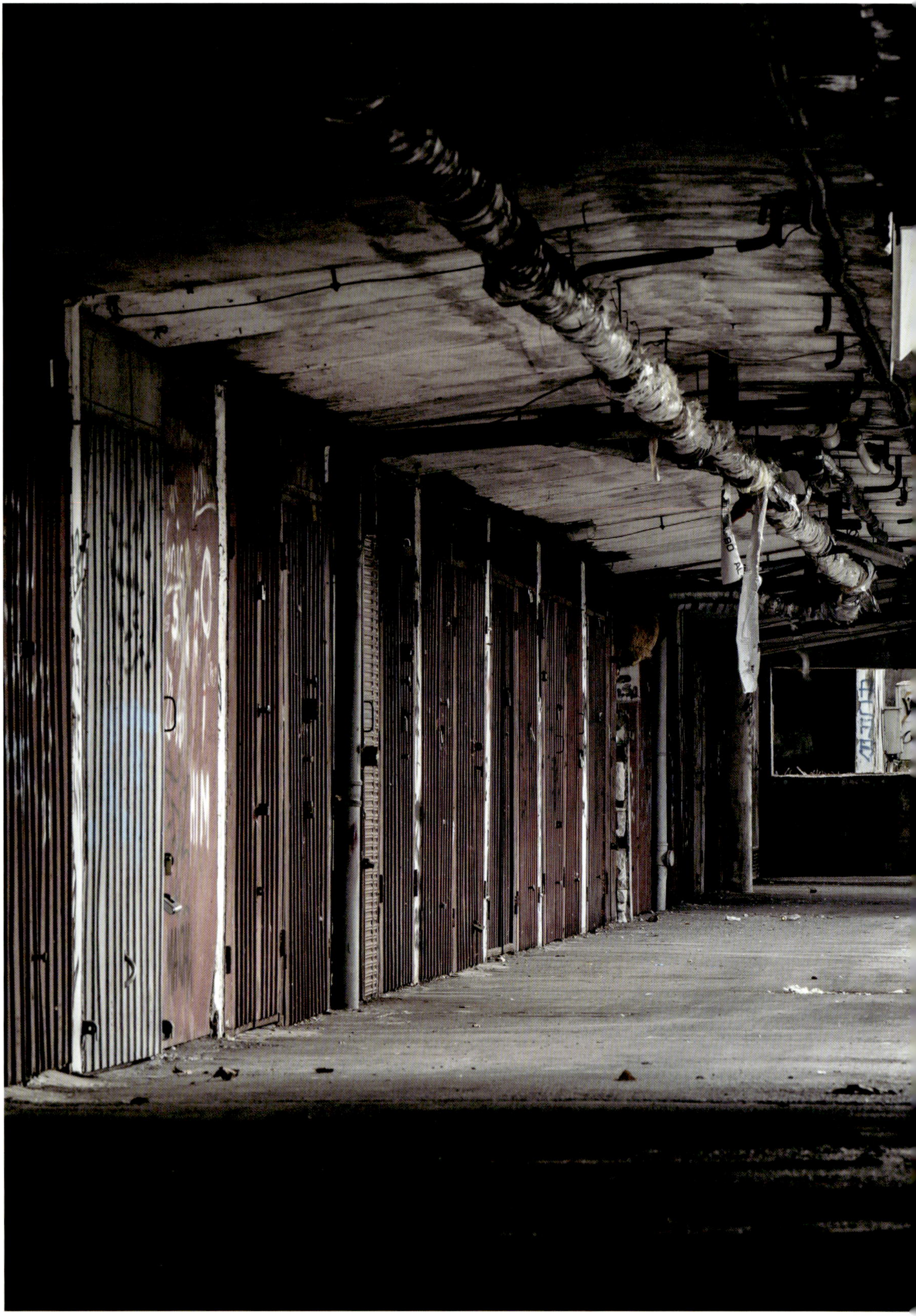

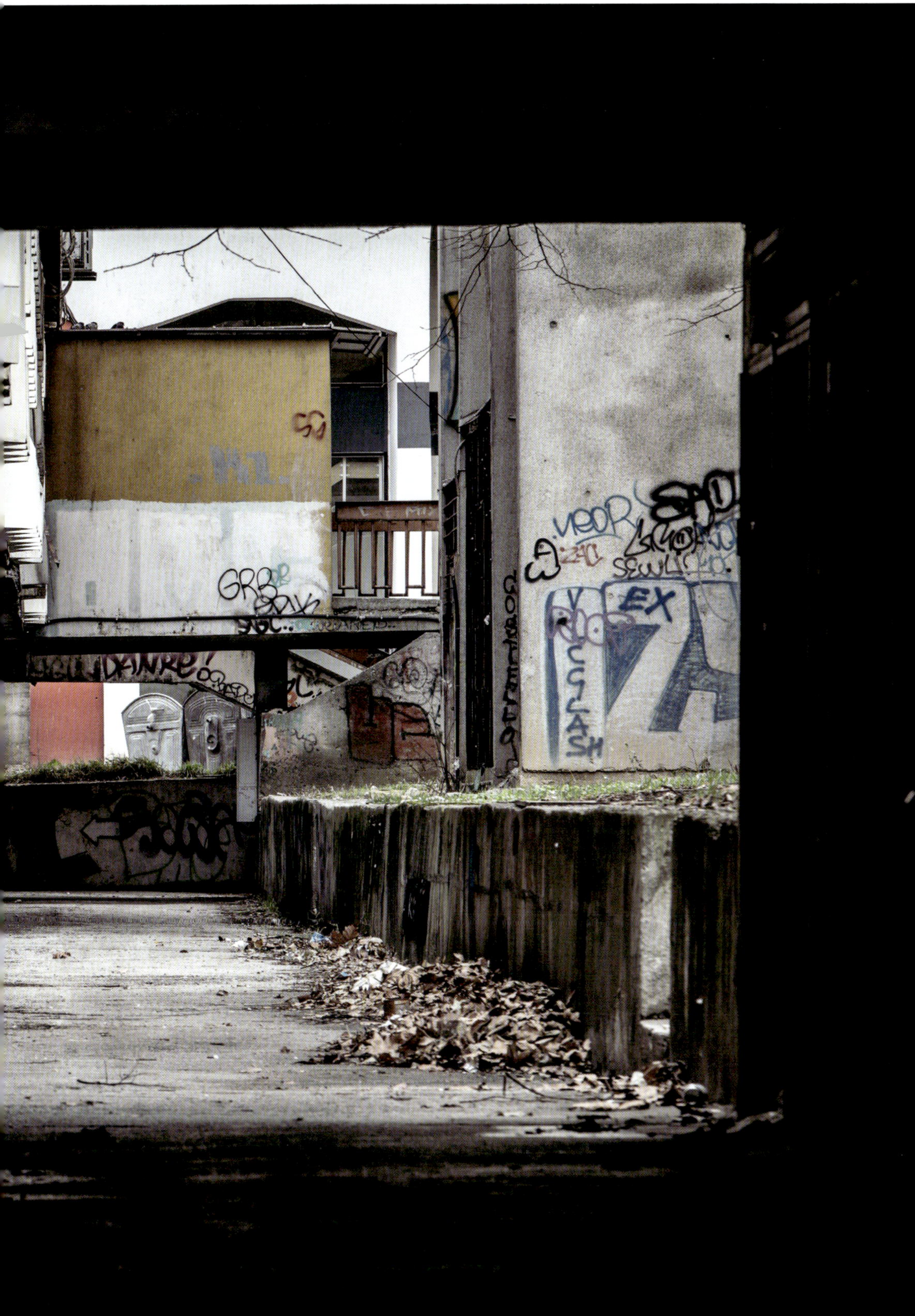

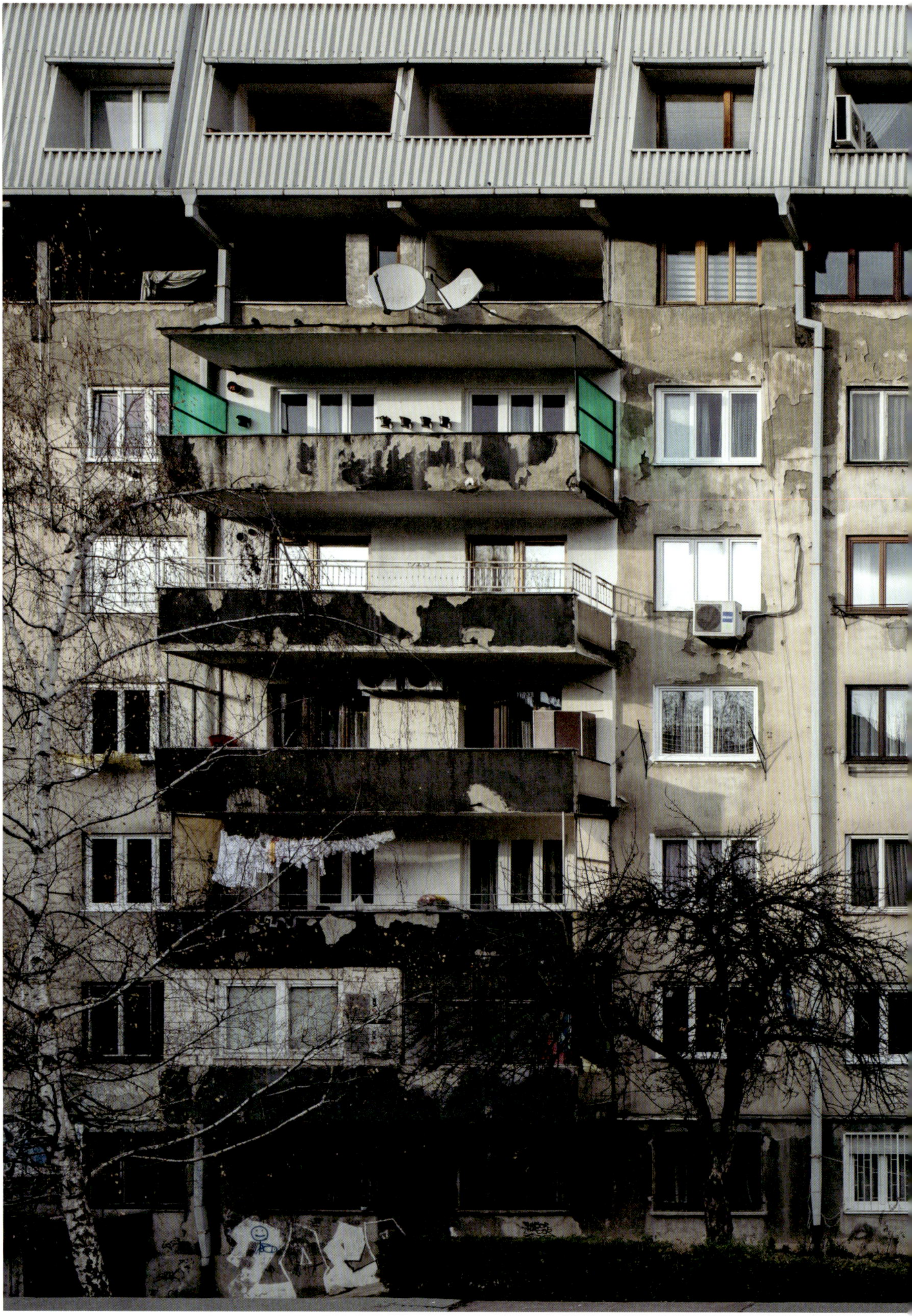

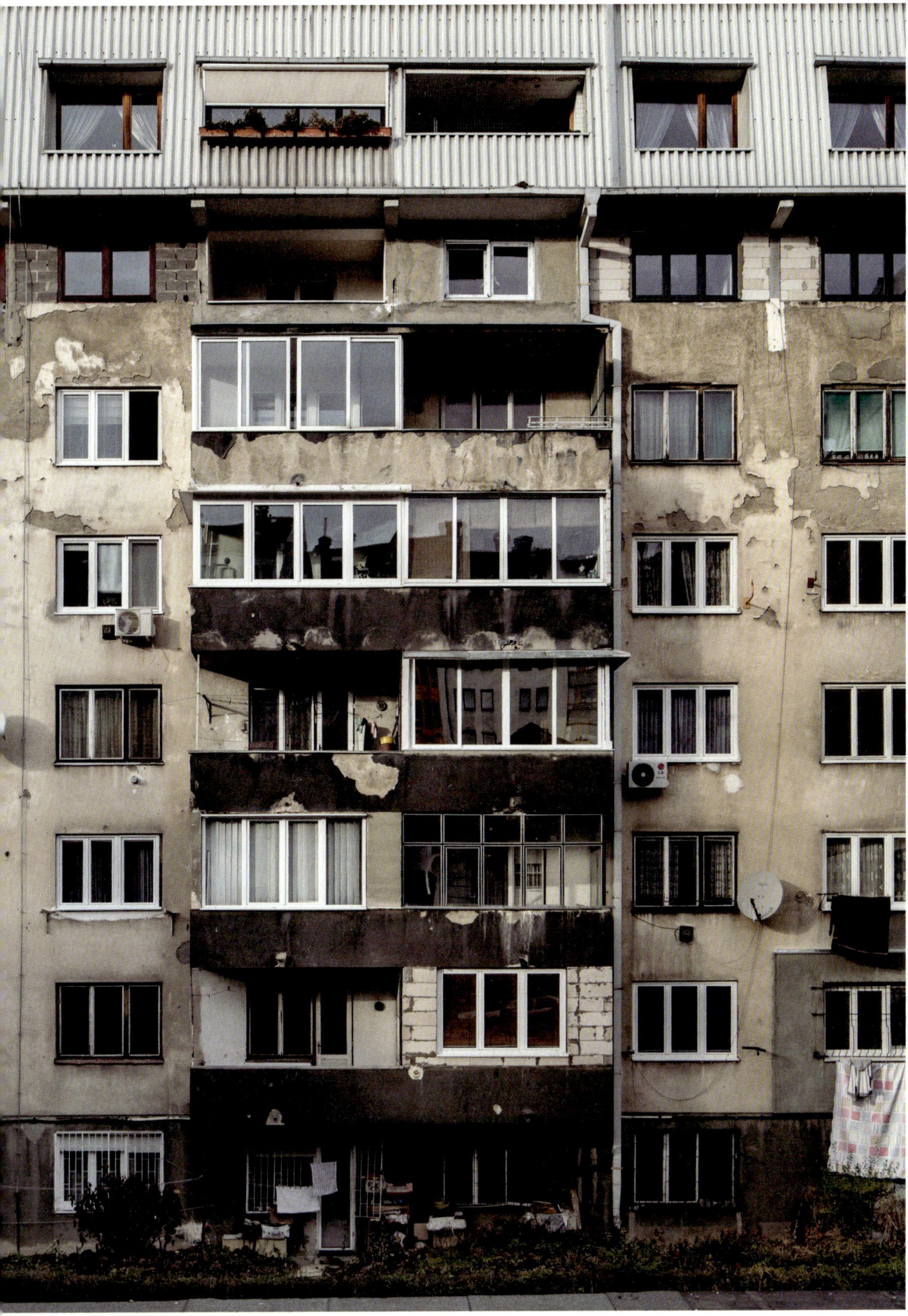

Previous spread
Sarajevo - Grbavica
Residential Building

Members of the 'Republika Srpska' Army's paramilitary formations committed crimes against non-Serb civilians. Part of the population of the Municipality of Novo Sarajevo was affected.

One member was charged and convicted of, among other things, raping fourteen women in different homes. Most of these were survivor homes.[21]

43°51'01.4"N 18°23'45.4"E

Opposite and overleaf
Sarajevo - Vogošća
Sonja's Restaurant and Guesthouse

Kon-Tiki Pension has been advertised by the Bosnia and Herzegovina Tourist Board as accommodation for tourists. During the war, Kon-Tiki Pension was officially used by units of Republika Srpska from 2 May 1992 to 8 July 1992. After taking control of Vogosca, a suburb of Sarajevo, Serbian forces took almost the entire Muslim civilian population to a Yugoslav People's Army barracks[22] in Semizovac.[23] From here the inmates were taken to various camps. One of them was Kon-Tiki Pension, also known as Sonja's Restaurant. It is located twenty to twenty-five metres from an old WWII bunker. The detention conditions were totally inadequate. The house was overcrowded, the prisoners were not given enough to eat and drink, and there were not enough places to sleep.[24] According to detainees, the 'soulless elite' came to this place in expensive cars: Dragan Vukanovic, Sinisa N, Miro Vujovic and others were given access to the Kon-Tiki 'women's prison' as a kind of reward, as well as a litre of brandy and half a kilo of coffee.

A particularly perfidious rape was committed by a group of twenty Serbs in the Kon-Tiki boarding house. Two girls, aged seven and thirteen, were raped in the presence of their mother. The girls died from the rape. Fifty women and children were held in the Kon-Tiki boarding house.[25] One of the detainees was present when two other Muslim girls were raped and killed by Serbian officers in front of a group of Muslim women. Two other Kon-Tiki inmates told *Newsday* (*Newsday* is a newspaper published in the United States) that they were raped 'in a public house' by UN officials and a Serb soldier. The Kon-Tiki was also visited by UN peacekeepers. The 'party guests' partied loudly and stayed late into the night. Among the visitors was Richard Gray, a senior New Zealand military observer who not only visited the Kon-Tiki but also the Park Hotel in Vogosca, where women were also raped.

43°54'10.7"N 18°19'46.6"E

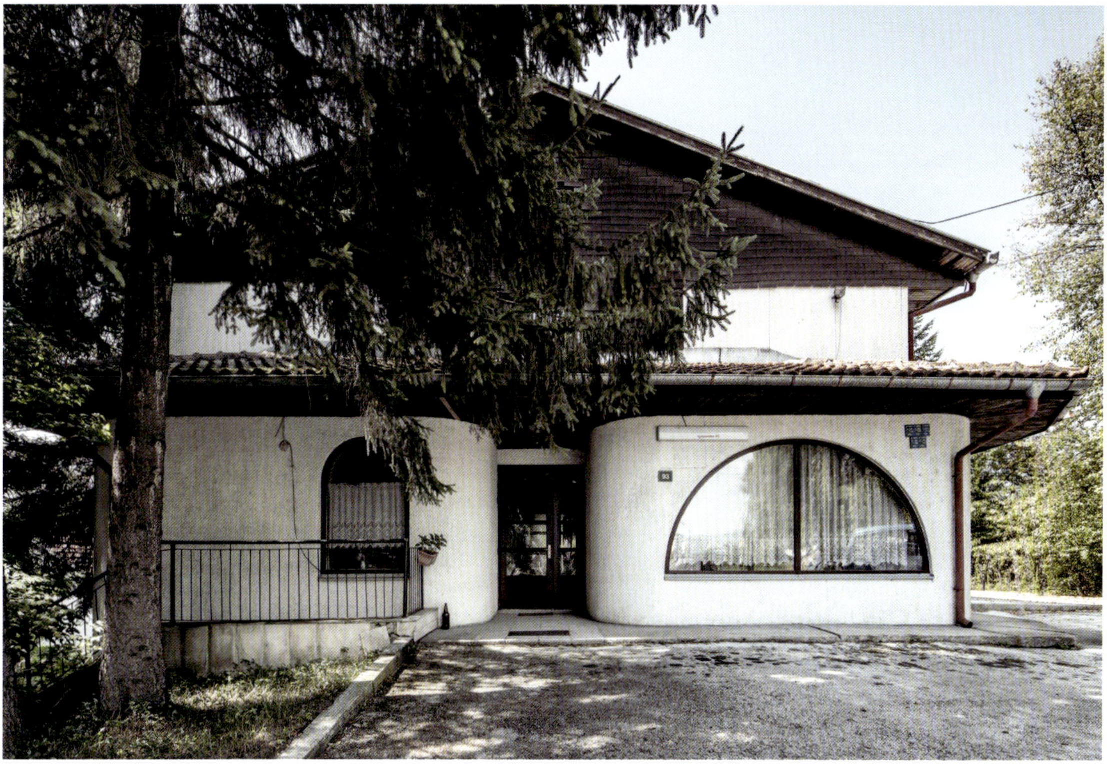

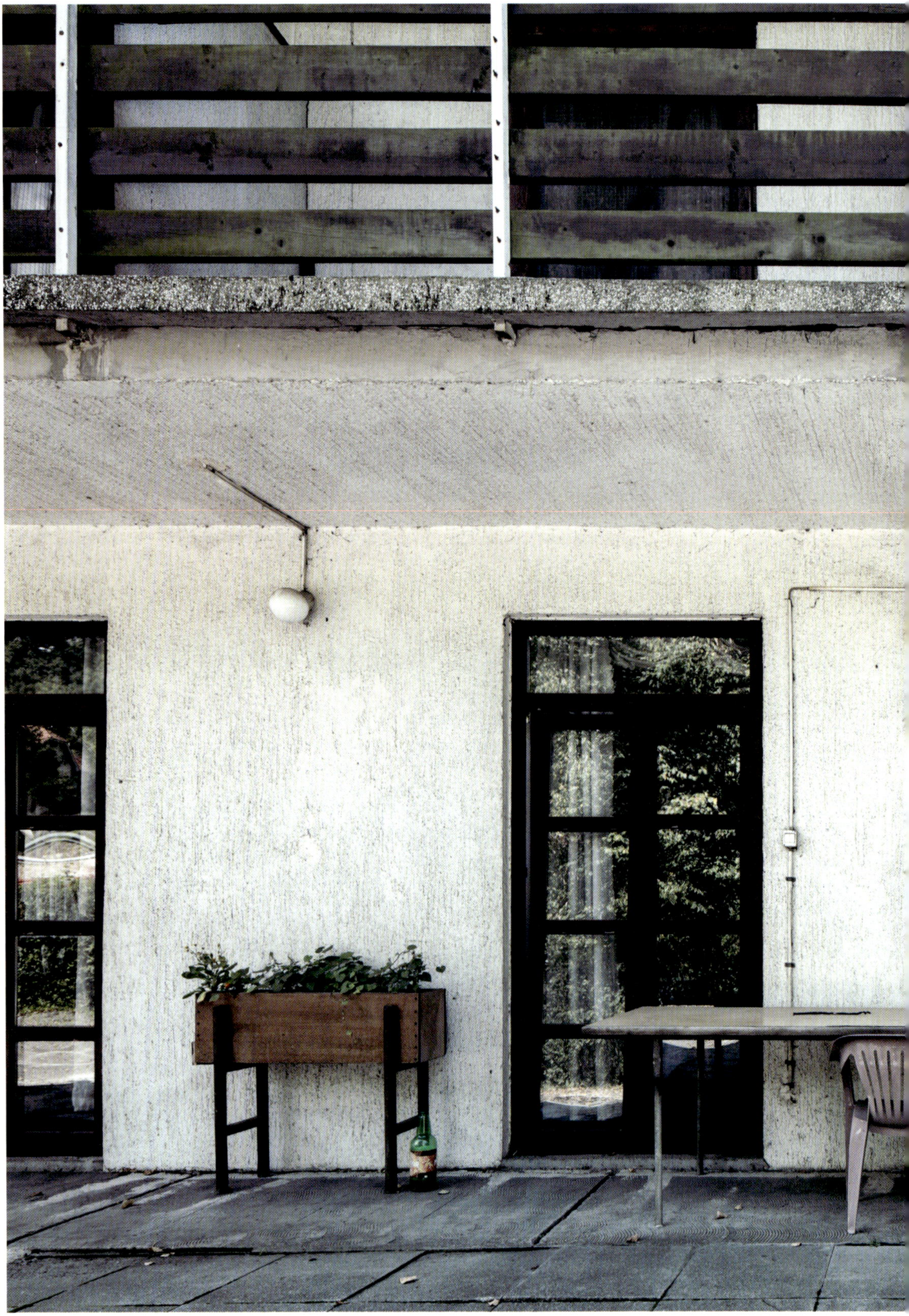

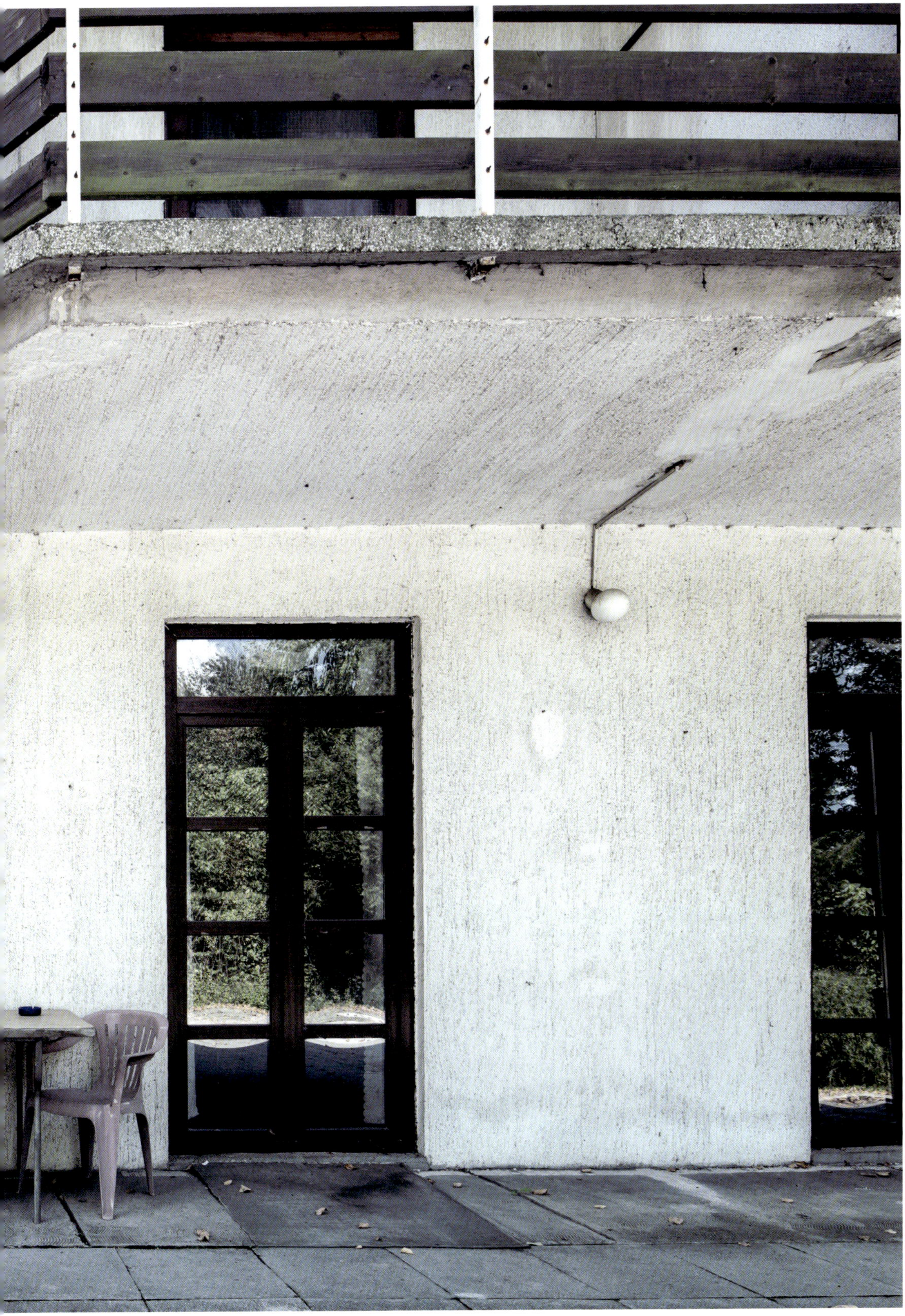

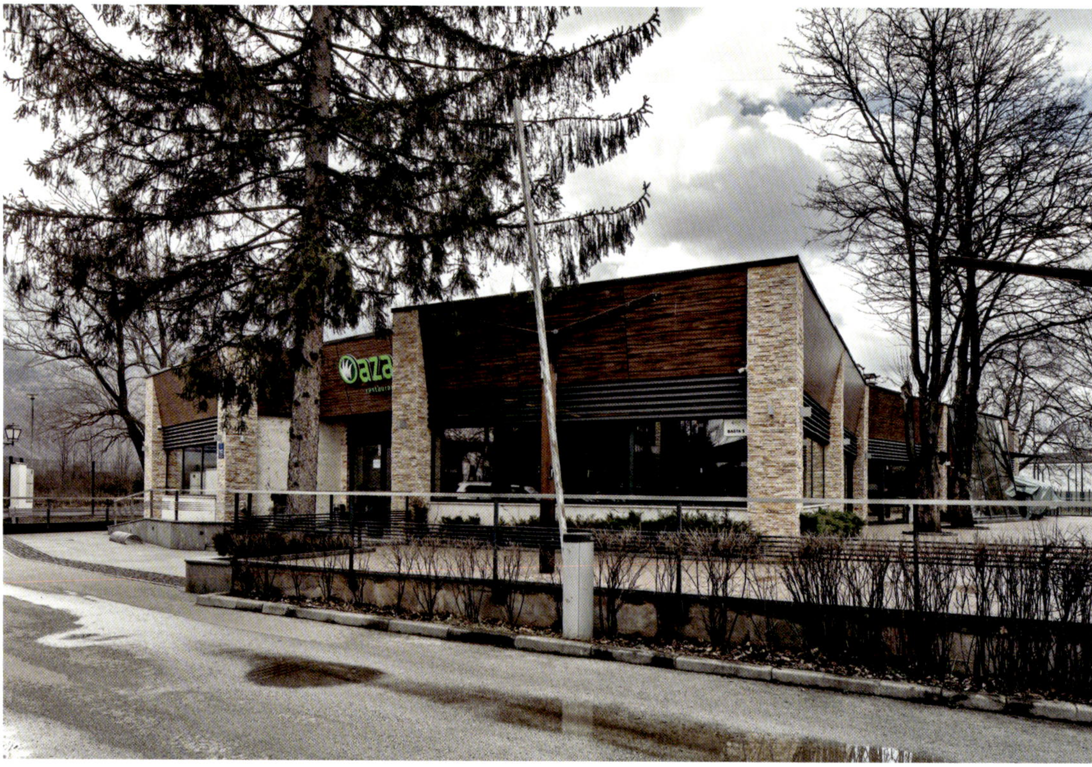

Left
Sarajevo
Now, Oaza Camping Resort

A detained Bosniak was brutally raped by a Serbian Army soldier over a period of three to four hours. After that he said to her, 'You will now give birth to a child of a Turkina New Serb, a Chetnik in the Serbian Republic!' After this rape, the woman became pregnant. After eight months, the woman was part of a prisoner exchange and later gave birth to a son.[26]

43°49'41.4"N 18°17'48.1"E

Overleaf
Ilidža
Šipad's Villa

After the Serbian Armed Forces took control of the Municipality of Ilidža, they mainly kept Muslim and Croatian civilians in twelve detention centres of the community.[27] One of the internment camps was Villa Šipad, once a representative entity of society for dealing with wood products and wood processing. The headquarters were located in the villa of the SDS for Ilidža, as well as the headquarters of the paramilitary formations of Arkan and Seselj. From 16 May 1992, prisoners were locked in the basement of the villa. The detainees were men, civilians, but also an elderly woman and a young woman aged twenty-eight. A witness later reported, 'Because I was bleeding profusely and almost unconscious lying on the ground, I could see that the young woman had been raped by three or four soldiers. She screamed and moaned. Then these soldiers pushed a metal pipe into her large intestines, through which they poured sand. The girl screamed terribly! The soldiers later disappeared from the detention room. The girl was bloody and bruised from the beatings. She approached me and asked me to untie her. Since my hands were tied behind my back, she helped me first and then I helped her. The young woman regained her strength and managed to dress. She got me later covered with a few bloody rags.'—testimony of a prisoner.[28]

43°49'25.7"N 18°17'58.9"E

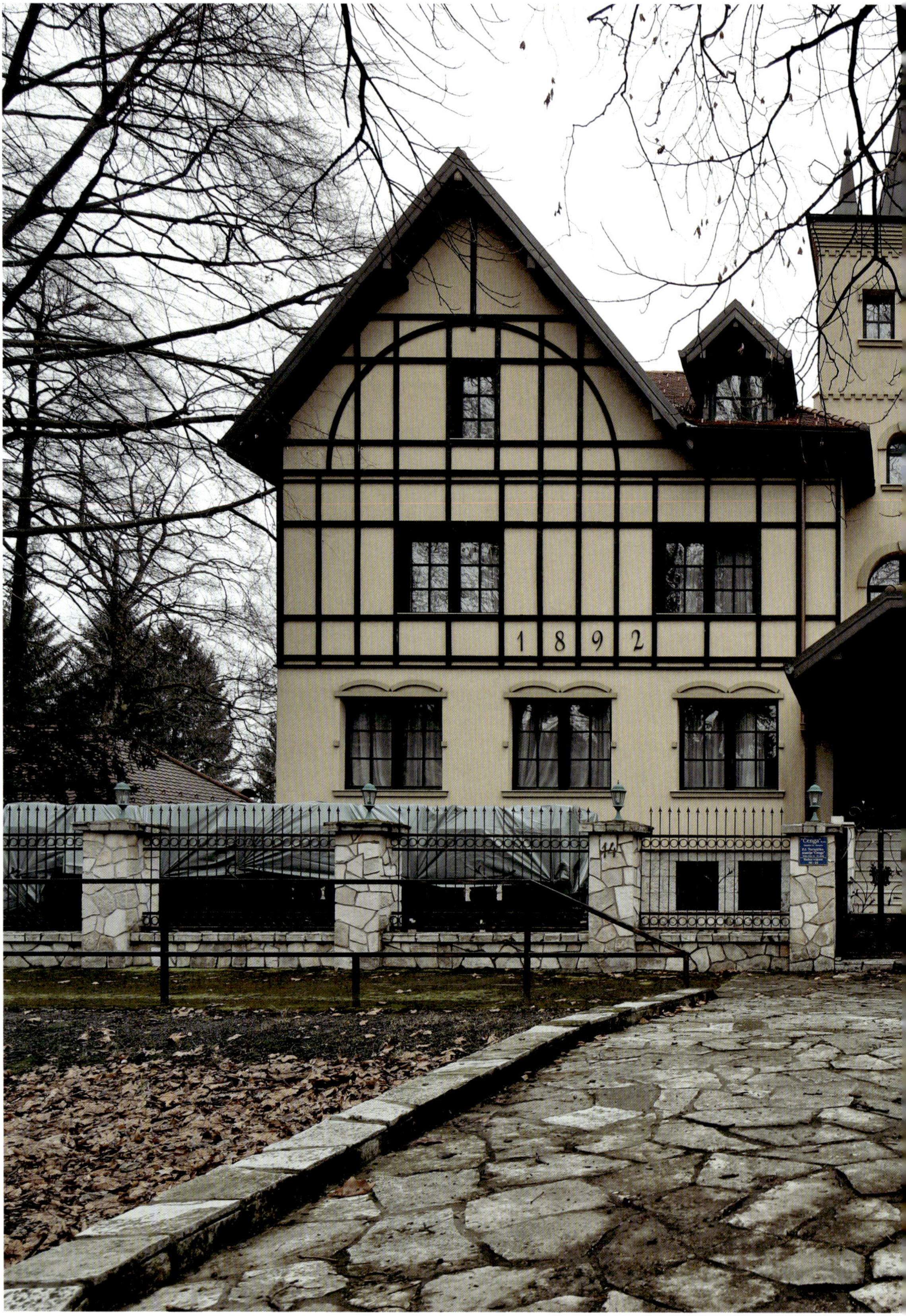
1892

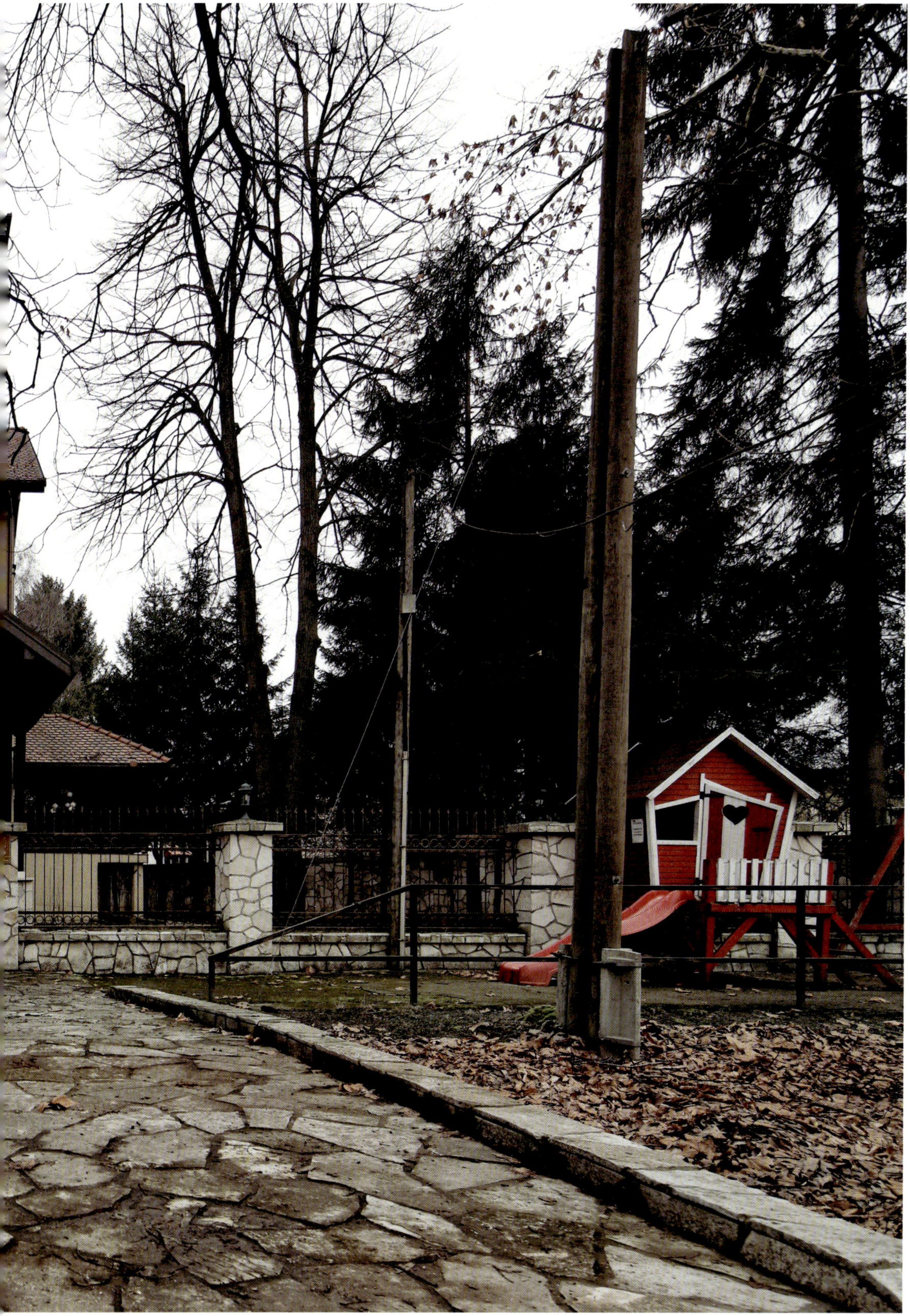

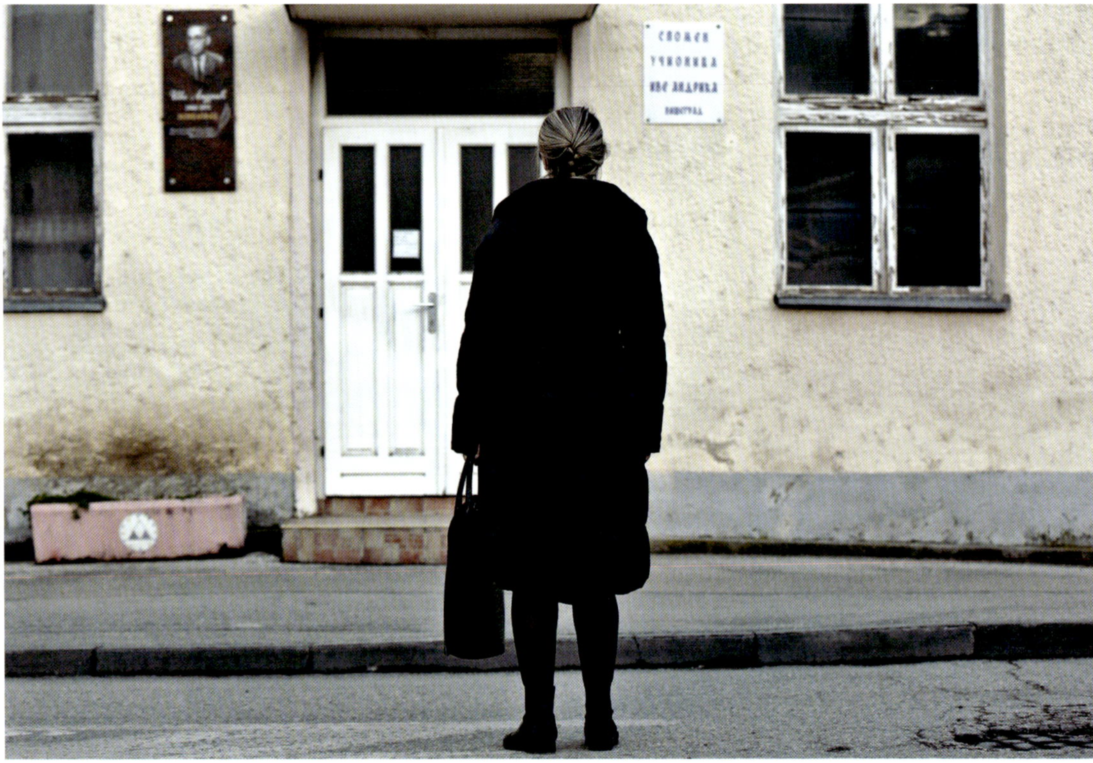

MIRJANA FROM VIŠEGRAD

'I, Mirjana, was born in 1961 in Sarajevo, where I lived happily, grew up, went to school and finished my university studies as a teacher. I loved Sarajevo but life took me somewhere else.

I was employed as a teacher in Konjic, Bradina, where I met and later married my husband. We enjoyed life with our two wonderful children until my husband passed away on 26 May 1992. He was murdered by soldiers in front of his loved ones. I buried him myself, dug him up again and later put him in a real grave. But life goes on...right?

On 7 December, I was taken to a detention centre in Musala-Konjic, while my children stayed in Bradina. They were locked in a school among crowds of detainees, with no food and no one they knew.

What I could not even imagine 'happened' to me in the Musala-Konjic camp. Suffice it to say: 'a woman in the camp.'

My sister, through her acquaintances, helped me to get back to my children. We were transferred to Sarajevo, Ilidža. We stayed there until Dayton and then moved to Višegrad.

The camp, the hunger, the fear of hunger created a new impetus for life in me. I don't ever want my kids to be as hungry as I was. I want them to be able to eat healthy. We live life in every moment.'

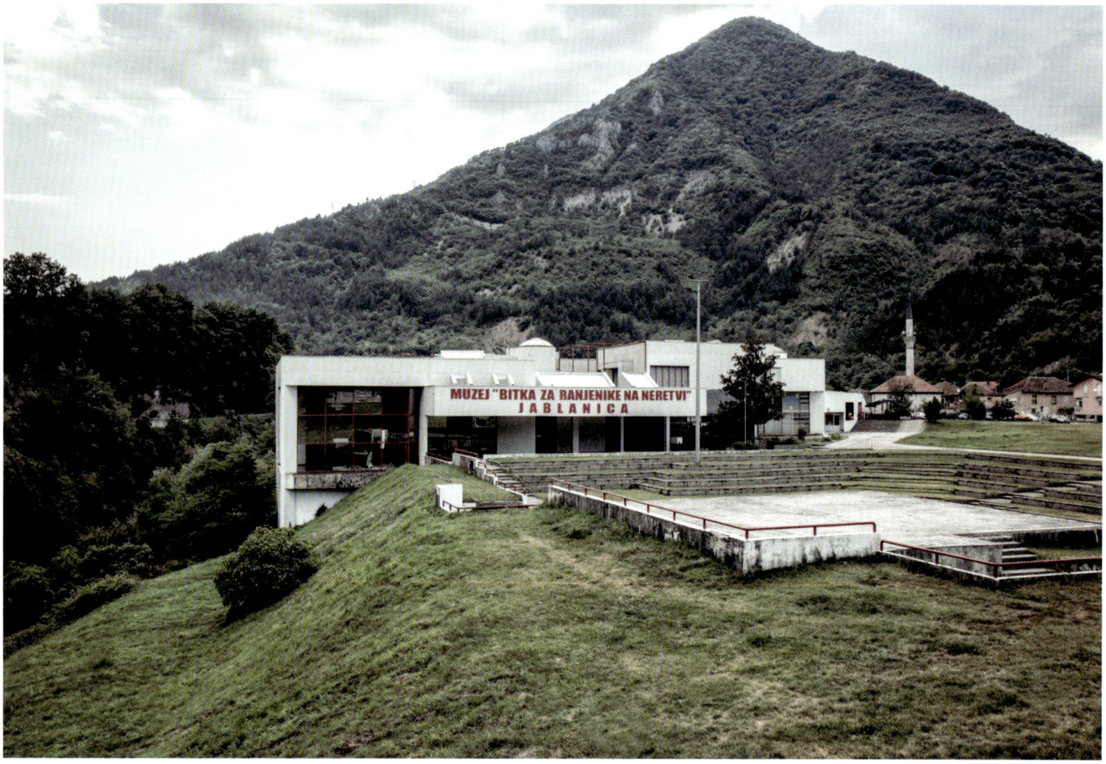

Jablanica

Museum of the Battle for the Wounded at Neretva River

The museum was under the supervision of the RBiH Army. It was converted into a detention centre on 15 April 1993 and closed on 22 March 1994. There were around 350 detainees, including from the village of Doljani near Jablanica—men, women, children, newborns and the elderly. The detainees were Bosnian Croat civilians, but there were also a number of HVO soldiers who were housed separately in the basement rooms.

The prisoners in the museum were accommodated in rooms of about 6 x 5 metres. There were about thirty people in each room. There were also seven separate rooms in which eighty-eight Croatian military, thirty-six HULDR (Croatian Association of Ex-detainees of Homeland War) prisoners were housed. They slept on the floor and couldn't shower. They had one meal—soup—a day, seldom had breakfast, and when they did, they were given some tea and a slice of bread. There was only one working toilet and two faucets, used by hundreds of prisoners.

Detainee A was locked in a room without lights. One night, Bojadzic came to the door and took away two women, a thirty-five-year-old and and a woman in her twenties. They returned a few hours later and other inmates said the two had been raped. Detainee A said, 'They just cried.'

Detainee AZ remembers the same incident on 28 July 1993, when two men came into the museum. Zeric: 'In the evening he came and pointed his finger at two women and said: 'You and you.' About three hours after midnight a soldier brought these prisoners back. They cried and were afraid.' The raped women were then taken to a war hospital in Jablanica.[29]

43°39'14.8"N 17°45'38.5"E

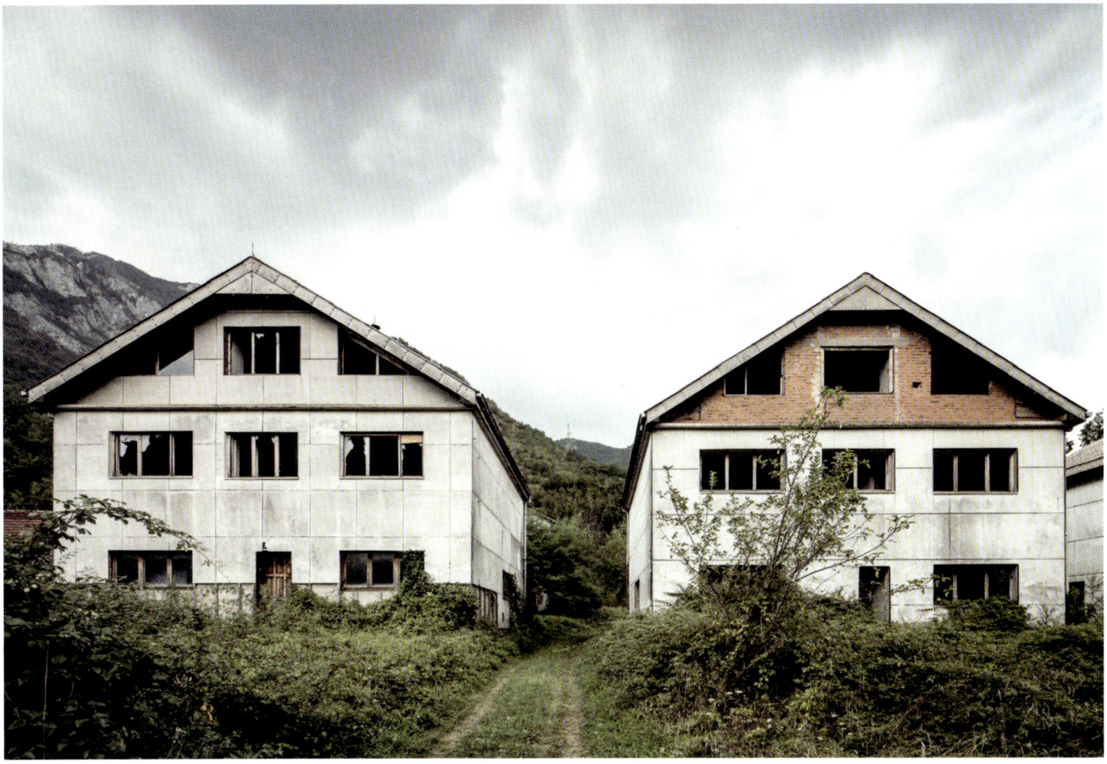

Donja Jablanica
Village, Rogić's Houses[30]

There were eleven detention centres in the entire municipality of Jablanica, holding between 692 and 891 Croatians. Control of the detention centre at Rogic's houses was in the hands of the Bosnian Army's special unit 'Zulfikar' under the command of Zulfikar Ališpago and Nihad Bojadzic, deputy commander.[31]

From 8 September to the end of November 1993, Croatian civilians and members of the HVO were imprisoned here.[32] In July 1993, two Croatian women were raped in the houses by soldiers from the unit mentioned above. One of the two women testified that she was taken into a dark room by a man. It was the soldier who had forced her to come along. 'I was scared... He said, 'We'll do it or I'll kill you.' He raped me.' She added that he raped her again in another room.[33]

43°37'59.0"N 17°45'20.9"E

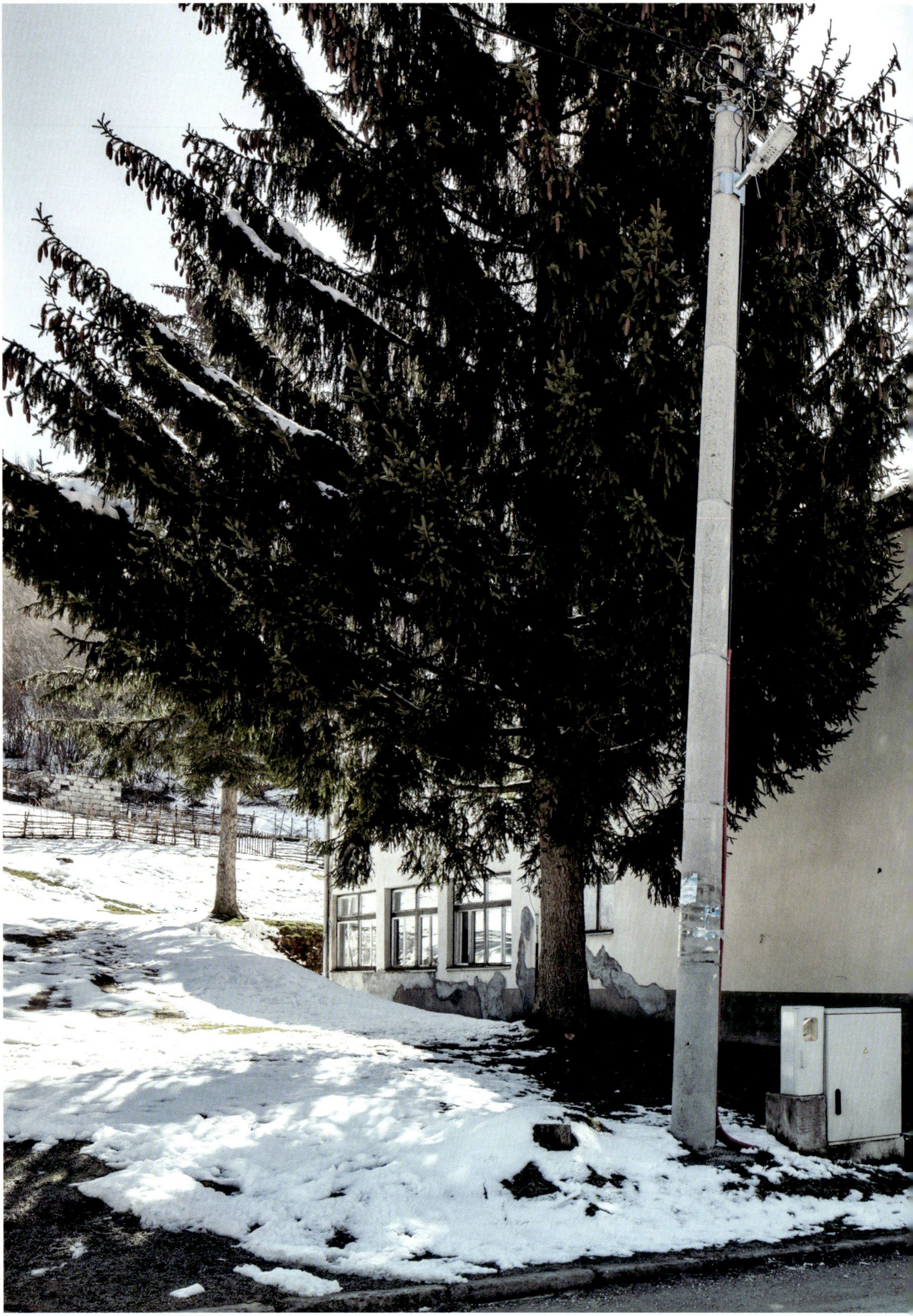

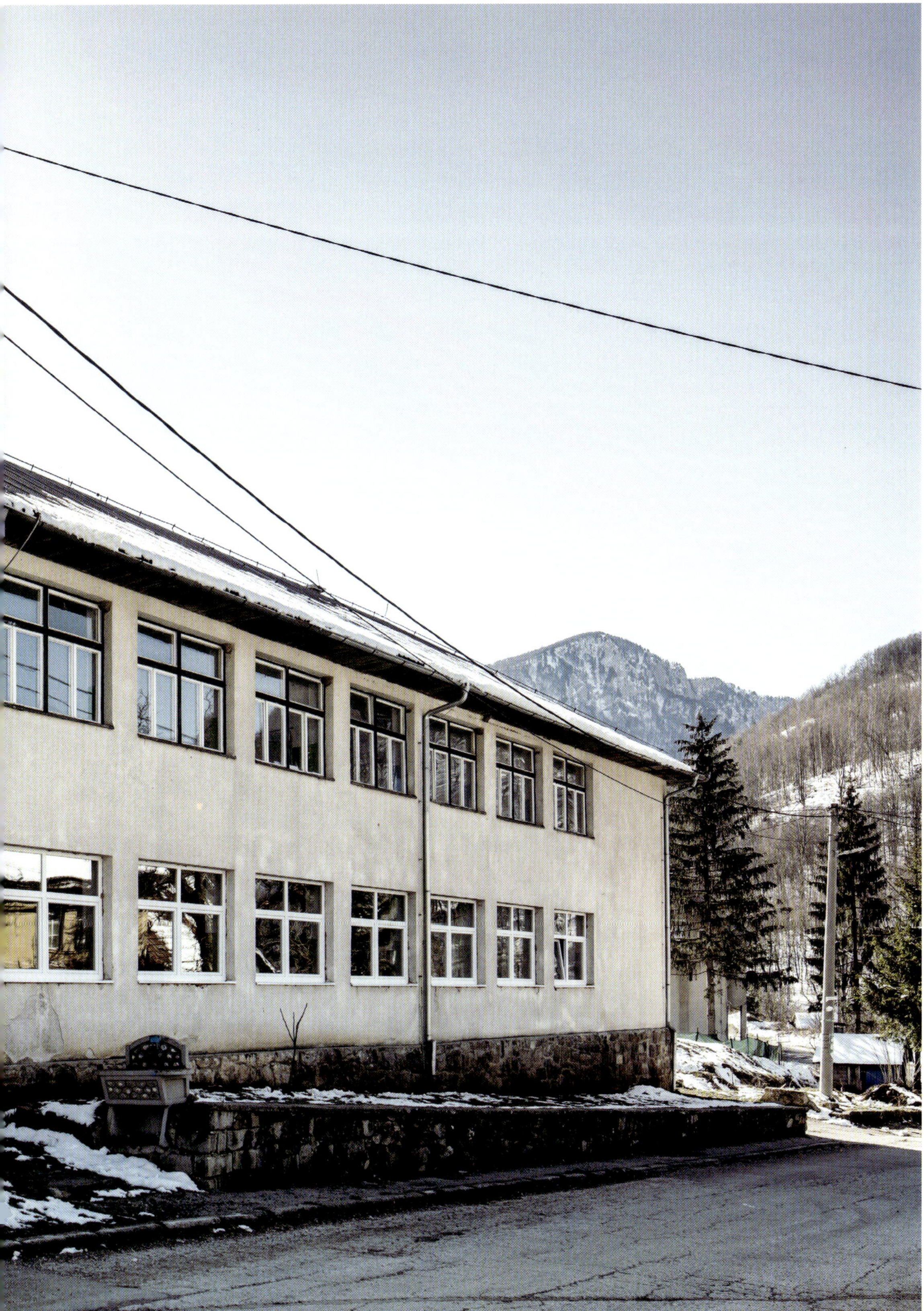

Previous spread
Bradina - Konjic
Elementary School

During the military operations of the Bosnian Territorial Defense Forces (TO), the Croatian Defense Council (HVO) and the Ministry of Interior (MUP), several members of the Serb population were arrested and imprisoned in barracks and warehouses. 'The Croatian aggressors murdered forty-eight people, 240 villagers were herded to the Celebici detention centre.'[34]

Women, children and the elderly were brought to this school. Soldiers confiscated jewellery and other valuables. They grabbed the breasts of young women and girls, pushed their fingers between their legs and raped them. On 13 July 1992, members of the Green Berets raped fifteen women. Male prisoners were also raped by soldiers.

43°44'38.3"N, 18°01'07.9"E

Opposite
Konjic
Sport Hall 'Musala' and Elementary School

The detention centre was under the administration of the RBiH Army. Serbian prisoners were housed on the first floor of the hall, Croats on the ground floor of the hall and in the changing rooms. About 900 Croats, 100 Serbs and about thirty members of the RBiH Army passed through the camp. The Musala camp operated from 10 May 1992 to 6 October 1994. In August, detainees S-3, S-2, S-4 and Đalto Ivica were taken from the locker room of the Musala sports hall and taken to the primary school next door, where they were ordered to strip naked. They were beaten all over their bodies, made to kneel, and forced to rape each other anally and orally.

43°39'03.5"N, 17°57'50.9"E

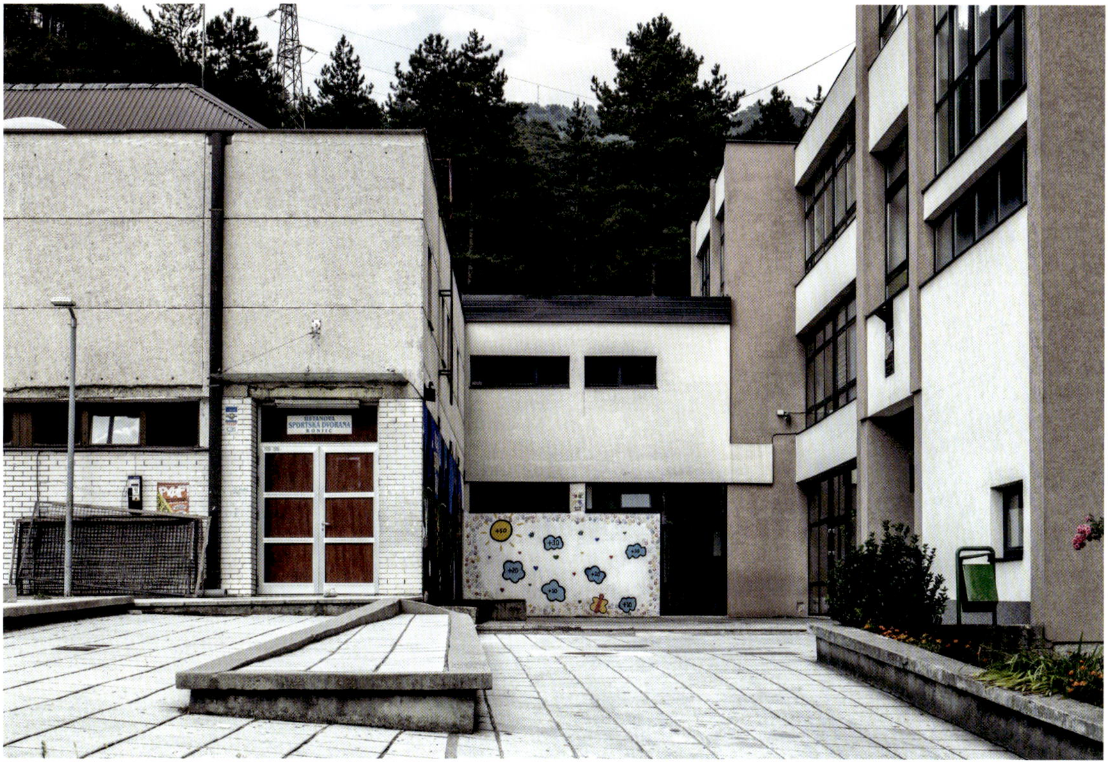
SPORTSKA DVORANA

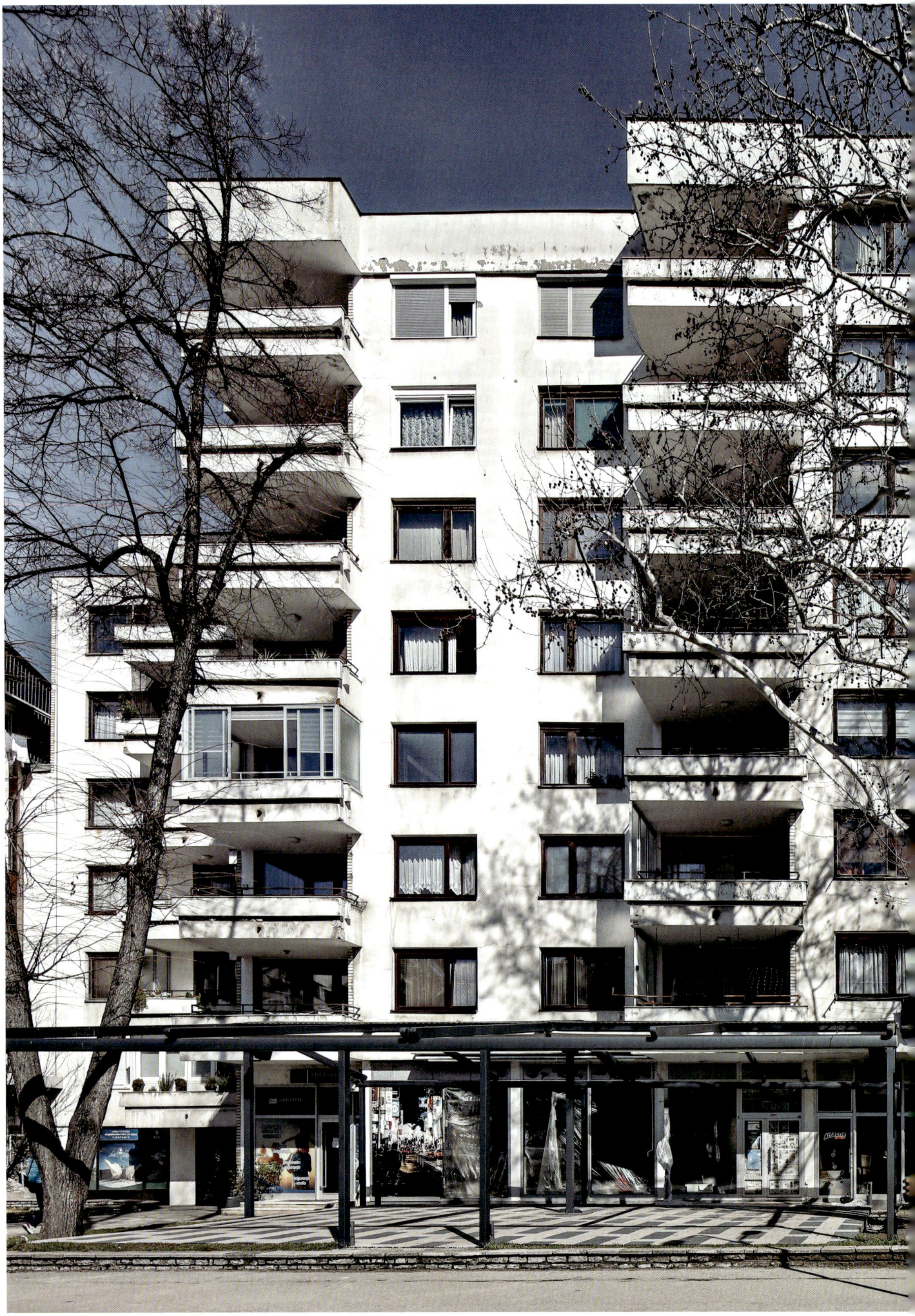

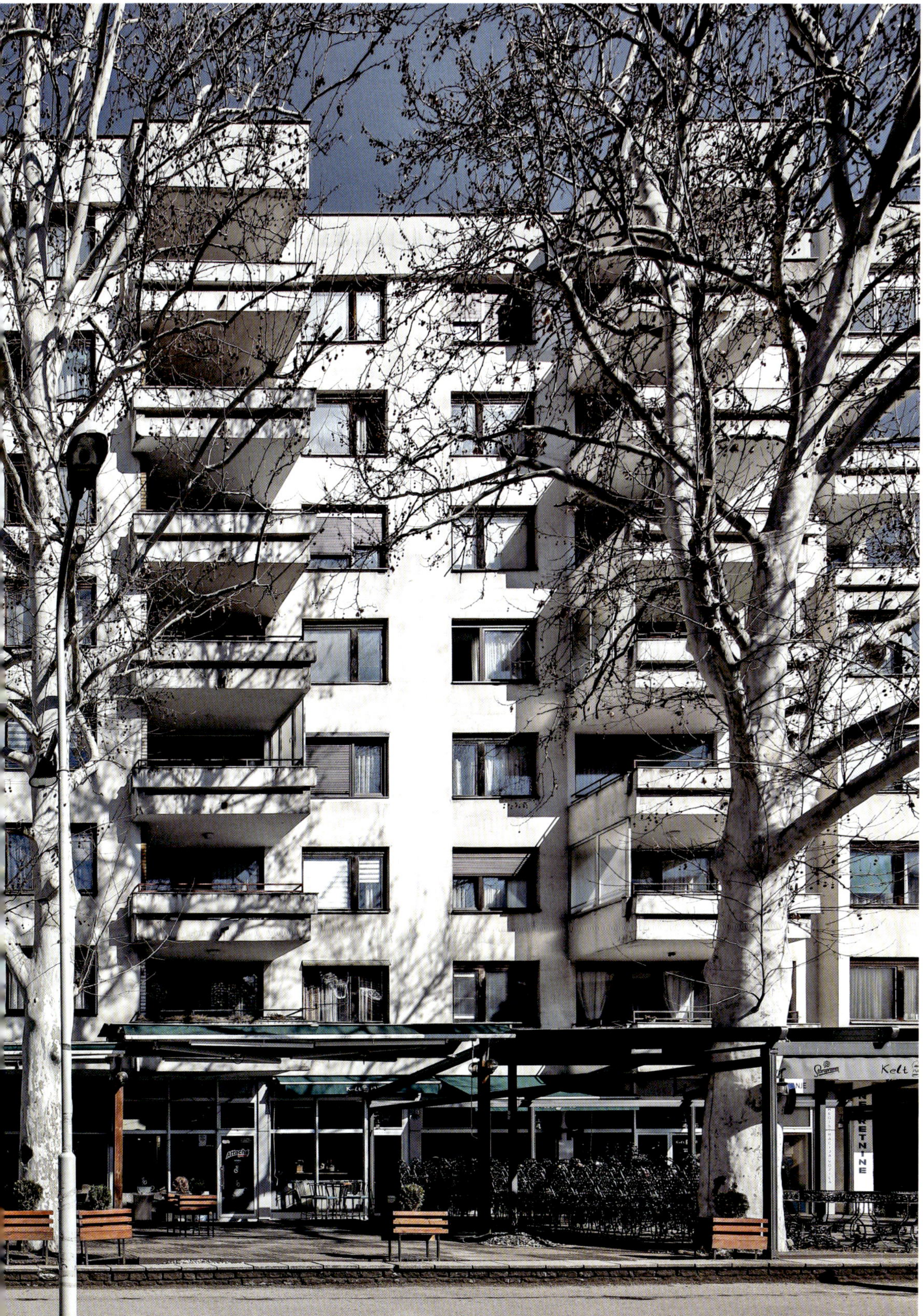
Kelt

Previous spread
Foča
Residential Building Lepa Brena

Apartments and houses where women were imprisoned were used as brothels by groups of soldiers, mostly members of paramilitary formations. One such place where Muslim women and girls were held was an apartment in this building called Lepa Brena. Radomir Kovac, called 'Klanf,' lived there. He was a member of the Dragan Nikolic unit in the Army of the Republic of Srpska (VRS). Jagoš Kostic, also a VRS soldier, lived with him in the apartment. Another apartment on the fourth floor was used by Radomir Kovac. With Kovac's consent, other soldiers also took girls and women there and raped them. In addition, captive women had to clean, cook, provide the men with food and drink, wash their clothes and carry out all the orders from Kovac and Kostic. They were not allowed to have any contact with the outside world. A neighbour, DK, sometimes brought them food when Kovac was absent for seven days or more. Kovac held girls and women captive in this apartment from 30 October 1992 to 25 February 1993.[35] [36] [37] [38]

43°30'28.0"N 18°46'28.0"E

Opposite
Višegrad
Old Police Station

Fifteen to twenty Muslim civilians were detained at the Višegrad Public Security Station. This detention centre operated until the end of June 1992.[39] The witness Bakira H was taken to the basement of the police station in April 1992. 'There was a large armchair, a bar, a couple of chairs and half the room was paneled. I saw Milan Lukic and Sredoje Lukic. I knew Milan Lukic well. He was holding a curved knife and told me to undress. I thought he was joking. But I could tell he meant it because he threatened me with the knife.' She did as she was told. She took off her pants and shirt and was left in only her underwear. Then she was raped.[40]
—Witness: Bakira H/Sarajevo

43°47'13.3"N 19°17'27.2"E

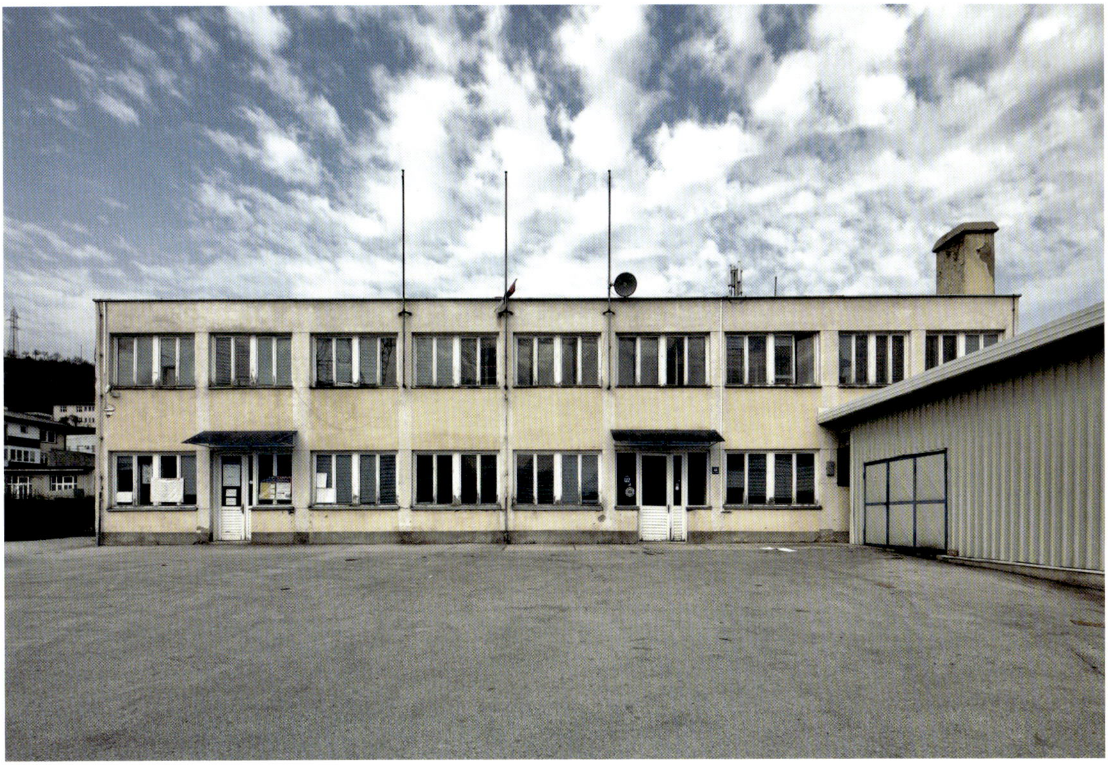

Overleaf
Foča
Football Stadium

The football stadium was not a place of detention; imprisoned girls/women from other institutions were brought to the stadium and raped there. A survivor now living in Australia testified: 'Around 12 August 1992, the evening before my release, two soldiers took me and another girl to the city's stadium. A large group of soldiers were waiting for us there, mostly Montenegrins and soldiers from Serbia. That night I don't know how many soldiers raped me on the stadium benches. The others stood and watched everything. I had fainted. That same night they took us to Buk Bijela, and the soldiers raped us there again...'[41]

43°30'16.4"N 18°46'42.6"E

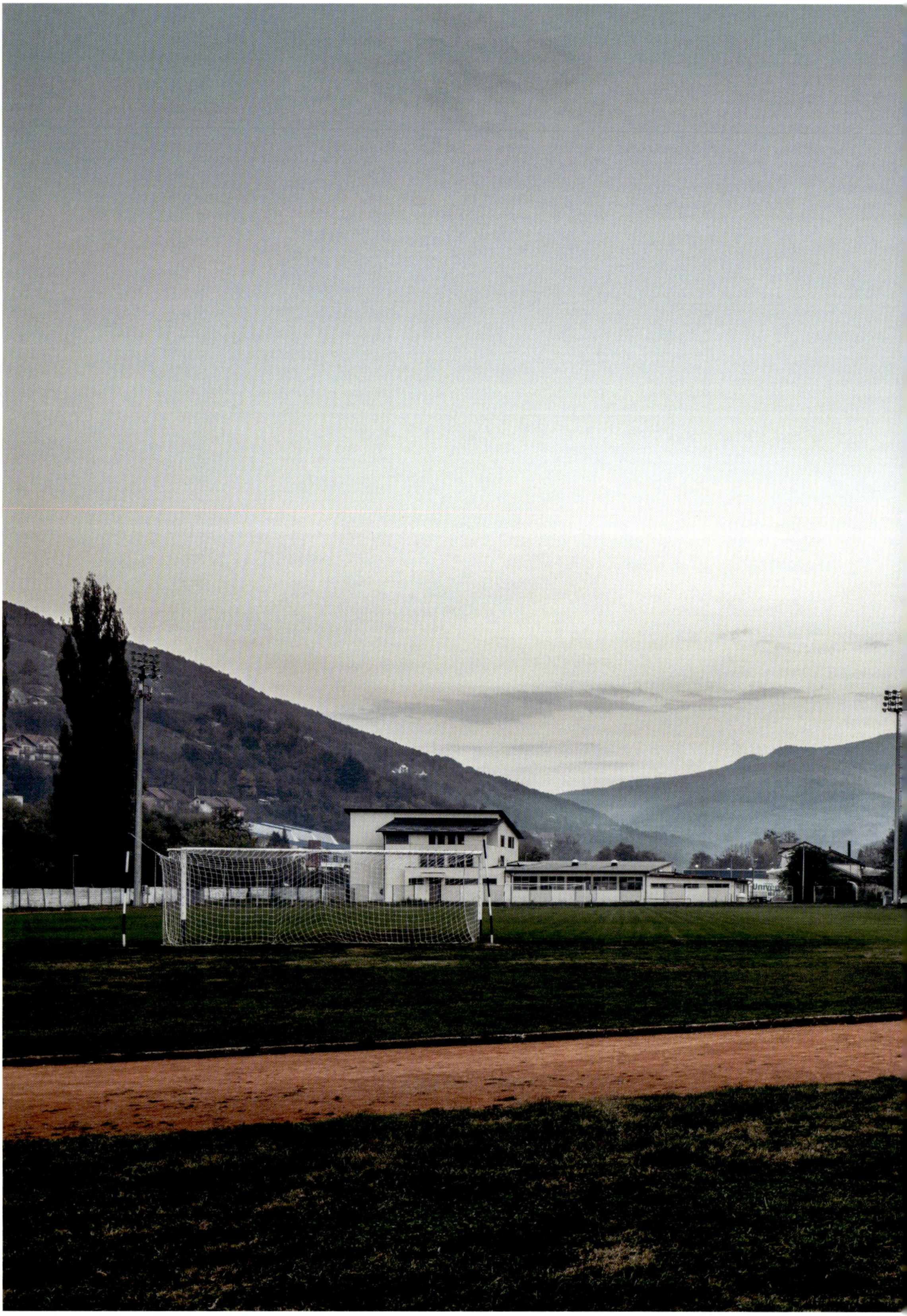

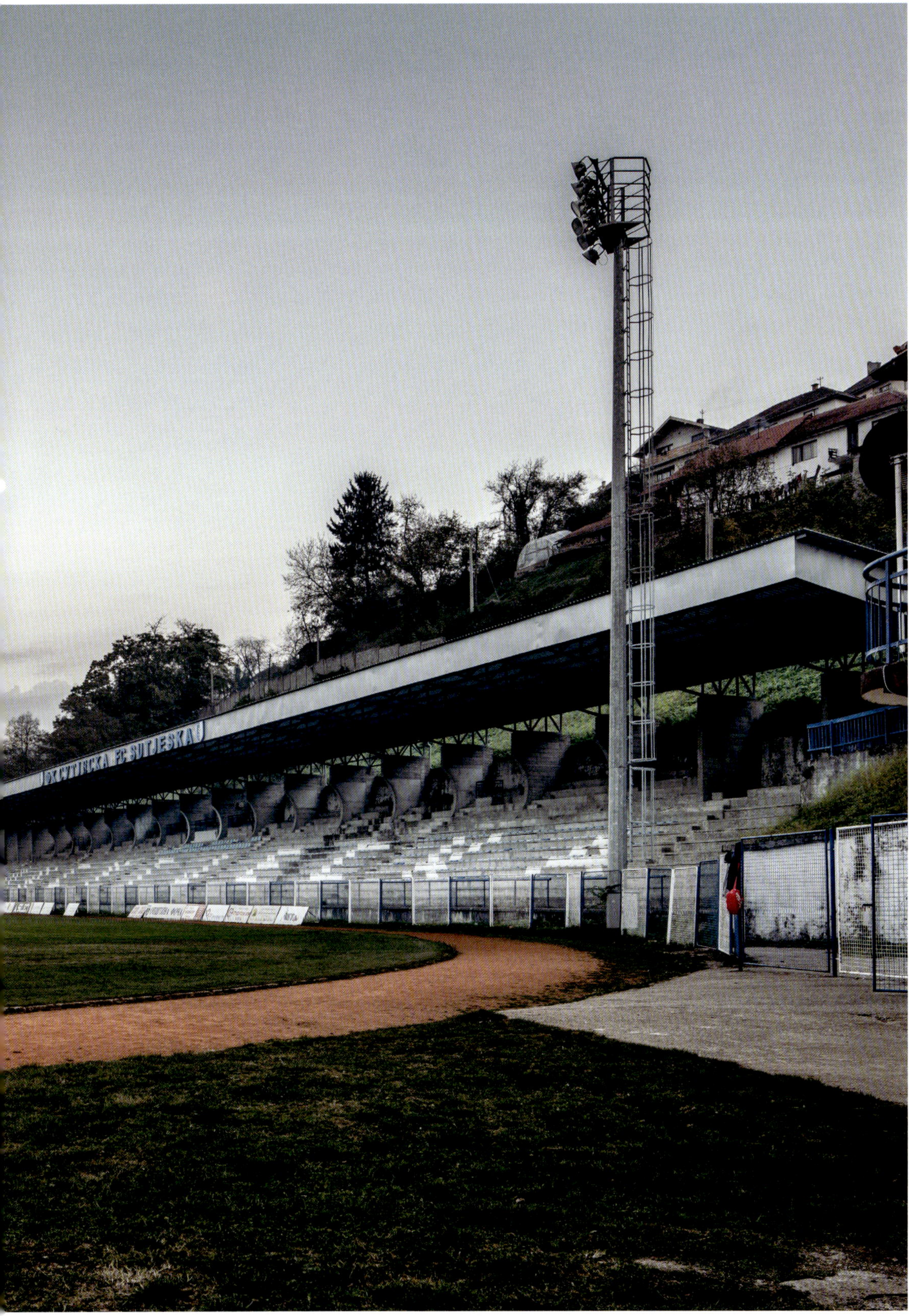
FC SUTJESKA

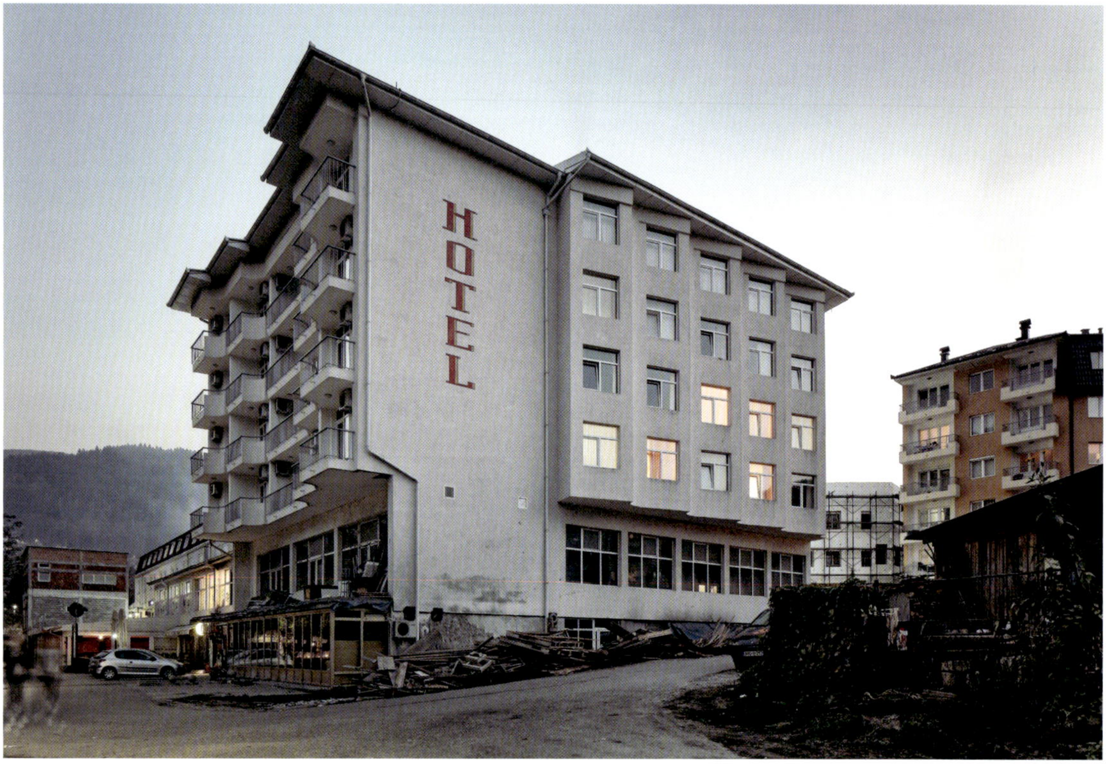
HOTEL

Left
Foča
Zelengora Hotel

Hotel Zelengora was the military headquarters of the Serbian Armed Forces. Bosnian Serb soldiers took Muslim women from Partizan Hall to houses, apartments or barracks and hotels such as Hotel Zelengora. On 13 July 1992, Janko Janjic took witness FWS-48 and two other female inmates to a house across from Partizan Hall and raped her there (vaginal penetration), while two unidentified soldiers raped the other two women in the same room. That same night, as soon as Janko Janjic had brought the women back to Partizan Hall, another military man, Dragoljub Kunarac, took the same three women to Hotel Zelengora. Witness FWS-48 tried to avoid further rapes and refused to go with him. He then kicked her and pulled her out. In the Hotel Zelengora, witness FWS-48 was housed in a separate room and both Dragoljub Kunarac and Zoran Vukovic raped her. Both perpetrators told her that she would now give birth to Serbian babies. Also in August 1992, Dragan Zelenovic and other soldiers brought witness FWS-48 to Hotel Zelengora. When they arrived there were many soldiers eating and drinking. Immediately thereafter, a person identified as Spomenko approached FWS-48, took her to an upstairs room, and raped her.[42]

43°30'29.8"N 18°46'35.0"E

Overleaf
Foča
High School

As of 3 July 1992, about seventy civilian women were detained in two classrooms at this school. Around 13 July 1992, all the detained women were transferred to the Partizan Gymnasium. The detainees were guarded and lived in an intimidating atmosphere with the knowledge and sometimes even direct involvement of the local authorities, particularly the police. Serbian soldiers and police officers, including Foča police chief Draga Gagovic, took out detainees and raped them. The inmates could not leave the facility because it was guarded, but the guards did not prevent the soldiers from entering. Witness FWS-95 (one of the detainees) once saw a security guard trying to prevent soldiers from entering the classrooms, but they told him that they had a document signed by Dragan Gagovic allowing them to enter the building and take women. According to what witness FWS-95 heard, the document states that soldiers need sexual intercourse to improve their fighting spirit. About two days after the prisoners were taken to the school, a group of soldiers came every night. They would select women and take them for hours, sometimes all night. The women were beaten, humiliated, raped and sexually abused 'in every possible way.' The selection procedure was as follows: soldiers entered the hall, pointed to a certain woman or called her by her first name. Then they took her to another classroom, raped her, and then brought her back. The soldiers threatened to kill the women or their children if they did not agree. Women who dared to resist were beaten.
—Witness FWS-48 was told that the soldiers were ordered to rape women.[43]

43°30'13.4"N 18°47'02.5"E

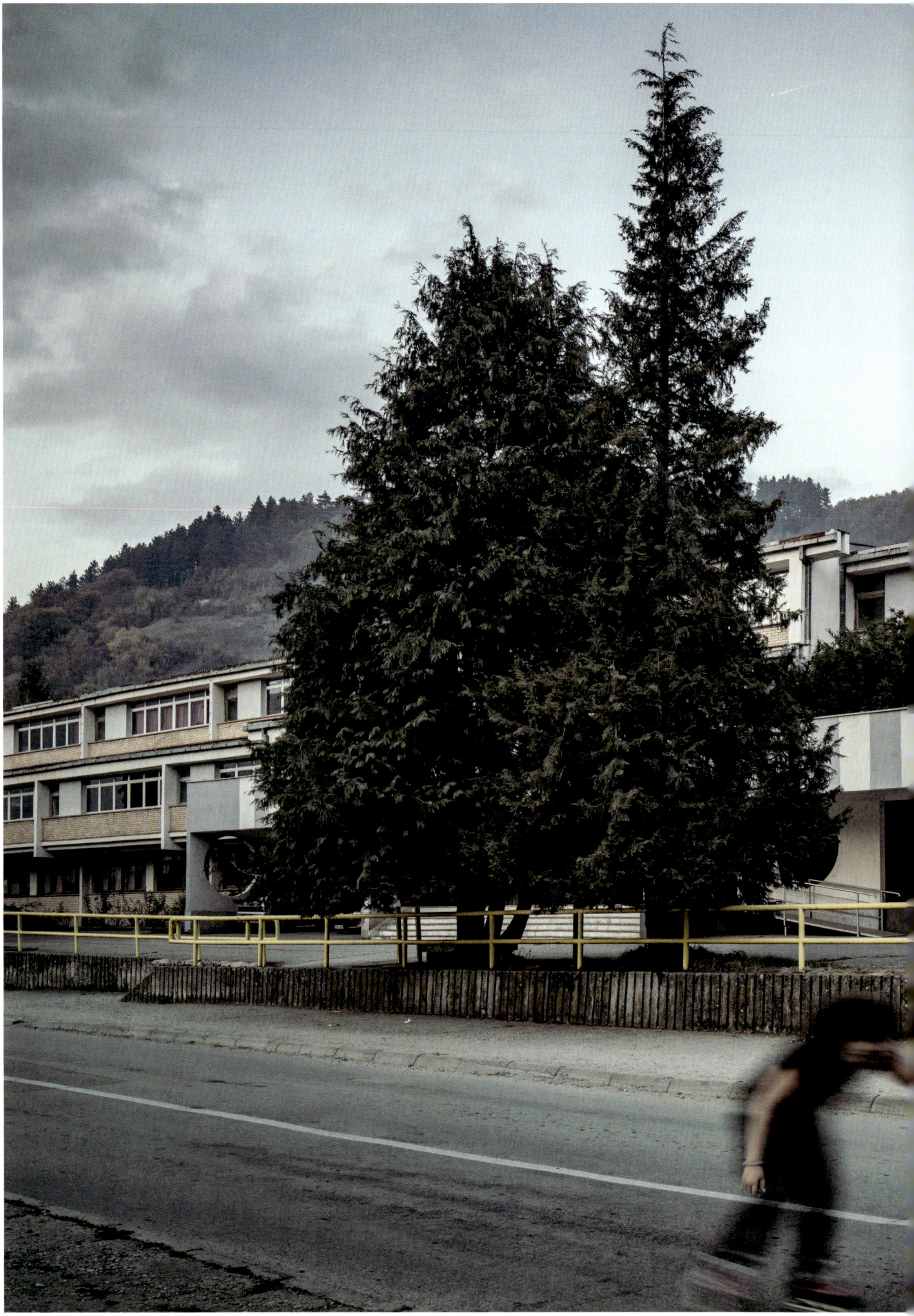

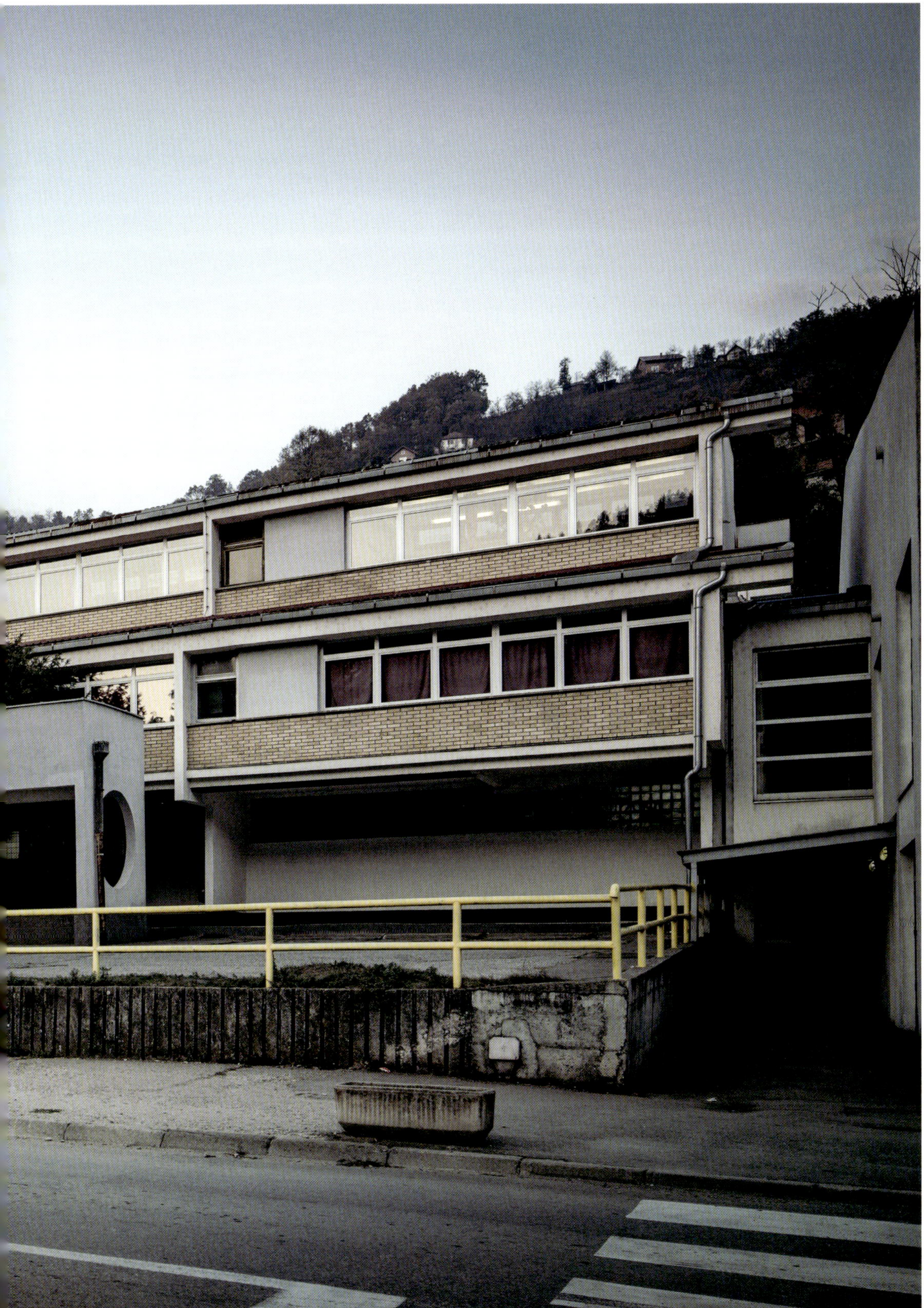

Opposite and overleaf
Višegrad
Vilina Vlas, Spa Hotel

The headquarters of Milan Lukic's (now convicted war criminal) paramilitary unit (Beli Orlovi: White Eagle) was stationed at Hotel Vilina Vlas near Višegrad, about five kilometres from the centre. Before the war it was used as a rehabilitation centre and thermal bath. After the war it was reopened as a spa hotel. During the war, from April to July 1992, it was a well-known and feared internment and rape camp. All rooms in the hotel were locked from the outside. The soldiers threw the prisoners pieces of bread, for example. They had to catch them with their mouths while their hands were tied, and the shackles were only released during the rape. In addition to the 'regular' rapes, women were also brought to this camp. They were 'carefully' selected for this camp brothel to give birth to 'chetnik' children. In addition, the soldiers only brought women to Vilina Vlas at night and allowed some to return home after the rape. According to one detained woman, younger girls in particular were taken to the hotel, while older women were taken to other places, such as squatted or abandoned houses, and raped there.[44] According to the report of the United Nations Expert Commission (Bassiouni Commission) to the Security Council, it was estimated that 200 women, mostly Bosniaks, were detained and sexually tortured in Vilina Vlas. Many of the women were murdered. Of those who survived, many later took their own lives. The bodies of the victims have never been found and are said to have been buried in unknown locations and then reburied again to cover any traces. Only a handful of female prisoners, fewer than ten women, survived, according to the Association of Women Victims of War, an organisation that works with women survivors and works to prosecute the perpetrators.[45]

43°49'13.0"N 19°18'30.0"E

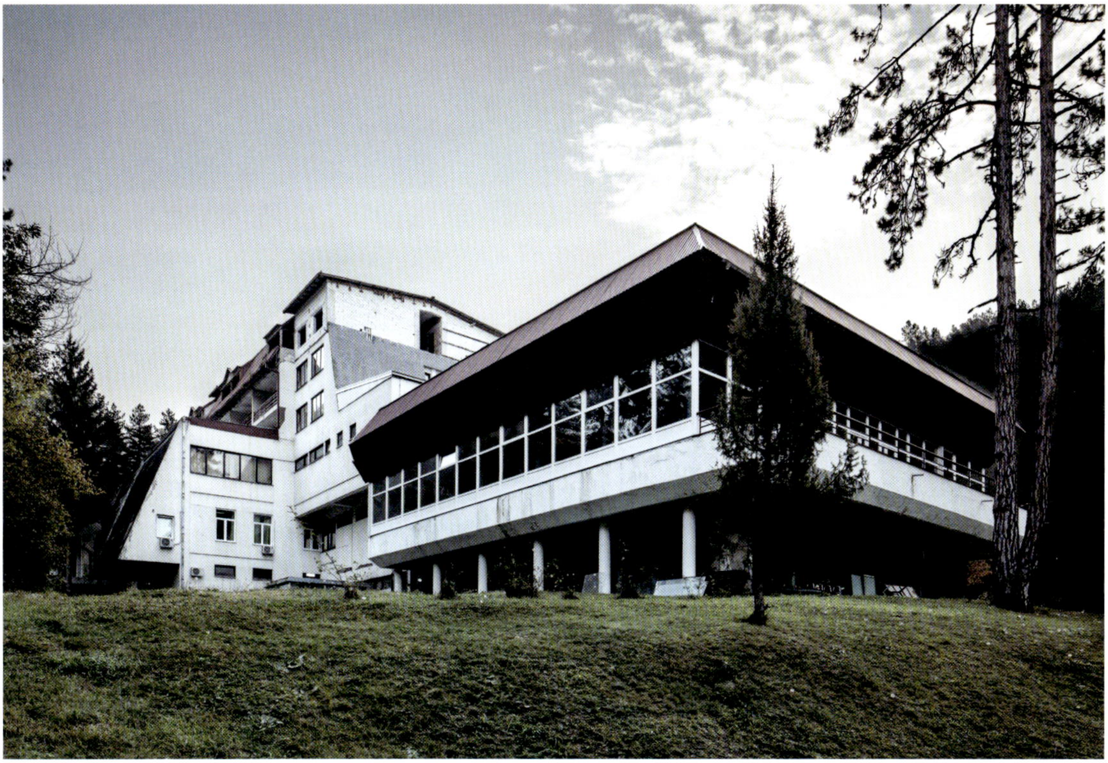

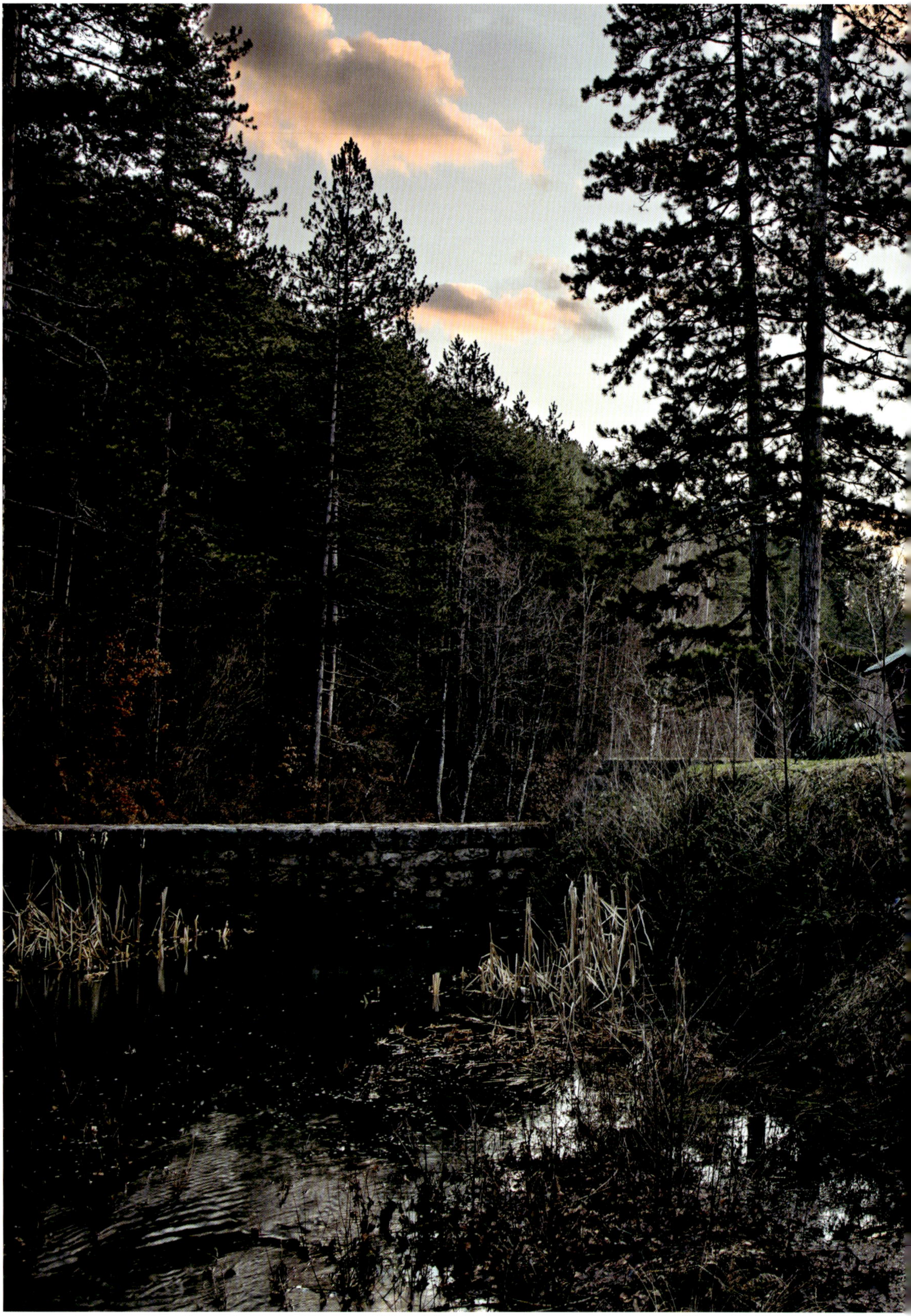

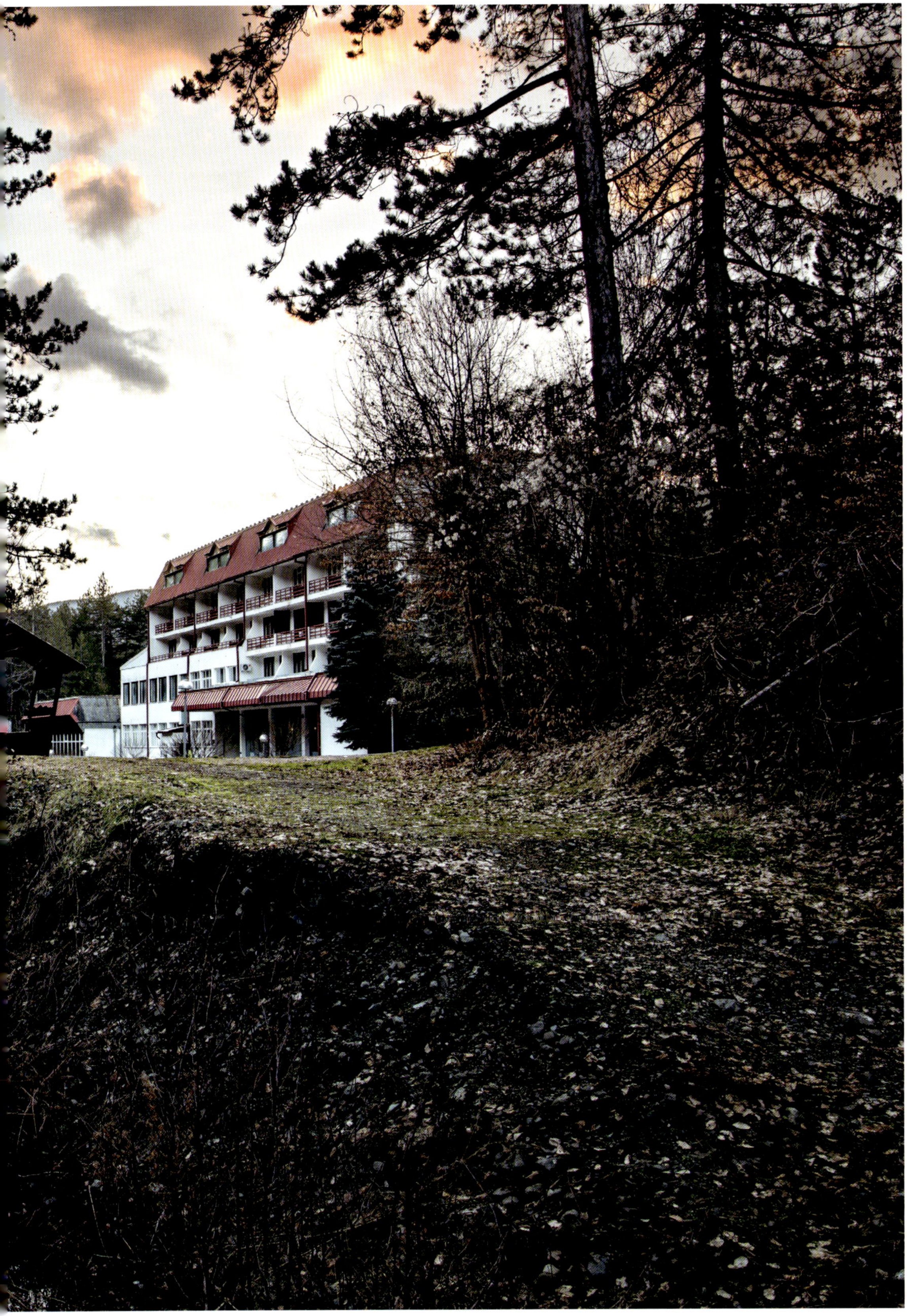

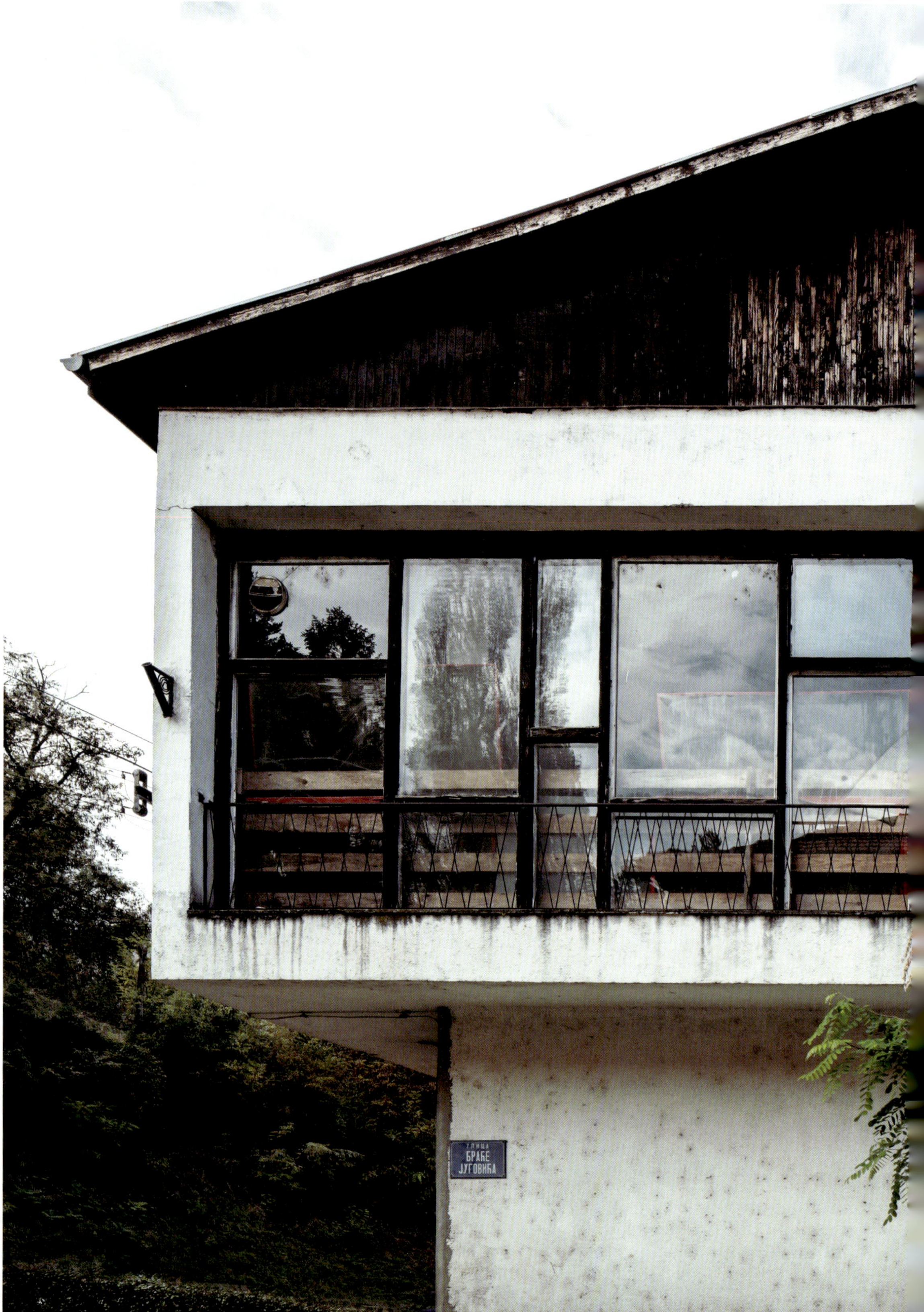
УЛИЦА
БРАЋЕ
ЈУГОВИЋА

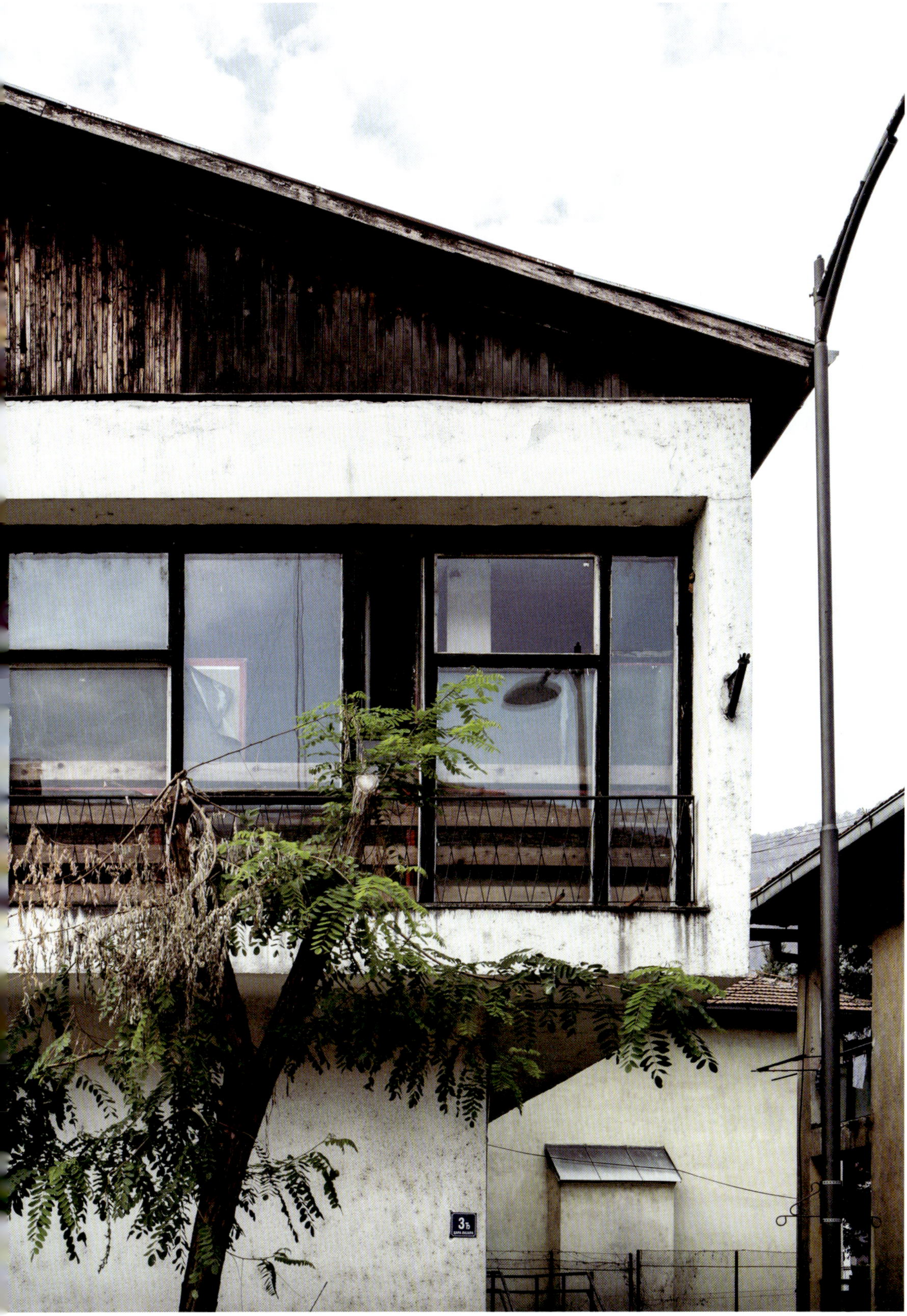

Previous spread
Višegrad
Fire Station

In the second half of June 1992, from various villages in the Višegrad area (like Žlijeb, Kuke and Vlahovici) around 150 Muslim civilians–women and children and around twenty men–were arrested by Bosnian Serb Army soldiers and held captive on the ground floor of the fire station. The fire station served as a detention centre and was managed by members of the paramilitary formations and the RS Army without a clear command structure. Here, too, girls and young women were systematically raped. According to witnesses, soldiers beat them with clubs, kicked them and ordered them to undress. They were raped in turn over a period of two to three hours. When they returned to the group, the women did not talk about it, but kept silent, even to those closest to them.

43°46'55.5"N 19°17'30.4"E

Opposite
Foča
Miljevina, Miljevina Motel

During the war, this motel was used as a meeting point for the local crisis unit tasked with expelling the non-Serb population of the community. In this building, girls and women were repeatedly raped. According to a source from the Bosnian court files, in June 1992 Nedo Samardžic, together with a group of soldiers, came to a Bosniak house. They took a young woman out of the house and searched it, put her in a car and took her to a room at Miljevina Motel and started beating her, inflicting many injuries on her. First, Samardžic raped her, causing her to pass out. She was then raped by Zoran and then held in the hotel for seven days. During this time, she was raped by other soldiers on a daily basis.[46]

43°30'47.2"N 18°38'47.0"E

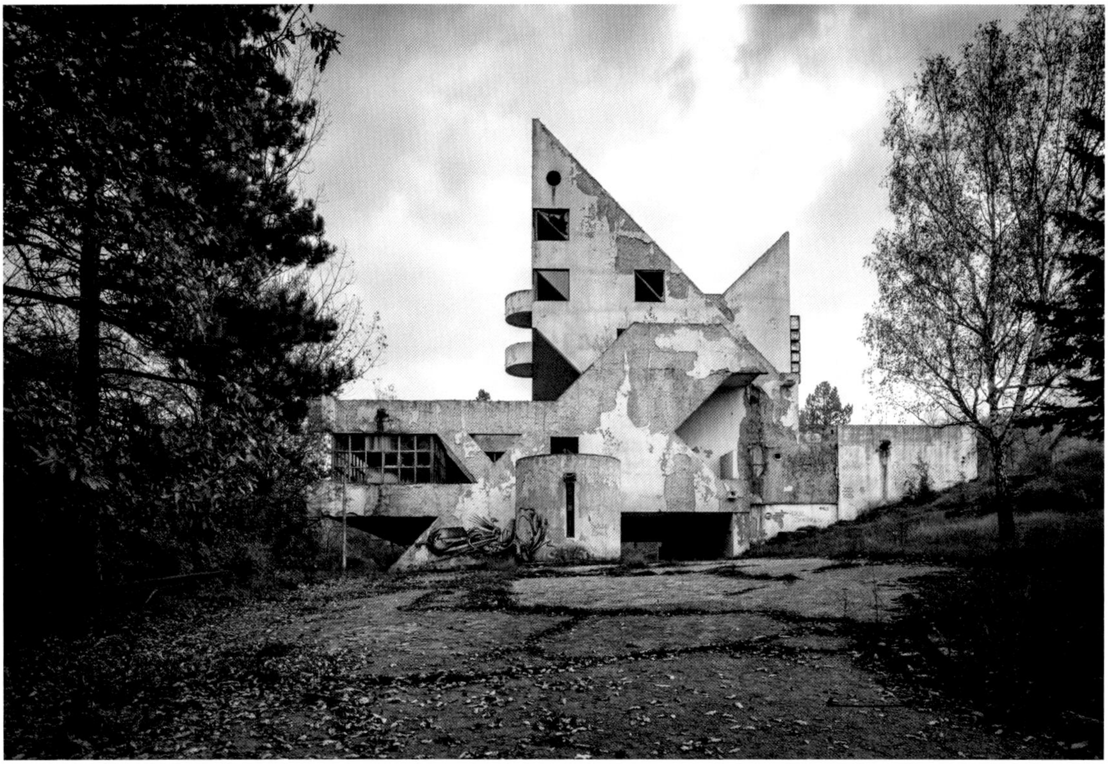

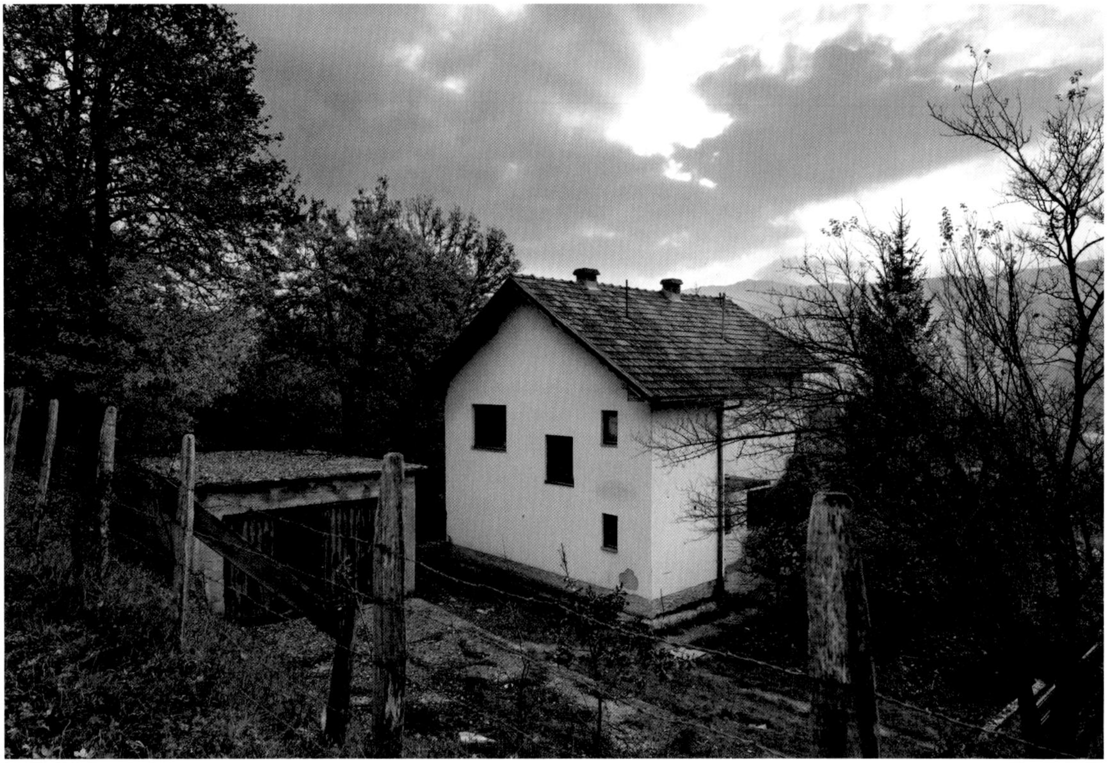

Left
Foča
Karaman's House

Karaman's house in Miljevina near Foča is named after its prewar owner Nusret Karaman. The house had two floors and two entrances. The ground floor consisted of a living room, bathroom and kitchen, while the upper floor had three rooms. The house was not quite finished and not furnished. Many apartments and houses where women were imprisoned were used as brothels, 'managed' and logistically organised by groups of soldiers, mostly members of paramilitary formations. This house was set up as a brothel in early August 1992 after Dragoljub Kunarac brought four women from the house on Osmana Áikica Street in Foča, house number 16, and handed them over to Pero Elez, commander of the Miljevina battalion. Its headquarters were in the hotel in Miljevina—very close to Karaman's house. Mostly girls, but also women from the Partizan sports hall and from the elementary school in Kalinovik were imprisoned here. The girls and women held captive could be raped by any soldier allowed into the house.

The prisoners had no medical help. Fear, frustration, insomnia and hunger were an integral part of life in Karaman's house. These women, too, had to do housework in addition to sexual exploitation—they cooked, cleaned and served Bosnian Serb soldiers. The soldiers often told them that they would kill them when they were done with them because they knew too much.[47 48]

43°30'52"N, 18°38'19"E

Overleaf
Foča
Buk Bijela

Buk Bijela is located below the road along the Drina from Brod to Miljevina. The buildings were accommodation for the construction workers of a hydroelectric power station for the construction of a dam. After the takeover of Foča and surrounding villages in April 1992, it was repurposed into a local military headquarters, which also served as barracks for Bosnian Serb forces and paramilitary formations. About 200 to 300 Bosnian Serb soldiers were housed in Buk Bijela. There was also an adjoining motel. In Buk Bijela, Bosniak residents of the surrounding captured villages were temporarily detained—women, children and the elderly who had been arrested in July 1992 in the municipality of Foča.[49] On the morning of 3 July 1992, the settlements of Trošanj and Mješaja were attacked by Serbs in camouflage clothes, several women and men were shot dead trying to escape, and the remaining civilians, including about sixty women, children and some elderly men, were captured and taken to Buk Bijela on foot.[50 51] During their several hours in detention in Buk Bijela, they were all lined up along the Drina River and guarded by armed soldiers. They were threatened with death or rape and humiliated. The soldiers separated the women from their children. The soldiers took every arrested civilian for interrogation. The interrogations focused on getting information about male villagers' hideouts and weapons depots. The women were threatened with murder and sexual assault if they lied. Several Bosniak women suspected of lying by the Serb soldiers were gang raped during or immediately after interrogation. For example, a woman was interrogated about her village and because she allegedly did not adequately answer the questions, she was taken to another room and raped by at least ten soldiers for two hours. She passed out after the tenth soldier sexually assaulted her. During another interrogation, a fifteen-year-old girl was also accused of not telling the truth. The interrogators stripped off her clothes, and then they all raped her. The first soldier threatened her by putting a gun to her head. During this sexual torture, she was in severe pain, followed by severe vaginal bleeding. Similar things happened to other women.[52] The women from the villages, Mješaja and Trošanj, after being held in Buk Bijela for several hours, were taken by bus to the gymnasium in Foča.[53]

43°26'33.8"N 18°45'20.9"E

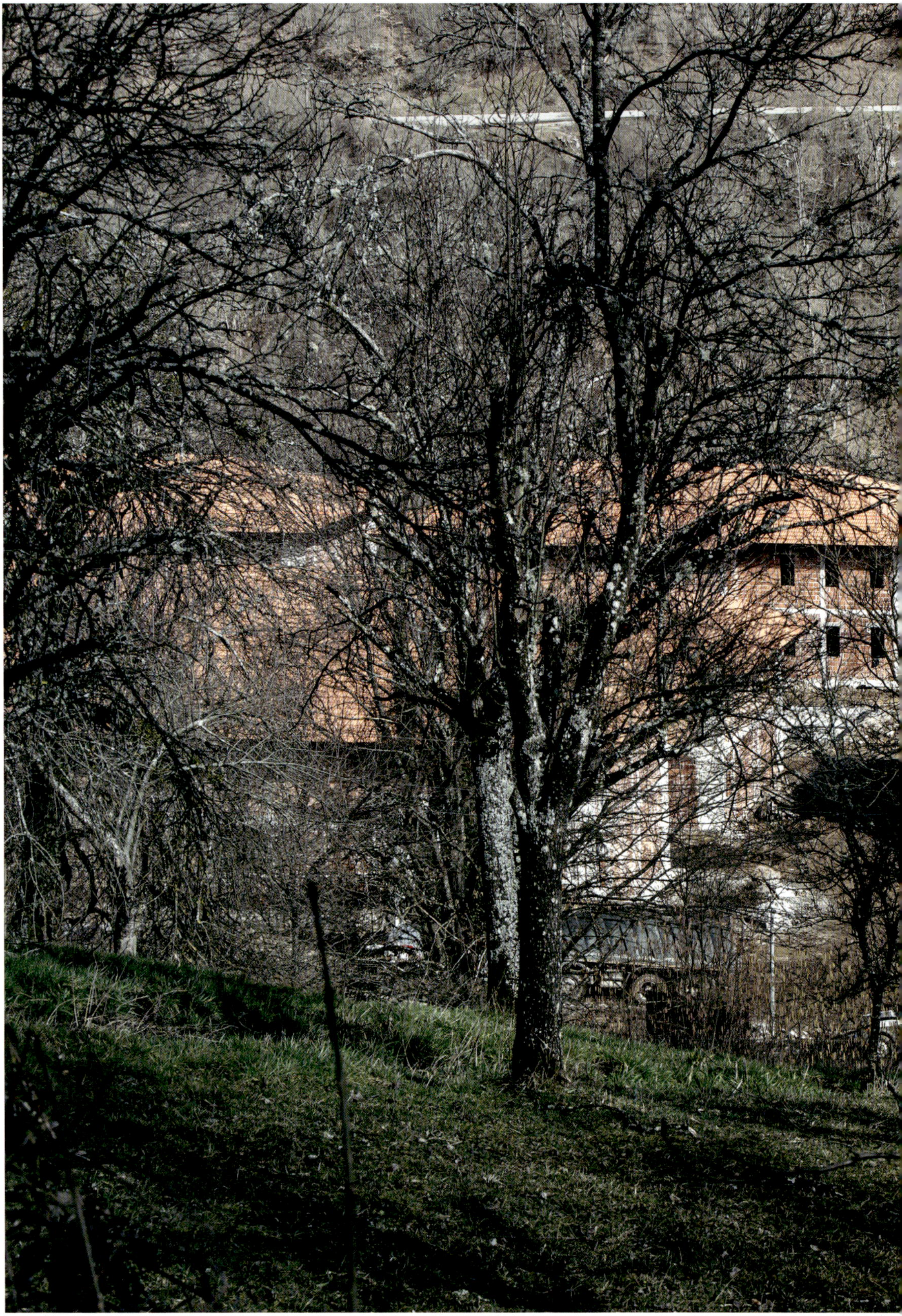

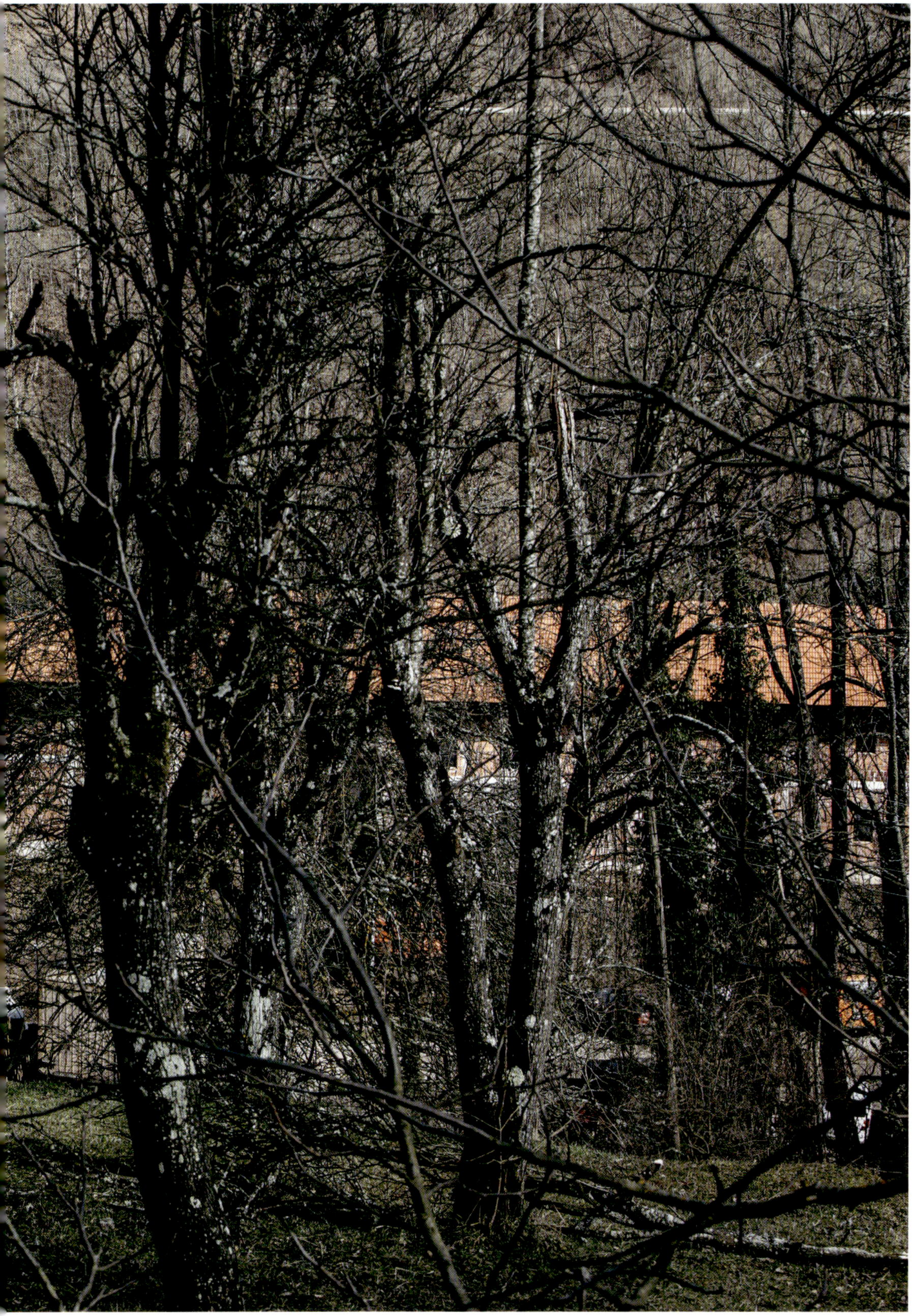

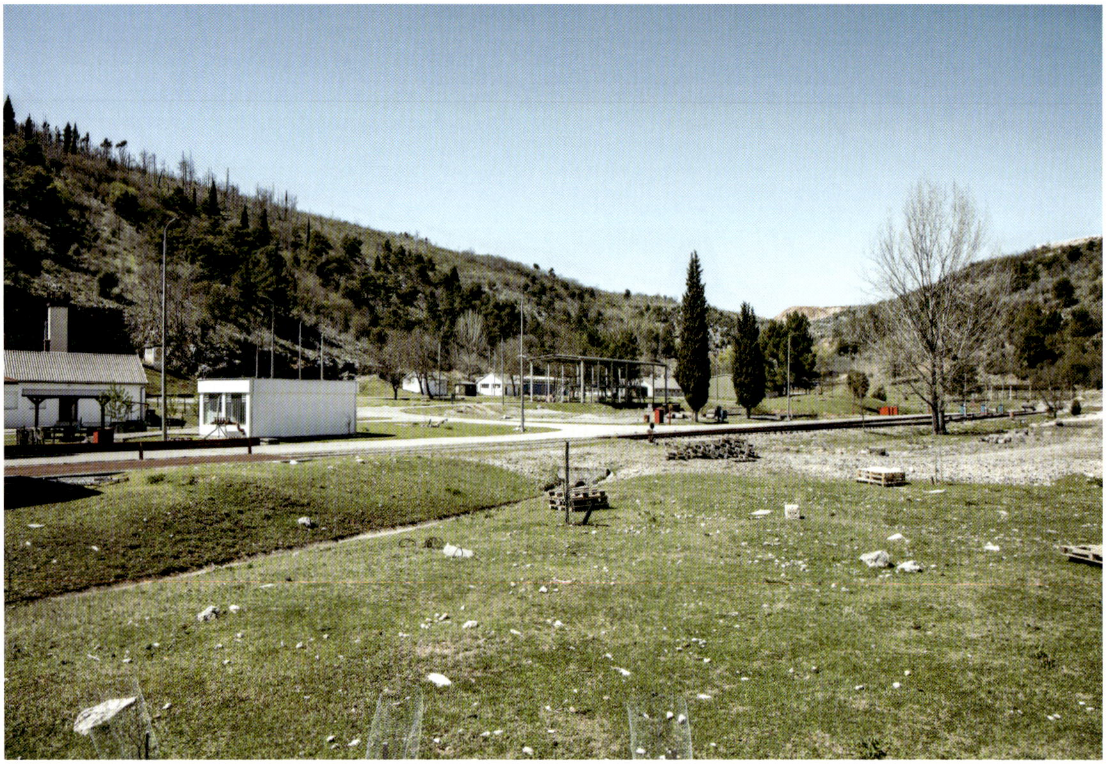

Left
Čapljina
Dretelj Camp

In May 1992, the Croatian Armed Forces (HOS) formed a camp in Dretelj for Serb civilians from Mostar and the surrounding area. From early May to 18 August 1992, at least 224 Serbs were imprisoned in this camp, 140 men and eighty-four women. The buildings of the former JNA (Yugoslav People's Army) were used for the camp. There was an administration building and some hangars on the site. Men were housed separately from women.

There was an ambulance and a doctor in the camp. However, the doctor did not treat the prisoners' injuries. S, a female prisoner was raped by several guards and other staff. Once they took her naked to a place where thirty soldiers were standing and forced her to insert a rubber rod into her vagina. Another detainee was taken to the manager's office. The guard forced her to strip, then beat her, pushed her to the ground, and raped her. She was raped more than thirty times by twenty-two men. One of the men who raped her was Ivan Medic, who was later, in April 2015, sentenced to seven years imprisonment.

43°07'30.7"N 17°42'30.0"E

Overleaf
Konjic
Čelebići Camp (ex Yugoslav People's Army hangars)

Čelebići was a large prison camp jointly operated by Bosnian Croat forces from April to December 1992. The camp was used by units of the Bosnian Ministry of Interior (MUP), Croatian Defense Council (HVO) and later Bosnian Territorial Defense Forces (TO). Here 400-700 Serbian civilians were arrested, beaten, tortured and murdered. From 15 June to early August 1992, Hazim Delic raped Witness A during an initial interrogation and repeated this torture over and over for the next six weeks. Other women were also repeatedly raped.

Some of these incidents are summarised below. Torture and rape of witness GC, a Serb woman from a village near Konjic, was taken to the Čelebići camp on 27 May 1992. Upon her arrival, Hazim Delic raped her twice in the presence of two men. GC said, '...he trampled on my pride, and I will never be able to be the woman I was.' In the months that followed, she was raped by various individuals on other occasions. GC lived in constant fear, she tried to commit suicide.

Hazim Delić was sentenced to twenty years in prison on 16 November 1998.[54] This ruling by the UN tribunal in The Hague is considered a groundbreaking decision on legal protection against sexual violence in armed conflicts. 'The Čelebići trial was thus a milestone in international law: it was the first time since the Nuremberg and Tokyo trials after World War II that an international criminal court had ruled on the concept of command responsibility. It was also the first time a court had recognised rape as torture and convicted an accused on that basis. To this day, the judgment of the Čelebići trial is mentioned in other judgments not only before the ICTY, but also before other courts dealing with war crimes.'[55]

43°40'49.7"N 17°53'22.3"E

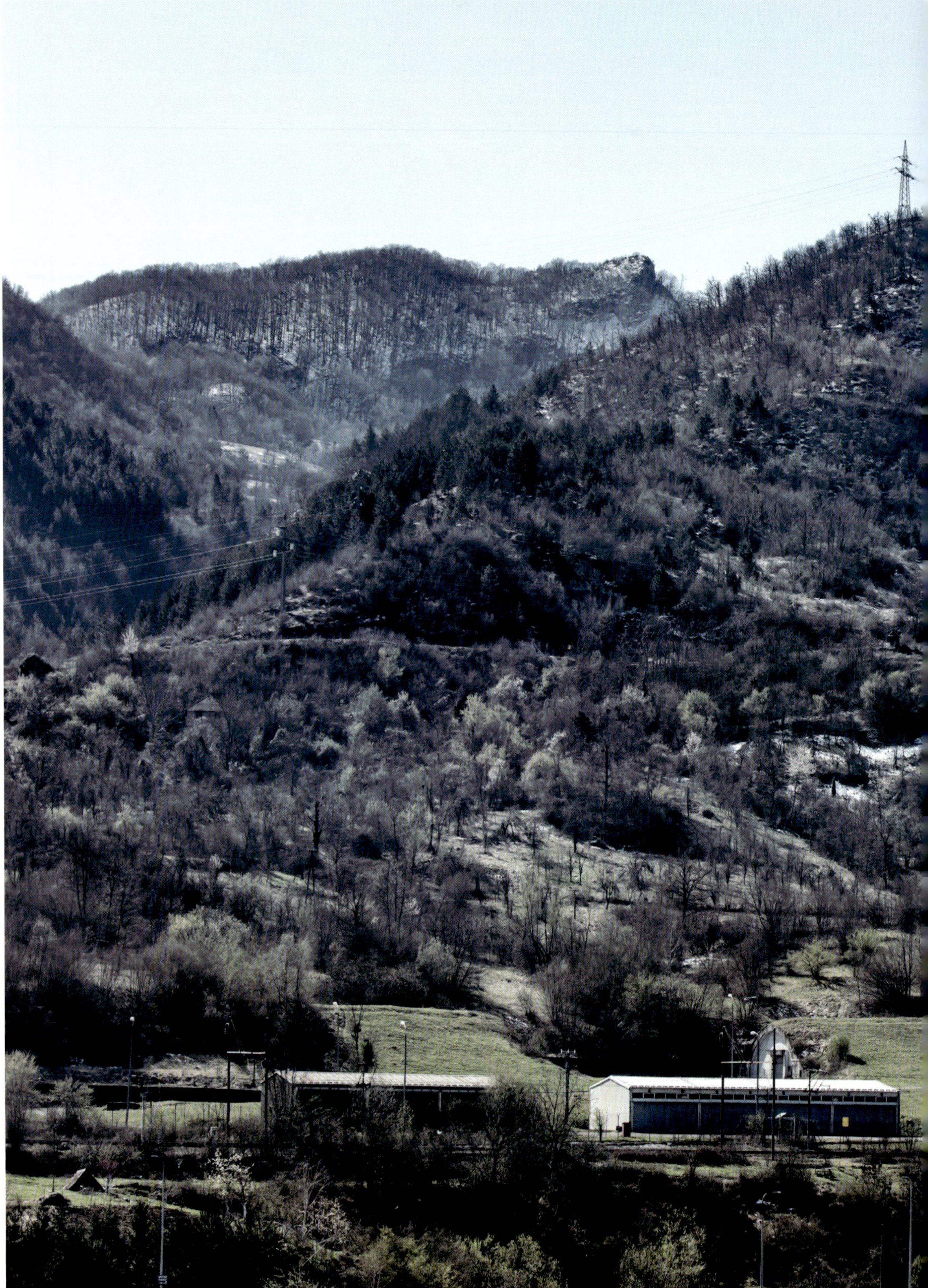

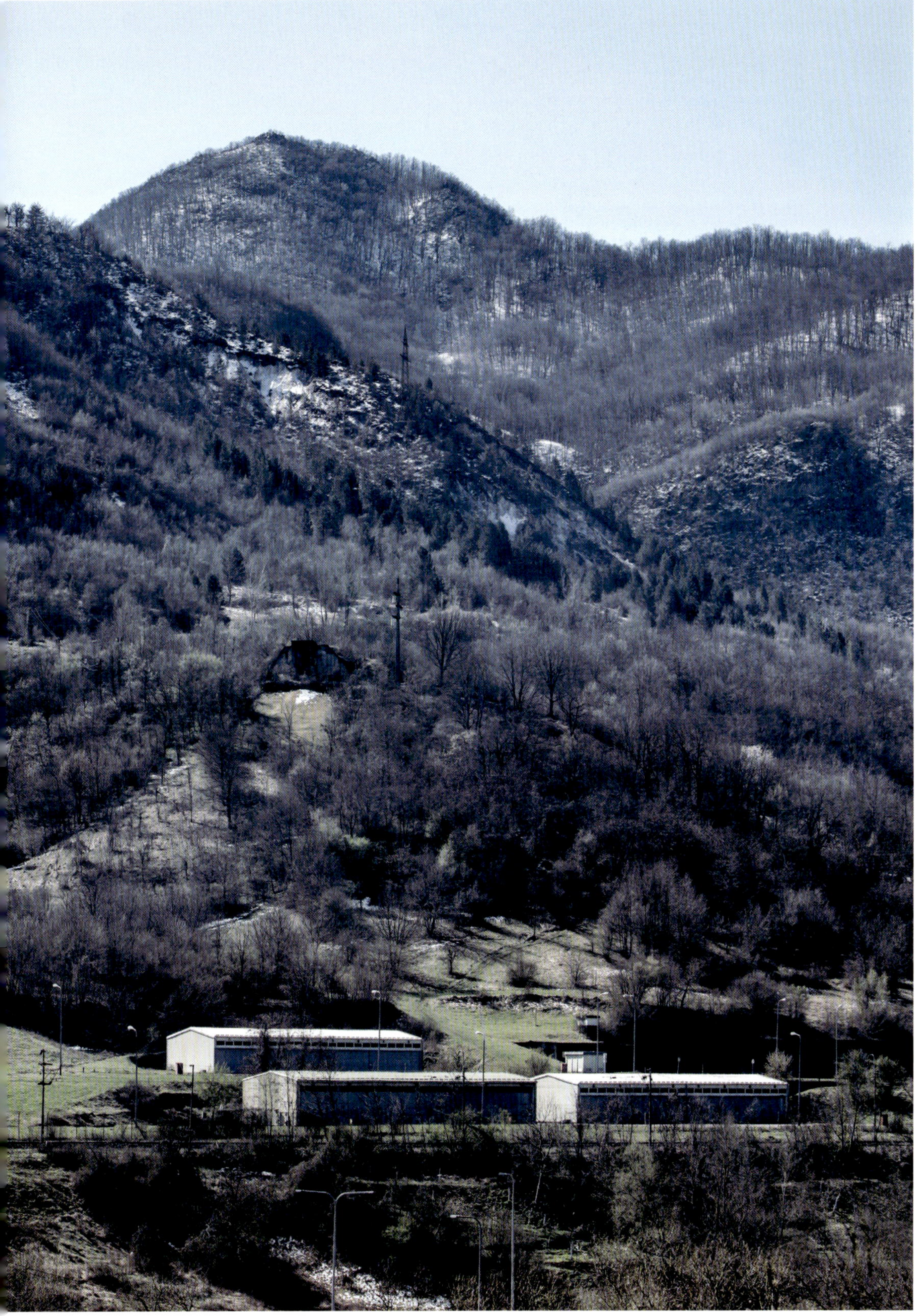

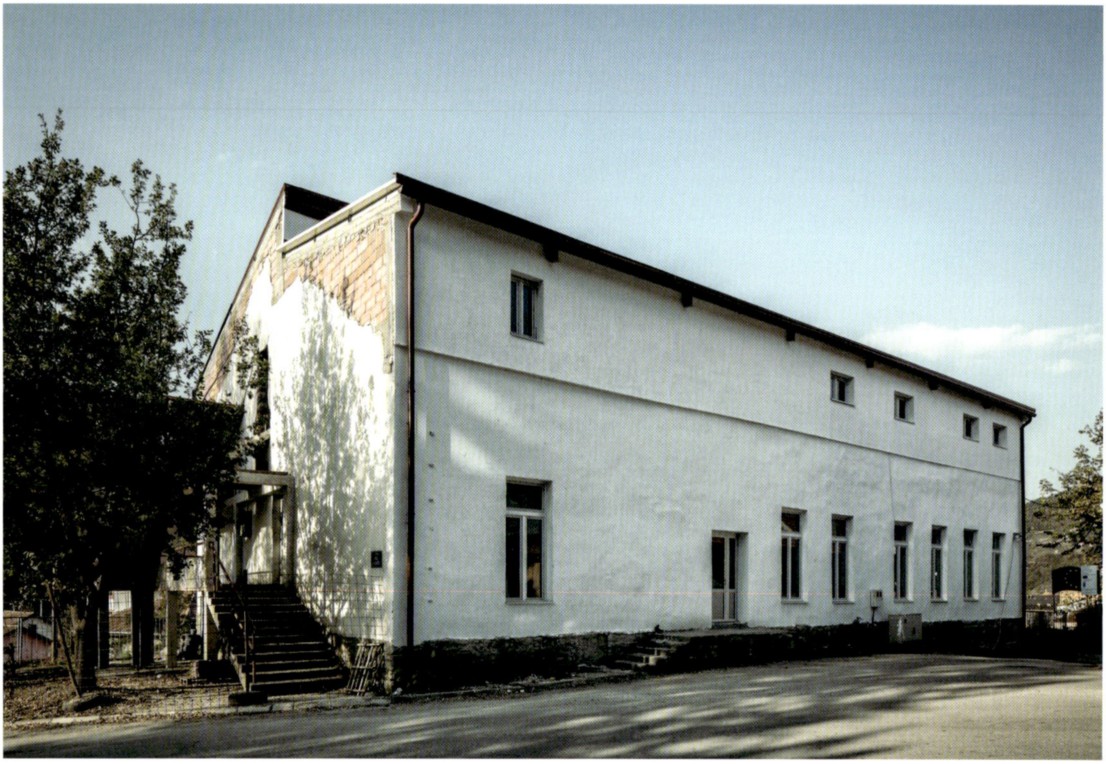

Foča

Sport Hall 'Partizan'

The Partizan gymnasium served as a detention centre for women. From 20 July to around 3 September 1992, women, girls, several children and elderly Bosniaks—over seventy in all—were forcibly imprisoned in this detention centre. Most of the women came from the above-mentioned high school centre, where they had already been held as prisoners. If they resisted or hid, the soldiers would beat and threaten them to obey. The building was secured by police officers reporting to Foča Police Chief Dragan Gagovic. Armed soldiers, usually in groups of three to five, came to Partizan Hall in the evening and took women away. Some women were taken from Partizan Hall by soldiers so many times that they couldn't remember exactly how many times they were raped. Witness FWS-95 made a rough estimate that she was raped approximately 150 times during her detention at the high school and Partizan Hall for approximately forty days.[56 57 58 59]

43°30'12.3"N 18°47'04.0"E

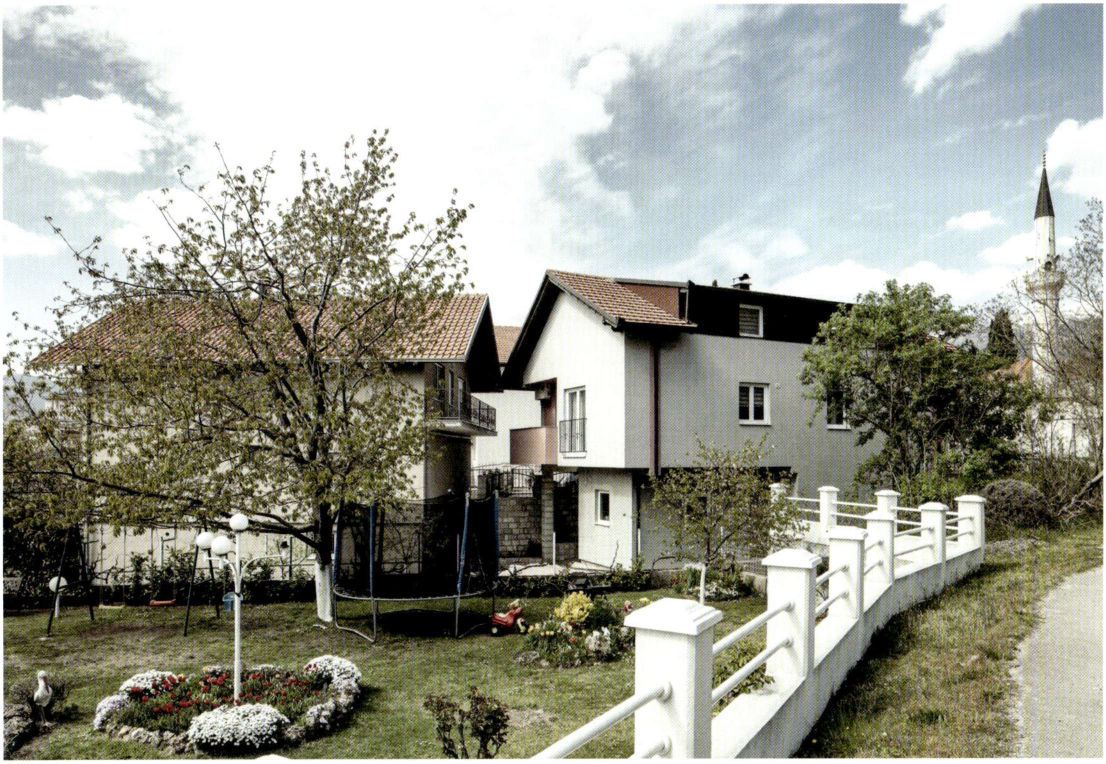

Potoci
Private Houses

RBiH soldiers raped Croatian women in these houses. These private houses border directly on a Muslim cemetery. The residents or owners had fled to Germany during the war and later returned to their homes. During the phase of the war when the alliance between the Croatian and Bosnian units broke down, the two parties became war enemies, fighting each other and terrorising the other's civilian population. The command of local units of the RBiH was established in these houses.

43°24'53.0"N 17°53'10.0"E

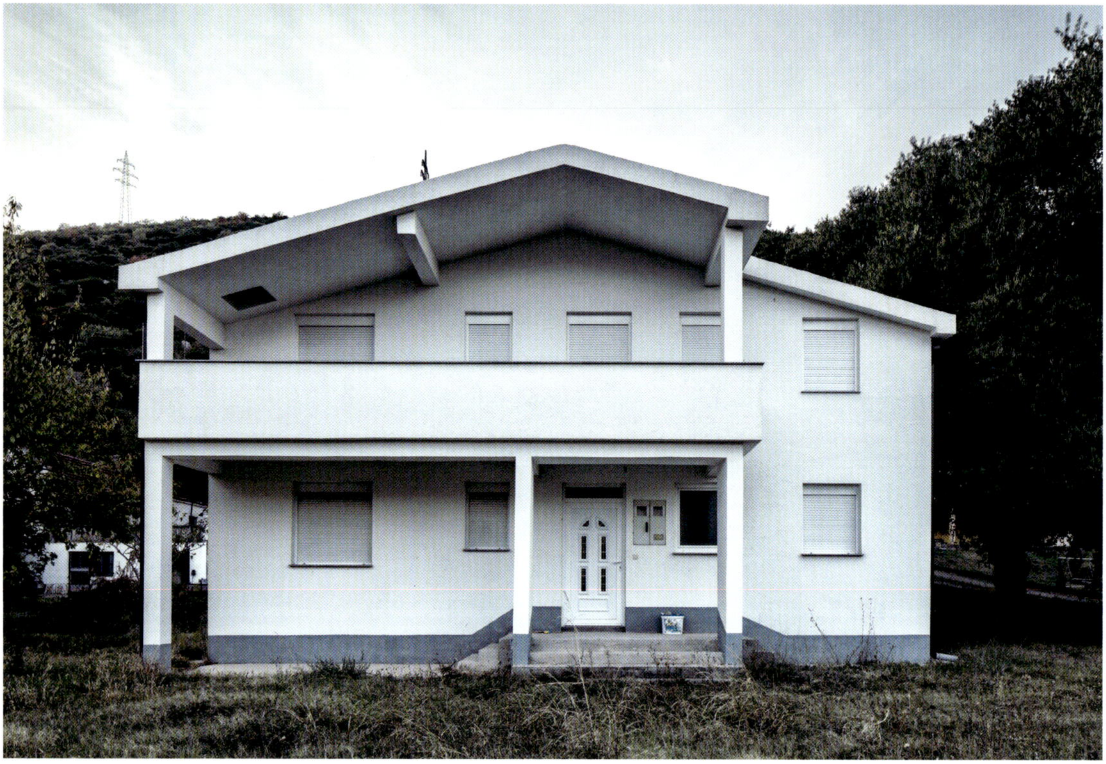

Left
Vojno - Mostar
Vojno Camp

Also near Mostar was the Vojno camp. Bosniak residents of the area and Bosniak soldiers were interned here by Croatian units. The camp consisted of private homes and garages. Women and children were held in two houses. One of the rooms housing women was 4 x 4 metres. Five women and eight children were imprisoned in this room. They slept on the floor without blankets. Another room housed twenty-two women and children. The conditions of detention were totally inadequate. Witness AM's testimony said: 'Mirko Vracevic entered the room where the women were being held and said that the woman who had made coffee for the soldiers earlier that day should come with him. He looked at me and led me into a twin room and told me to undress and lay on the bed. I had to do it since he was armed. He committed a sexual act.' Witness F spoke of what she had endured. 'When I entered the room, it was full of soldiers. A man who wore an earring in his left ear took me to another room and ordered me to undress. When I said I didn't want to do it, he ripped my shirt off and hit me. Then I passed out. When I woke up, I saw another soldier next to me and heard him say, "Emir, let me have her... Give her to me, Brekalo."' Another witness said Vracevic raped a girl, more than forty times and minors were sexually abused. 'I know that three minors were raped in Vojno,' she said. 'Brekalo introduced himself and asked Witness D, who was holding her child, to go out with him. When she said she couldn't go because of the child, he threw the child on the ground and dragged her out. When she came back later, she cried. When they went to the toilet together, she told my daughter that she had been raped,' said witness K.

43°24'53.0"N 17°52'10.0"E

Overleaf
Potoci
Aerial view

Here you can see the landscape of Potoci. What can no longer be seen are the front lines of the war and the protective trenches that ran over the adjacent mountains in the foreground on the right of the picture. Thirty-eight men interned at the Potoci camp were killed on these front lines.

43°24'57.0"N 17°53'24.0"E

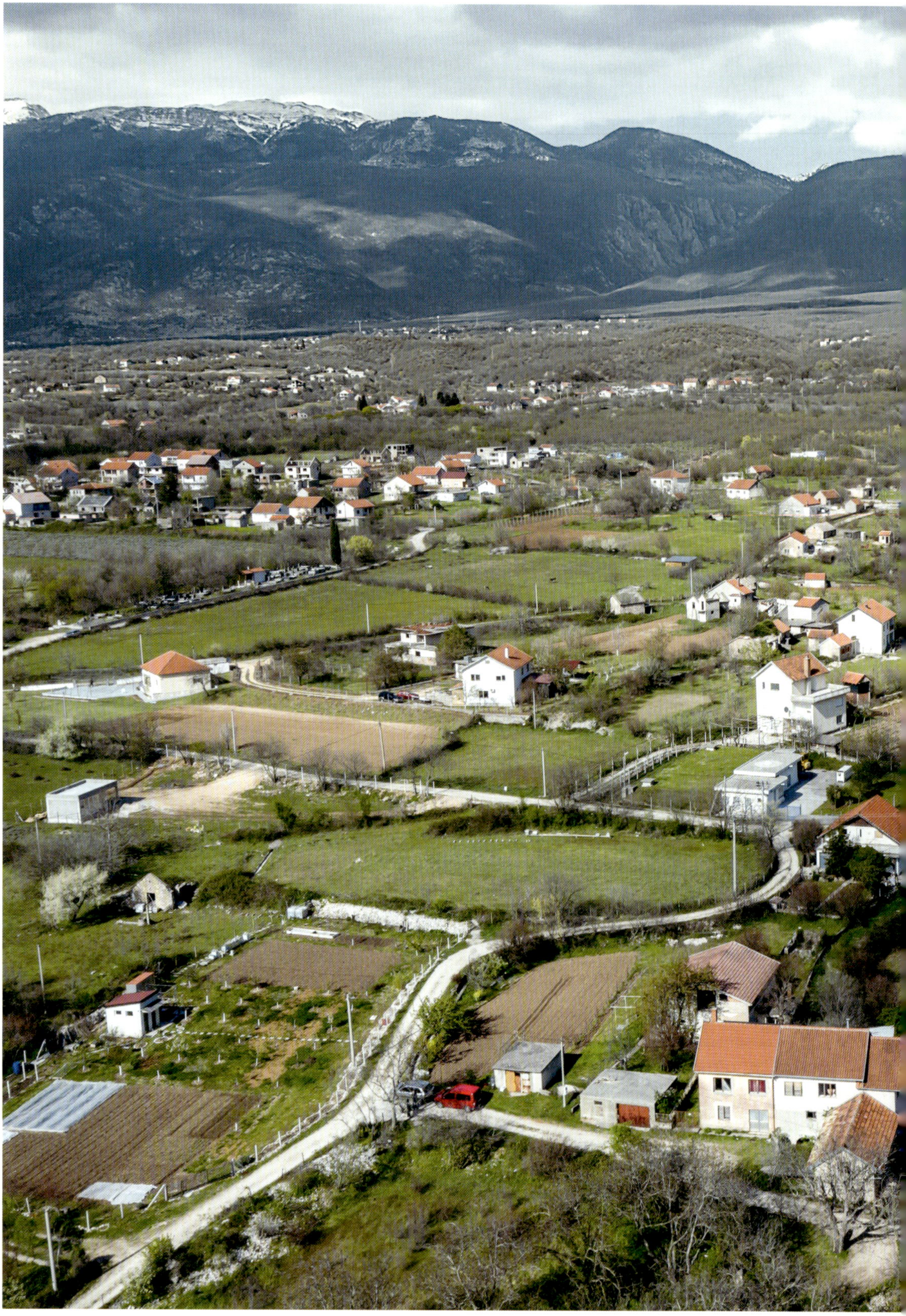

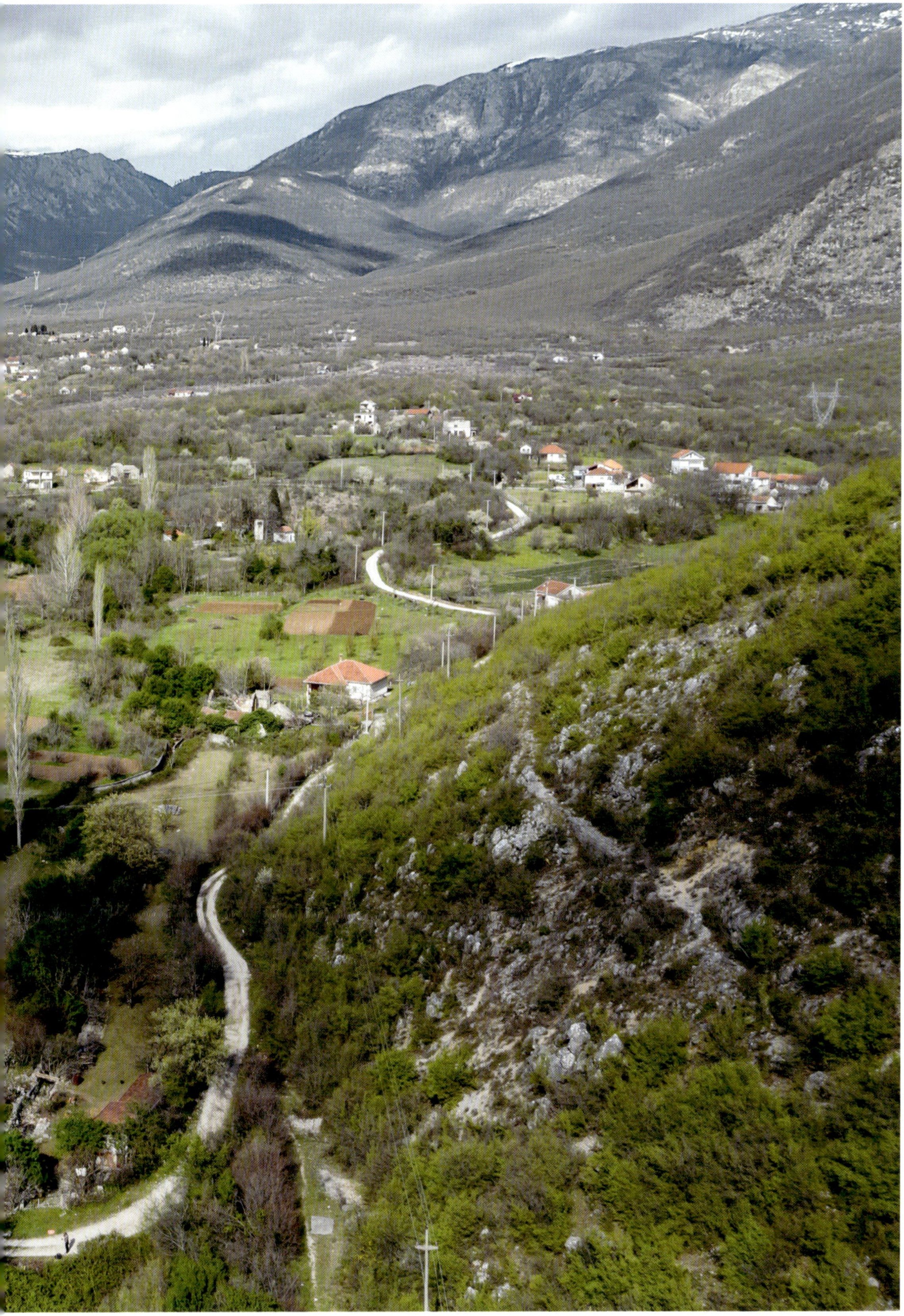

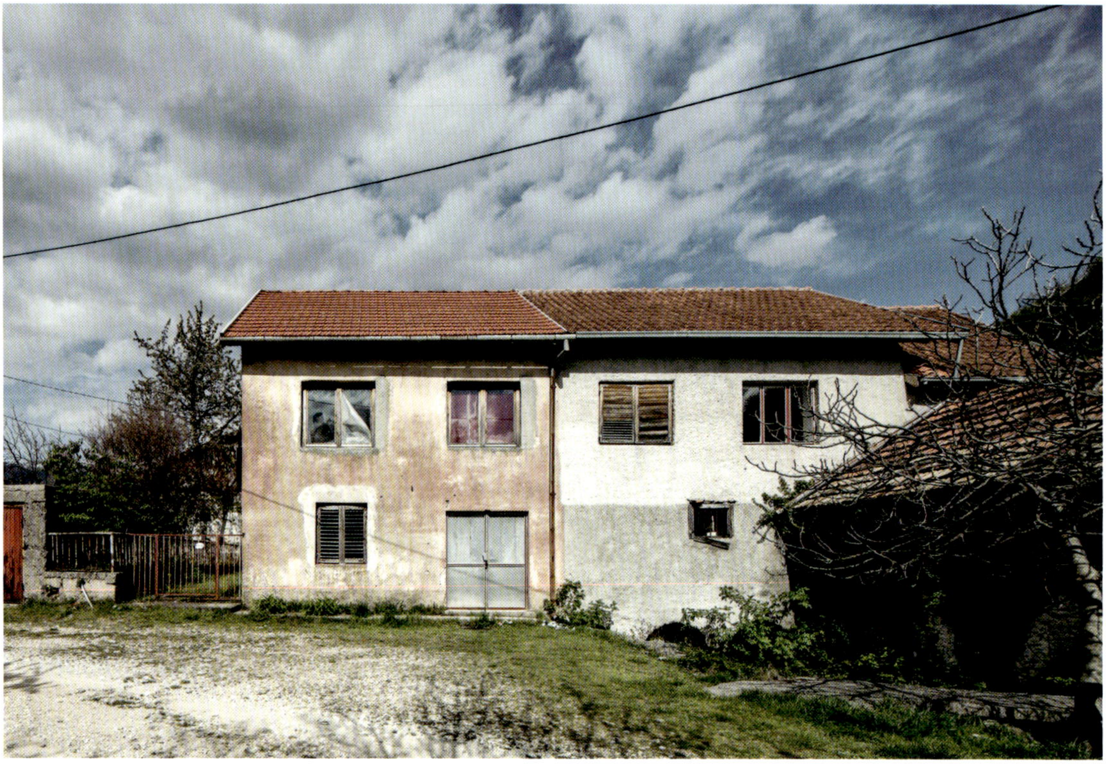

Above and opposite
Potoci
Old Mill, Skender's House

In the old mill in Potoci near Mostar, known as Skender's House, around 100 Croatian civilians and soldiers, including women and children, were detained under the control of the RBiH Army. They were subjected to psychological and physical abuse, and the men were used for forced labour at the front.

While the men were sent up the mountain to dig the trenches, women in the camp were believed to have been raped. On their return, the men noticed a completely different expression in the women.[60]

43°24'57.0"N 17°53'24.0"E

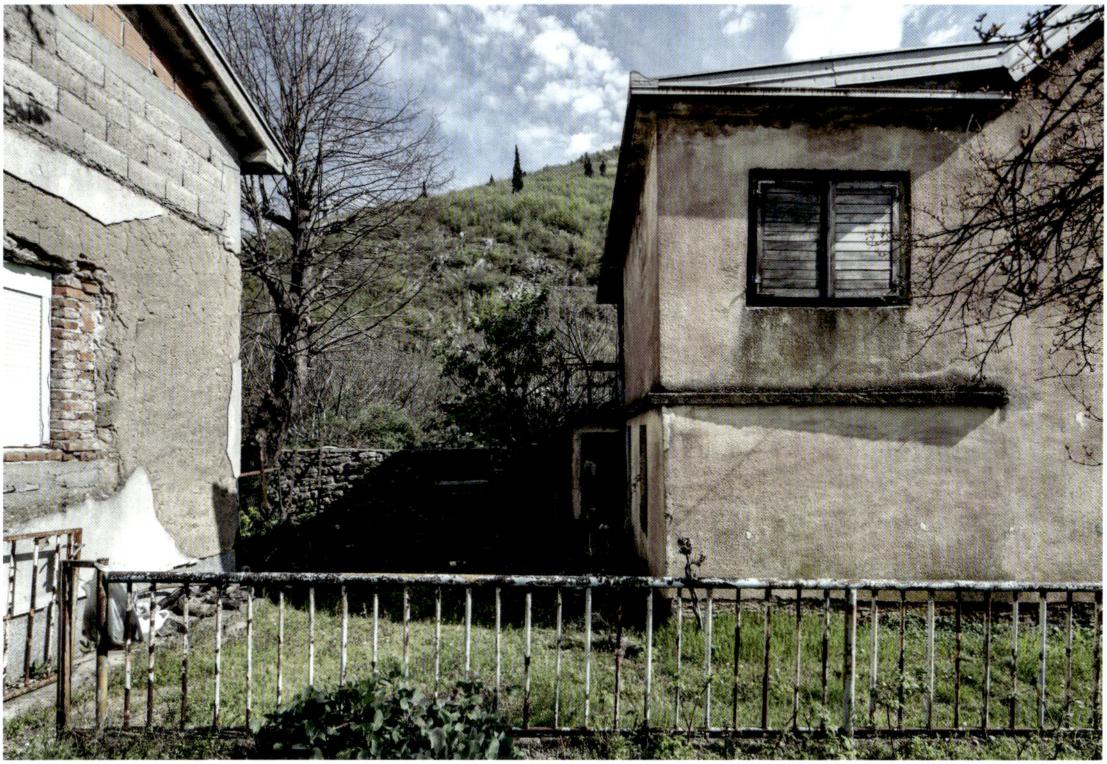

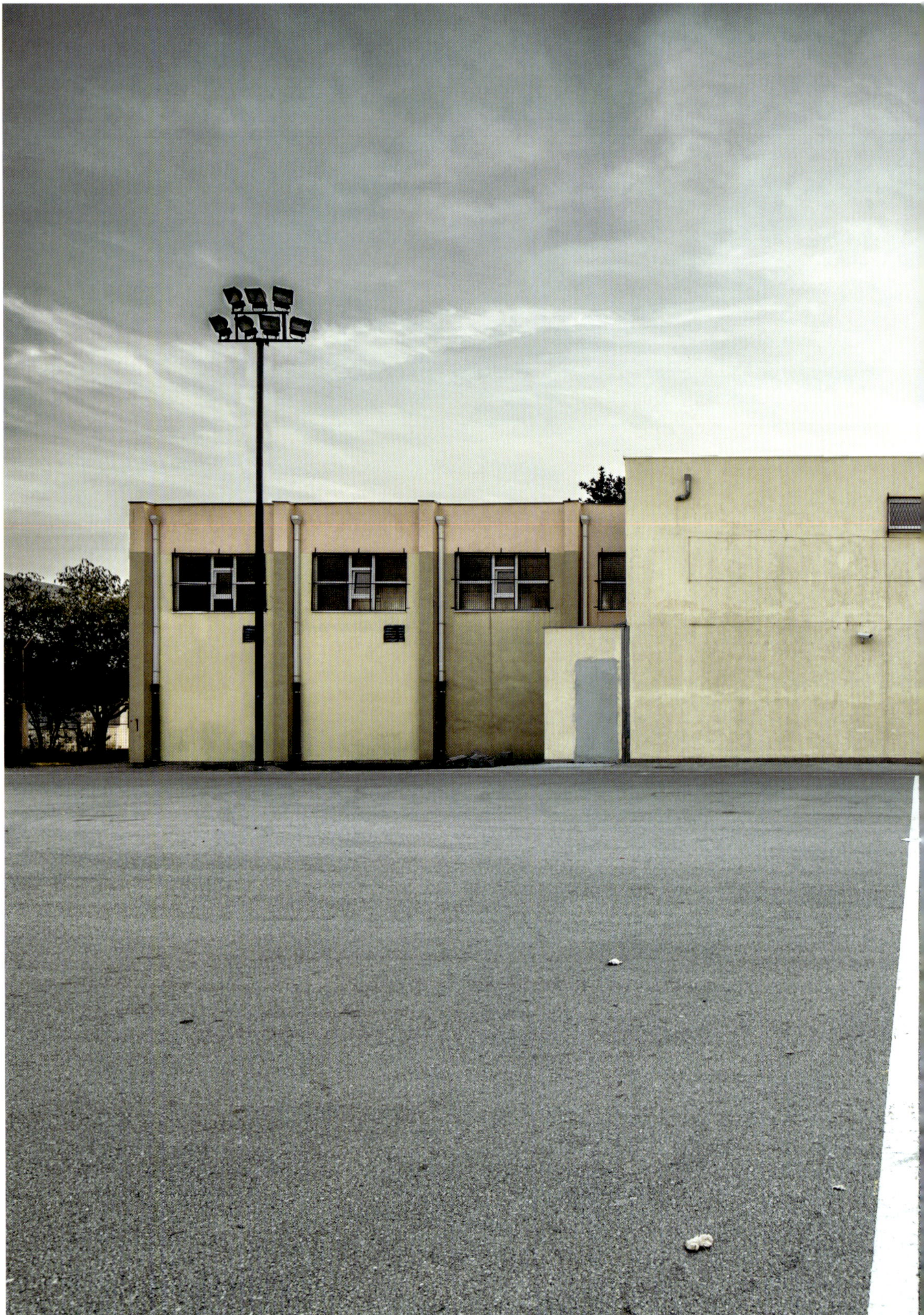

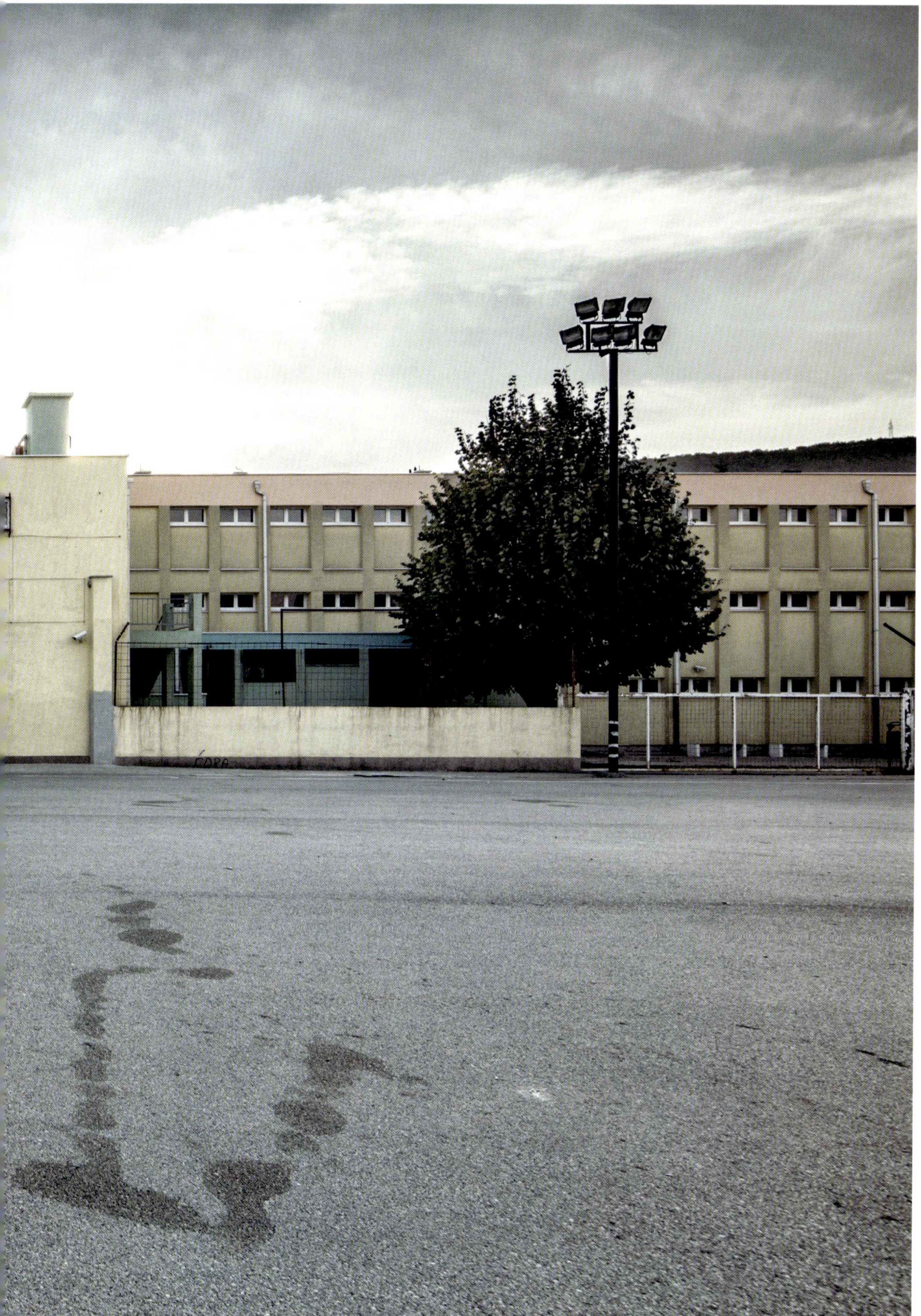

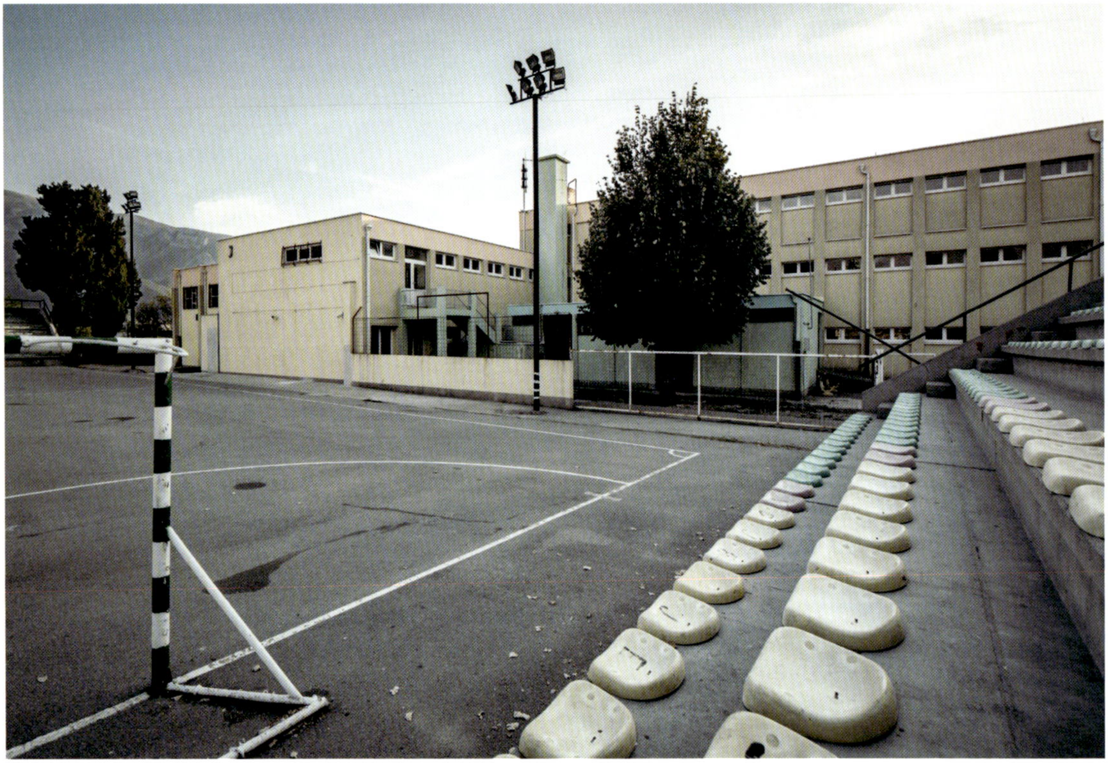

Previous spread and Left
Mostar
Elementary School

The elementary school in Potoci served from 22 July 1993 to 2 December 1993 as a detention centre for Croatian men and women. The facility was managed by members of the 49th Mountain Brigade of the RBiH Army. The primary school prisoners were Croatian Civilians, mostly residents of Potoci and Vrapcici near Mostar. About 100 inmates, men, women, the elderly and children, were housed in the school's gymnasium for about 150 days. The hall was about 24 x 12 metres. The inmates were forced to sit and sleep on the concrete floor since the wooden floors had been removed. There were reports of women being raped, and men were also physically and mentally tortured here. The witness ZZ stated that there were occassionally women who were taken away from the school, but did not speak about what had happened to them when they returned. The detainee AG said: 'For me, my stay in the camp was hell because, as a mother, I witnessed how my twenty-two-year-old daughter was subjected to sexual violence. She was taken away several times and brought back in the morning. Imagine this pain, the pain and insecurity of me as a mother and the pain of her father. Although it was obvious at the time what was happening to her and what they were doing to her, one tries to console oneself by wanting to believe that the worst might not have happened. When they brought my daughter back, she was silent, she didn't say anything, but I saw what condition she was in, her eyes gave her away. She recently testified in a trial that she had been raped several times by Ibrahim Demirovic. She was his slave to protect herself from other soldiers, as other women had to experience who had to experience being raped by several soldiers in a row. I don't think she has said everything today either.'[61]

43°24'47.4"N 17°52'37.3"E

Overleaf
Brčko
Detention Camp Luke (Harbor Facilities)

Camp Luke existed from 7 May 1992 to 9 July 1992. From the end of May to the end of June 1992, several hundred prisoners, mostly Muslim men between the ages of twenty and sixty, and some women, were interned at camp Luke. Most of the detainees were civilians. It was led by Goran Jelisic, who was captured by western troops in Bosnia in 1998 and later had to answer in court for the most serious war crimes, including genocide, rape, torture, robbery and looting. According to witnesses, Jelisic boasted that he had killed ninety-seven Muslims and planned to kill ninety-seven more. Jelisic called himself 'the Serbian Adolf' in reference to Adolf Hitler and his policy of genocide. On 14 December 1999, the ICTY sentenced Goran Jelisic to forty years in prison for committing crimes against humanity and violating the laws of war.[62] Other perpetrators, including Ranko Češić, were later charged and convicted by the ICTY. According to prisoner ST001, rapes were also committed in the camp. Shortly after arriving at the camp, she was first raped when Češić forced her into a car, drove her to a bridge, and raped her there. He said it was a pleasure to rape another 'Balija' woman (a swear word for a BiH Muslim woman). On a second occasion, ST001 was taken into a room and saw a Bosnian Serb soldier standing over a naked woman who was lying on the floor buttoning her pants. ST001 was then raped by two men whom she identified as Žućo and Makivija Stojanovic. She testified that after another rape by Makivija Stojanovic, she contracted a bladder infection, developed a high fever and was 'delirious or in a coma' for two days. Her hair suddenly turned gray and she lost a lot of weight.

44°52'12.0"N 18°48'36.0"E

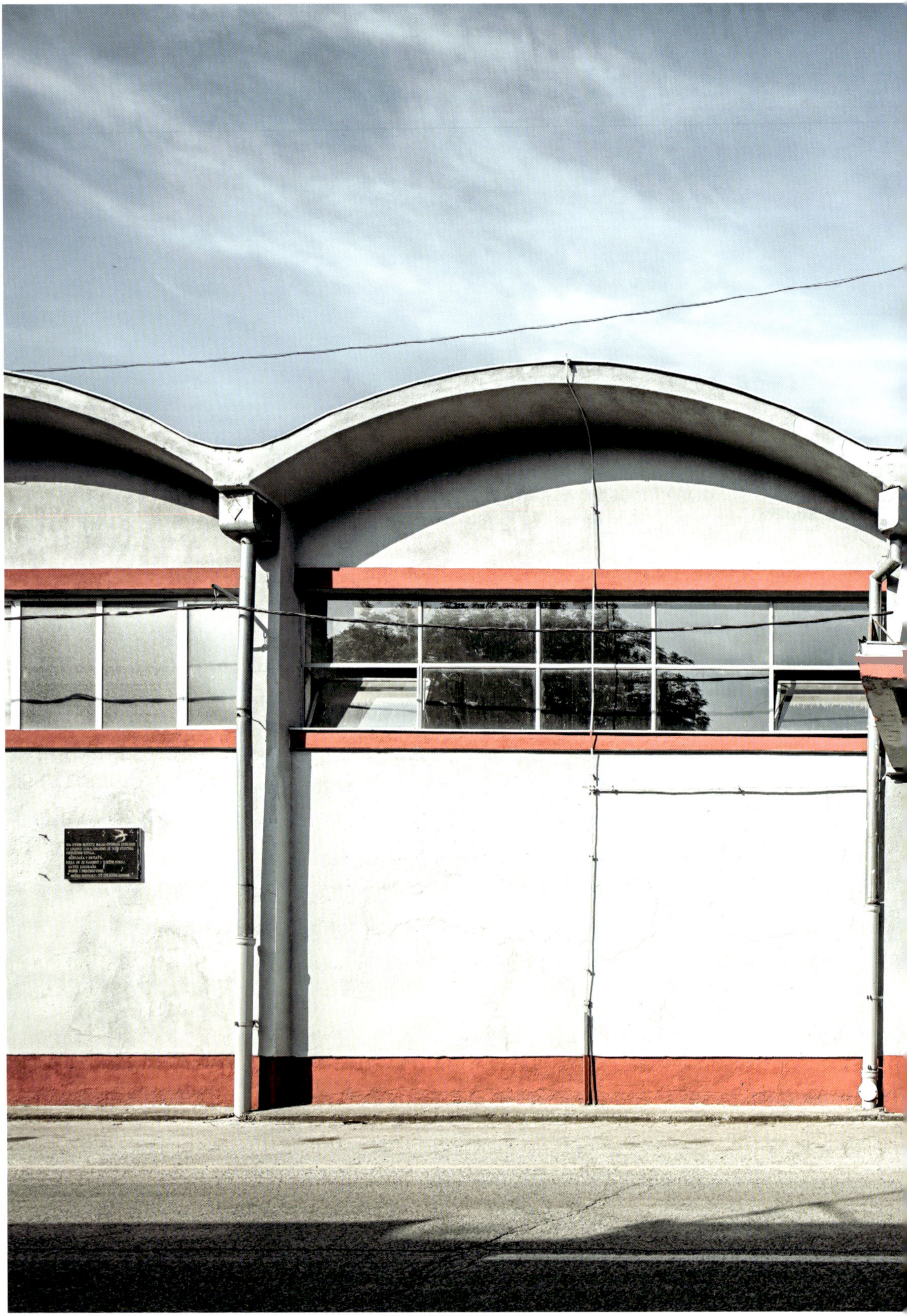

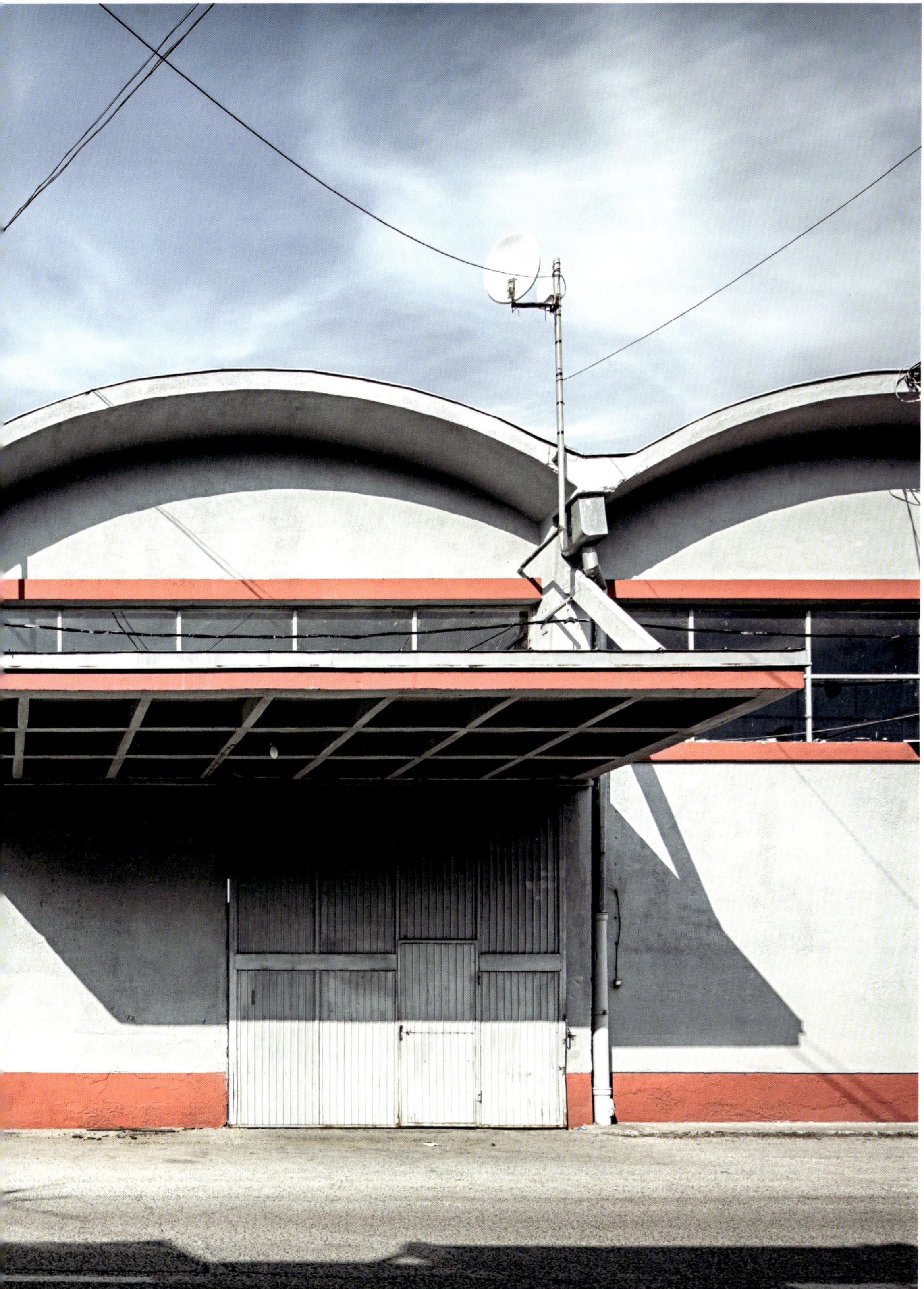

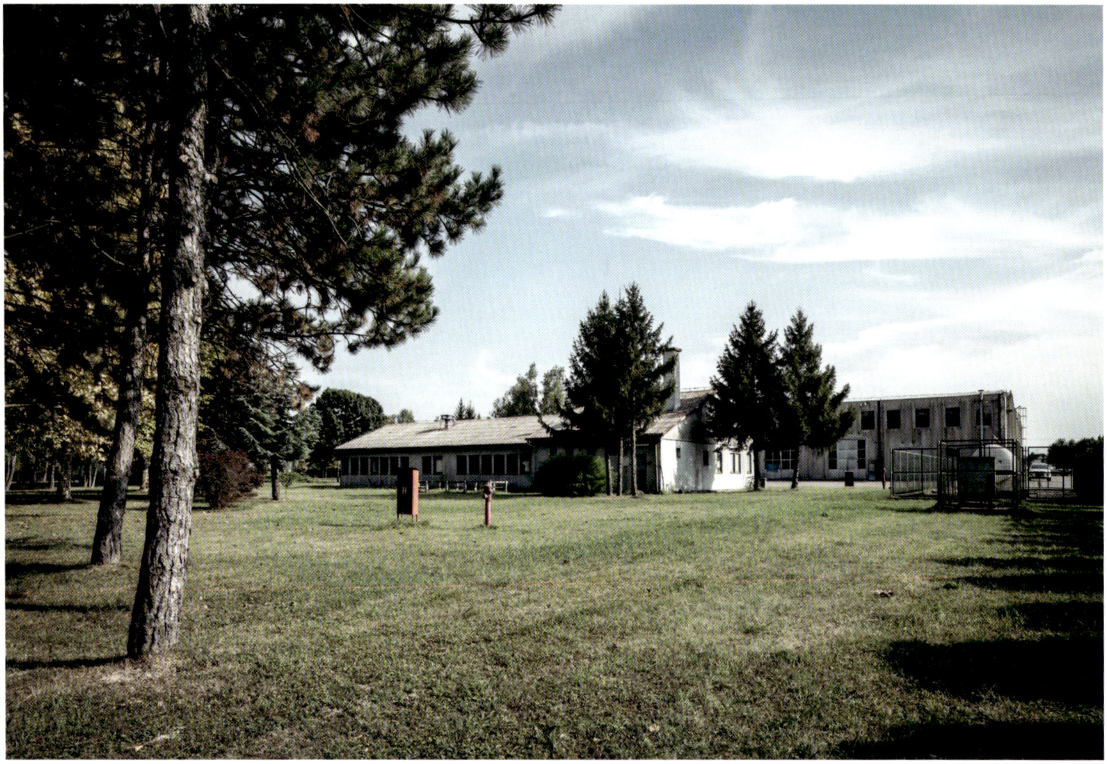

Brčko

Laser Bus Company

This detention centre, located about two kilometres outside of the city, was under the control of the Serbian Army and police. From 5-7 May 1992, a total of 200 Muslim and Croatian men, women and children were arrested here by local Serbs in uniform. The men were accommodated in the restaurant of this company. In the room next to it were a dozen women of different ages. A woman, who was a mother of two children, was raped in front of her own mother.[63]

44°51'04.7"N 18°49'06.8"E

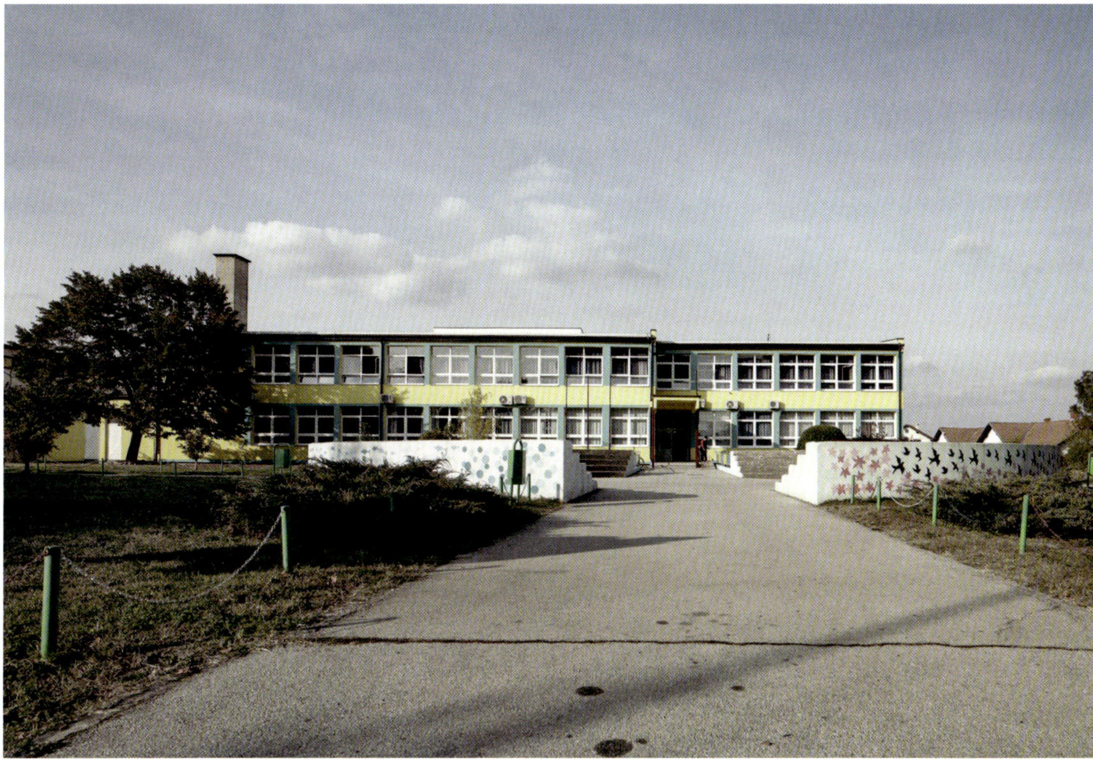

Odžak
Elementary School

The school was set up as a detention centre from 8 May to mid-July 1992. Around 700 Serbian civilians were held in a sports hall and in fifteen classrooms. Men were accommodated on the ground floor, women and children on the upper floor.[64] Witness AB3 relates that they were once forced to organise a 'wedding party.' In addition, they 'gifted' them musical instruments. DN, a man living with a mental health condition, was the 'groom' and the 'bride' was a woman from Modriča wearing a veil. Another inmate was assigned the role of 'best man.' The guards applauded the 'wedding party,' but the 'newlyweds' looked miserable and helpless. Then they took the newlyweds to a room (a school changing room) for the 'honeymoon' where they were forced to have sex in the presence of the camp staff. After several days of confinement in these school classes, women and children were moved to private houses.

45°01'01.0"N 18°19'39.0"E

Overleaf
Odžak
Strolit Factory

Before the war, steel structures for vehicles, machines and industrial equipment were manufactured in Strolit. The factory was under the control of the Croatian Defense Council's military police during the war and was used to detain 100-200 Serb civilians from 8 May 1992 until mid-July 1992.[65] There were few women, no more than ten, who were used for house and office work. The prisoners were beaten with axes and batons. Some of the men and women were sexually abused.[66]

45°00'06.0"N 18°19'39.0"E

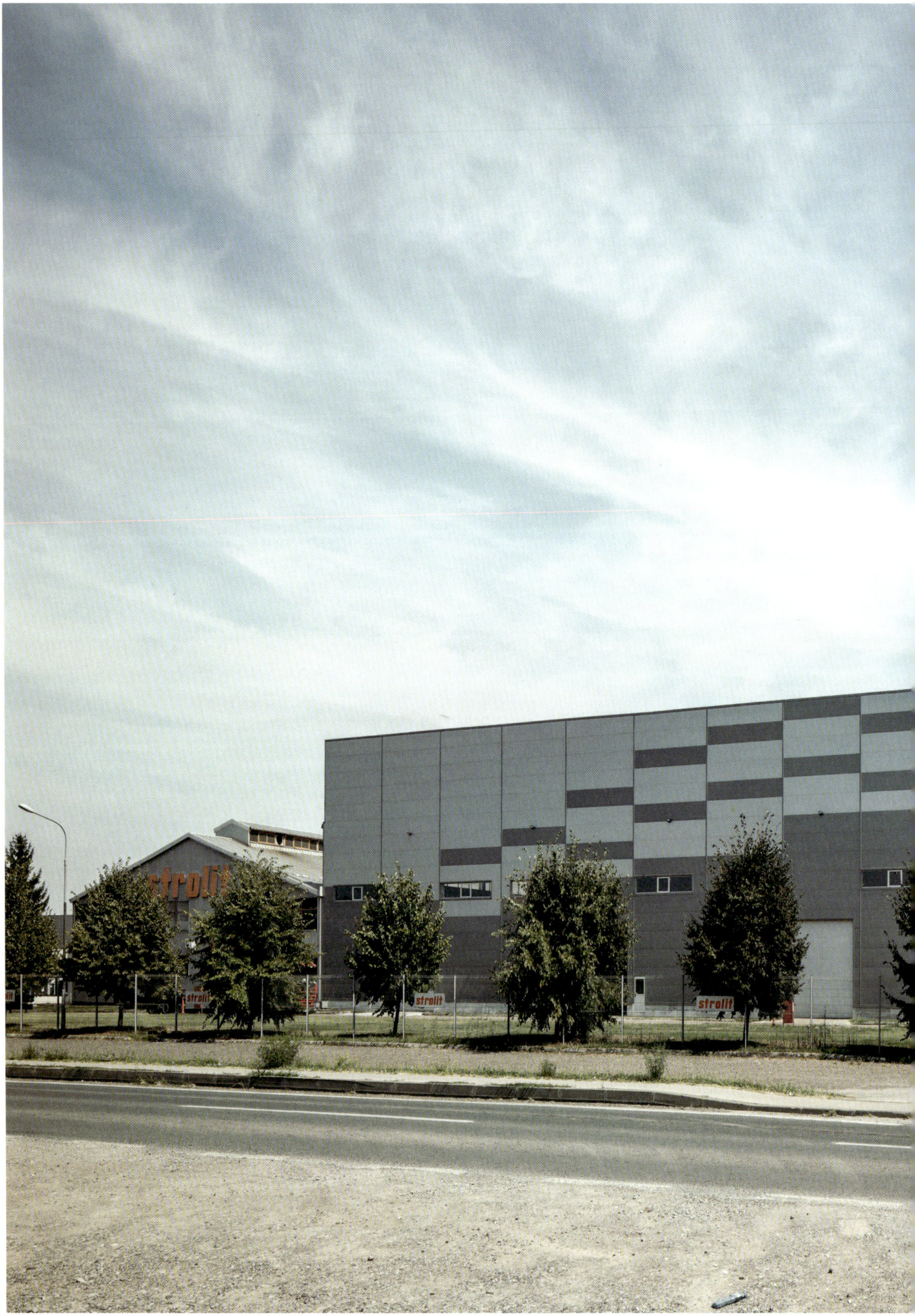
stralit
stralit
stralit
stralit

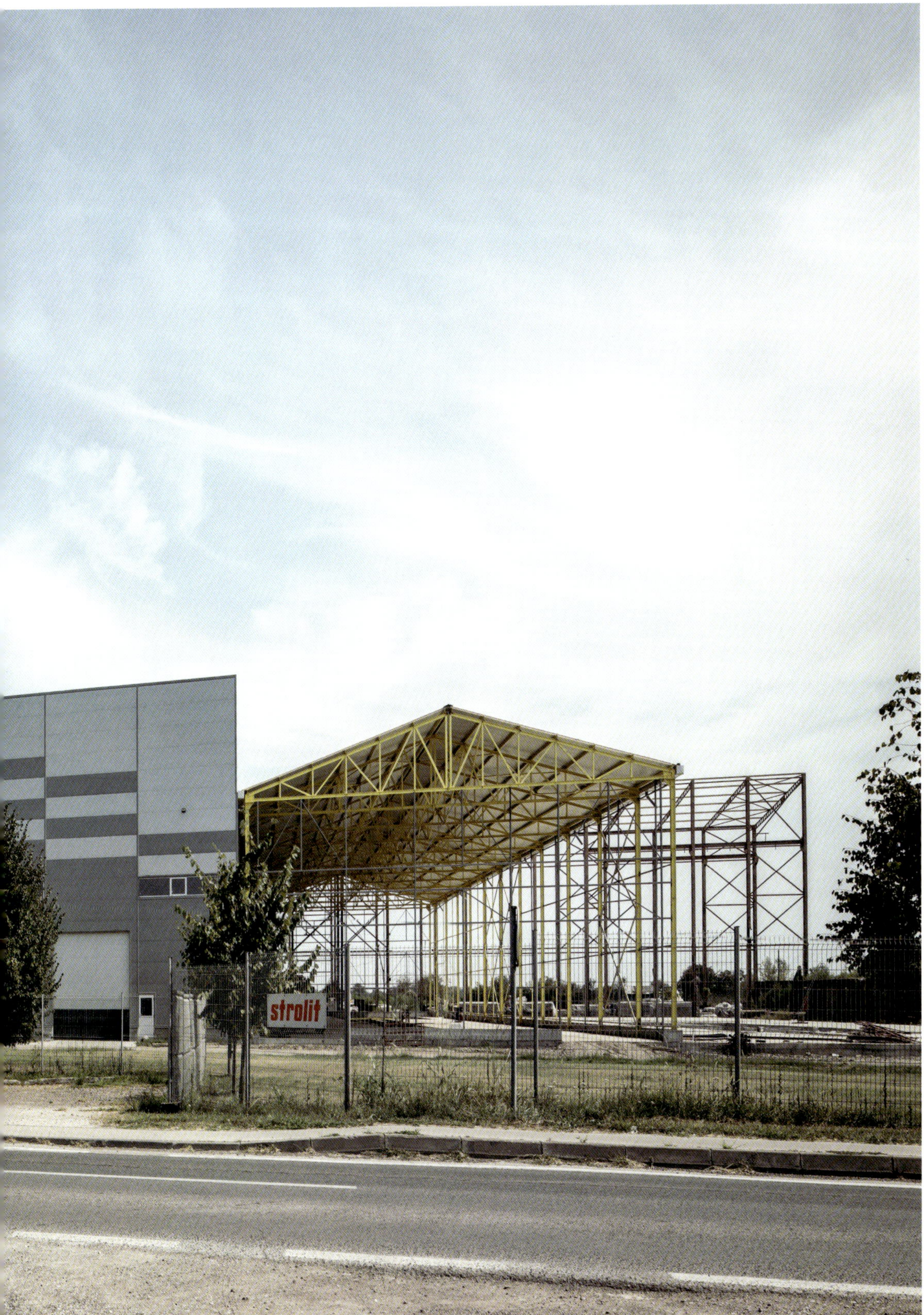
strolit

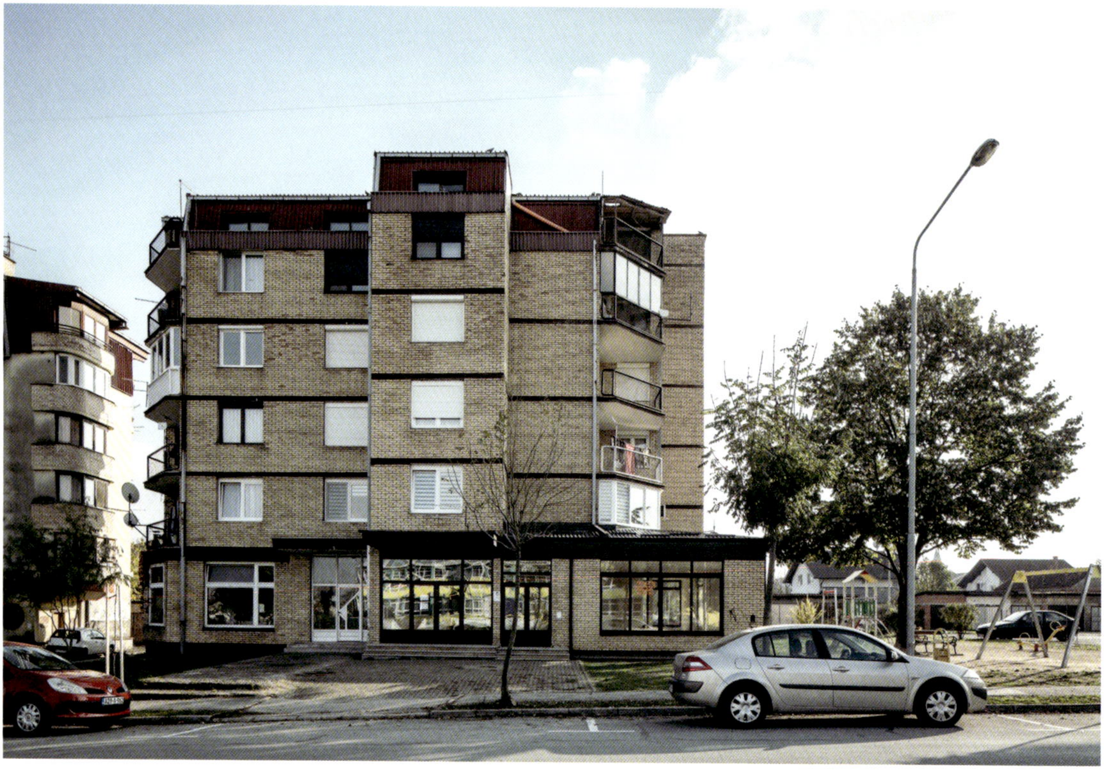

Odžak
Residential Building 'Hanka' (opposite the Elementary School)

ML and three other women, along with five to six children were taken to the residential building 'Hanka' opposite the school. In this apartment ML was raped for the first time by members of the 102nd Brigade of the Croatian Defense Council (HVO).[67] An excerpt from the judgment of the Court of Bosnia and Herzegovina against the accused Jozo Đojić (HVO) states: *Four men came at one point, including Jozo Đojić aka Koza, who was armed and in uniform. ML explained that Jozo and a certain Bekrija ordered them to undress after their children were taken from them. Jozo threw her son on the floor, after which he repeatedly raped her vaginally and anally and forced her to give him oral sex while her son was present. He beat her, pulled her hair, cursed, and threatened to slaughter her son and husband. She reported that he was taking breaks 'so he could keep going.' She said the rape lasted two to three hours, but it felt like an eternity. She stated that another woman was raped in the apartment. After that, Anto Golubović Verinitially took her back to elementary school. Then to a house where she found two other women. 'The same things happened, the same sexual violence by Anto Golubović.'*[68]

45°00'59.5"N 18°19'39.7"E

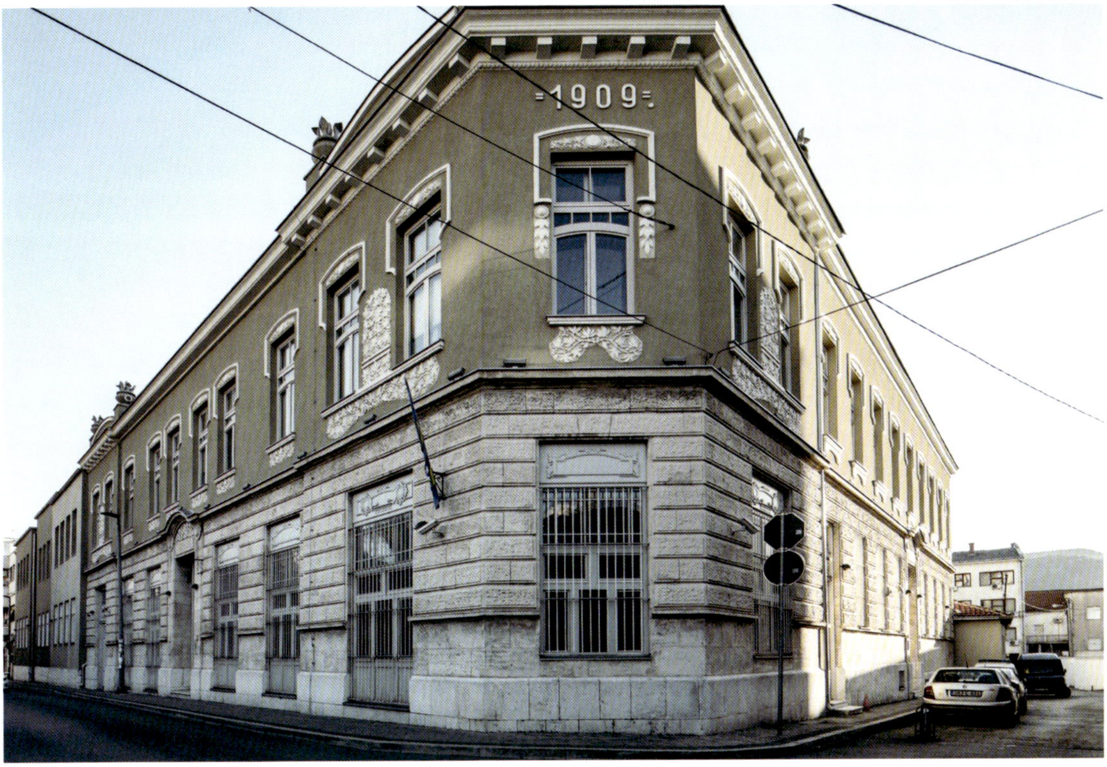

Mostar

Former IV. Elementary School, now Municipal Court

During the period of the Bosniak-Croatian war, the Fourth Elementary School on the left bank of the Nerwas in Mostar served as a prison for prisoners of war from 21 January to 1 October 1993. The prison was operated by the Military Police and Army of Bosnia and Herzegovina and operated until 19 March 1994, when the last detainee exchange took place.

Two hundred and twenty people were held here. Croatian civilians from the Vrapčići and Bijelo Polje areas and members of the Croatian Defense Council were brought here.[69] One of the women detainees explained: 'In Mostar we had to go through the cordon of civilians who beat us with anything they could find handy. The head of the camp was Mirsad Čupina, and he allowed civilians to come to the prison to beat us. Slobo Marić was a guard who separated women from the group so they could be raped.'[70]

43°20'31.8"N 17°48'51.8"E

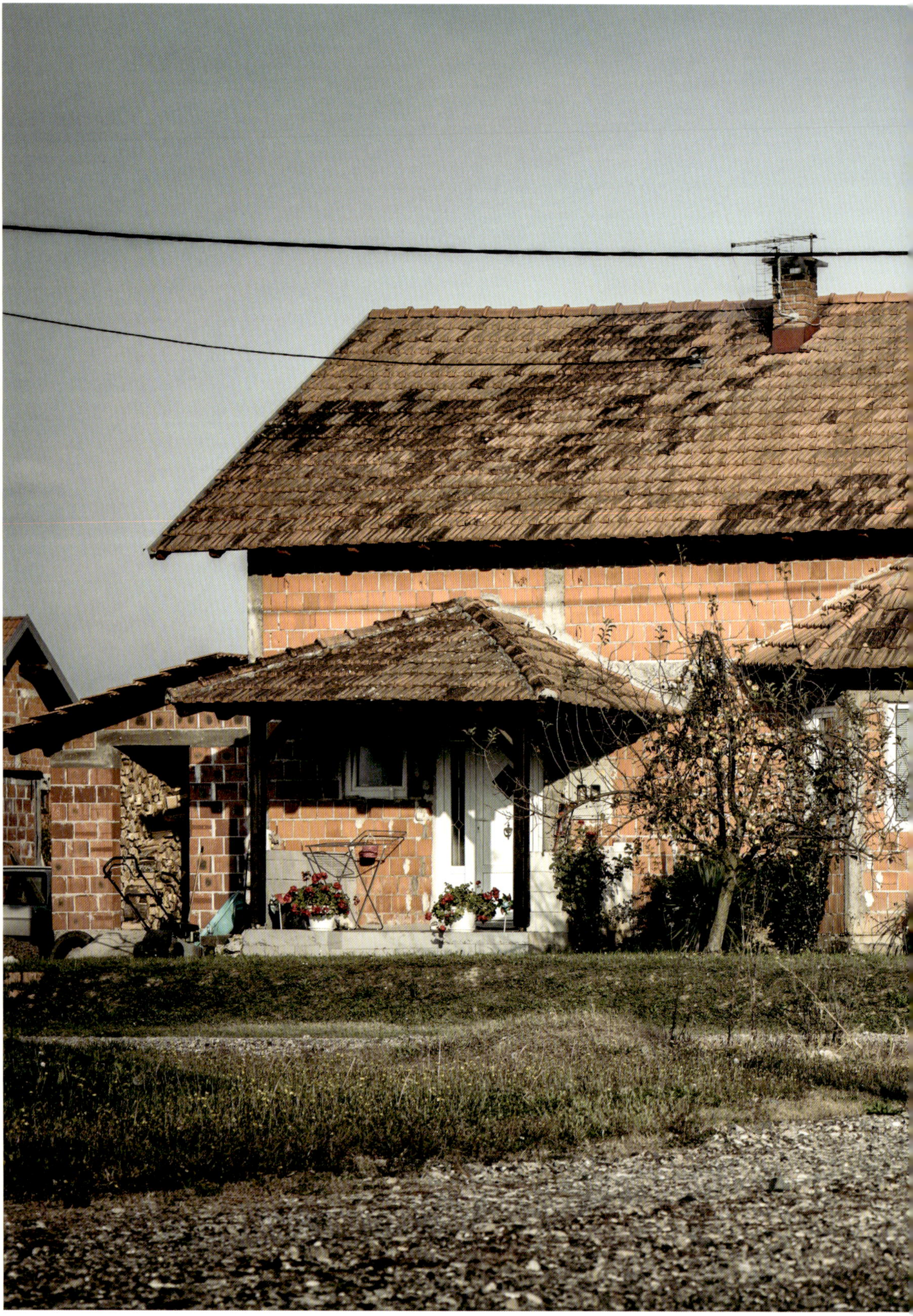

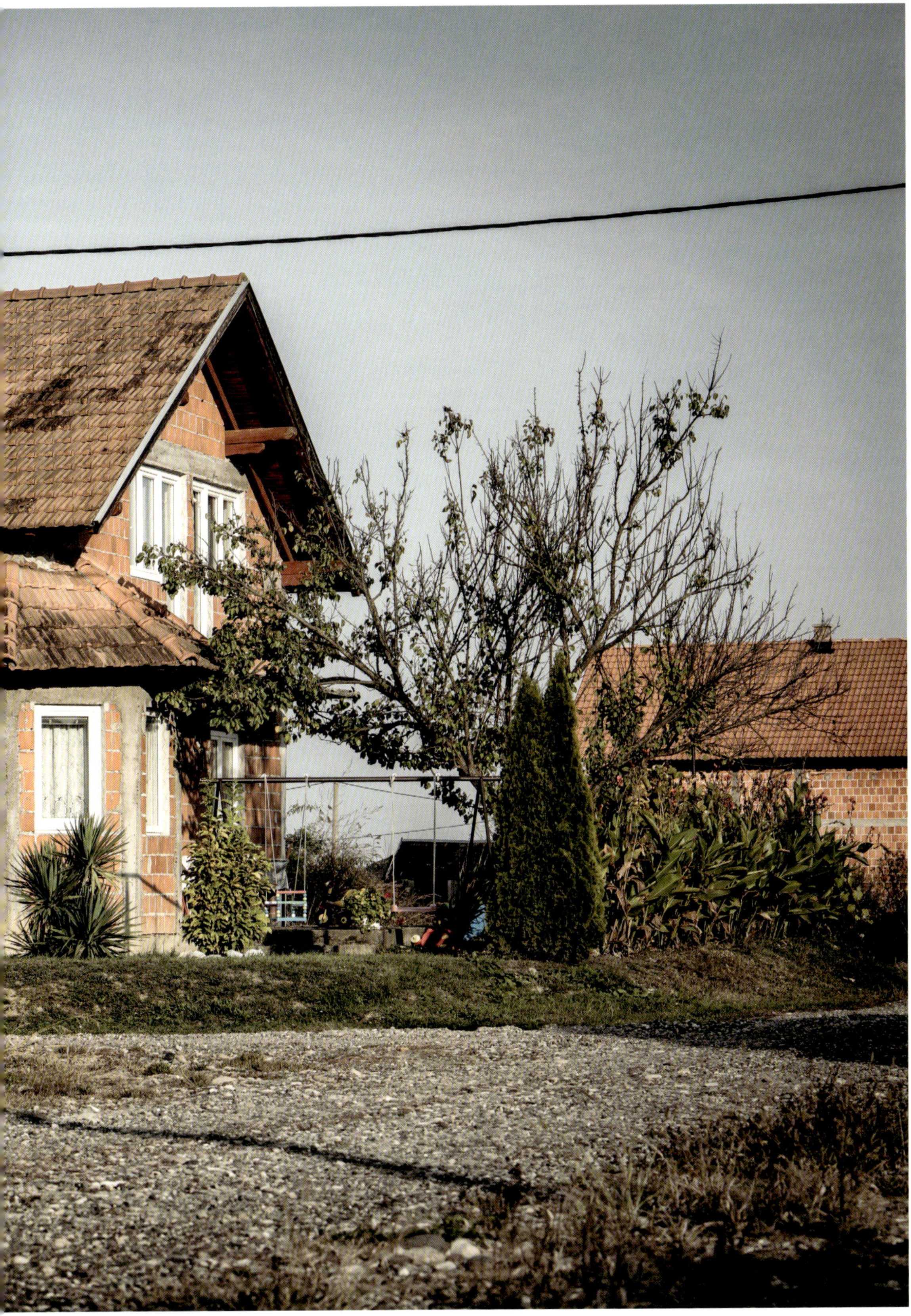

Previous spread
Republika Srpska - Odžak
Posavska Mahala

After the witness ML was raped in an apartment of the 'Hanka' building, she was arrested with four women from Odžak[71] and two other women from Derventa and brought to a private home in Posavska Mahala. She lived here in captivity for almost three months and was raped every day. She and the other women had little to eat. They lived in constant fear of death. They were promised their husbands would be released from the camp if they slept with the Croatian unit soldiers. ML often asked to be killed because she was convinced she could not survive the abuse. The answer was, 'If we kill you, we can no longer satisfy ourselves.' After three months of torture, they took the women in a van to the military headquarters in Modriča. From there they were transferred to the Croatian village of Lještrak near Novi Grad. ML and her son went to Serbia, to Mohor, near Zaove. Because of the threats she faced there as a Catholic, she only stayed three months. Her two-year-old son was with her the whole time and was an eyewitness to everything that happened to her.

45°03'15.4"N 18°19'13.4"E

Opposite
Republika Srpska - Novigrad
Stables

Bosnian Serb women and children have been detained in this building by 102 HVO Brigade. From here they were taken out to be raped.[72]

45°04'40.0"N 18°19'04.7"E

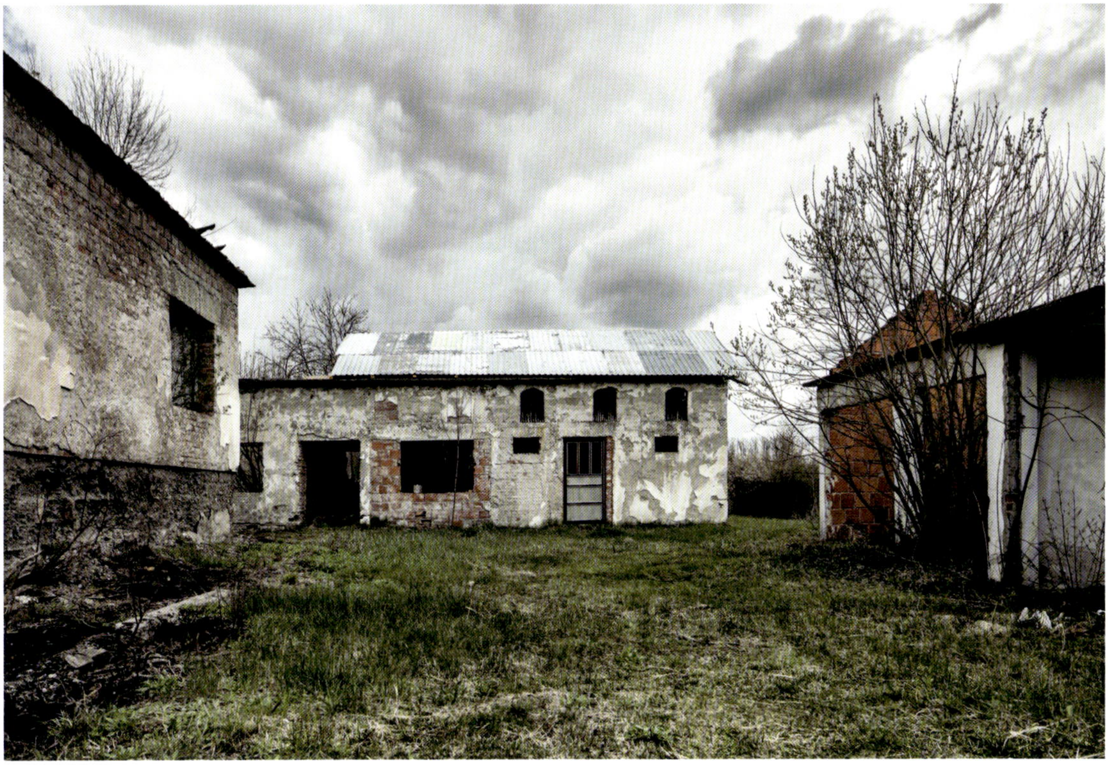

Overleaf
Republika Srpska - Novigrad
Private House

45°04'40.0"N 18°19'04.7"E

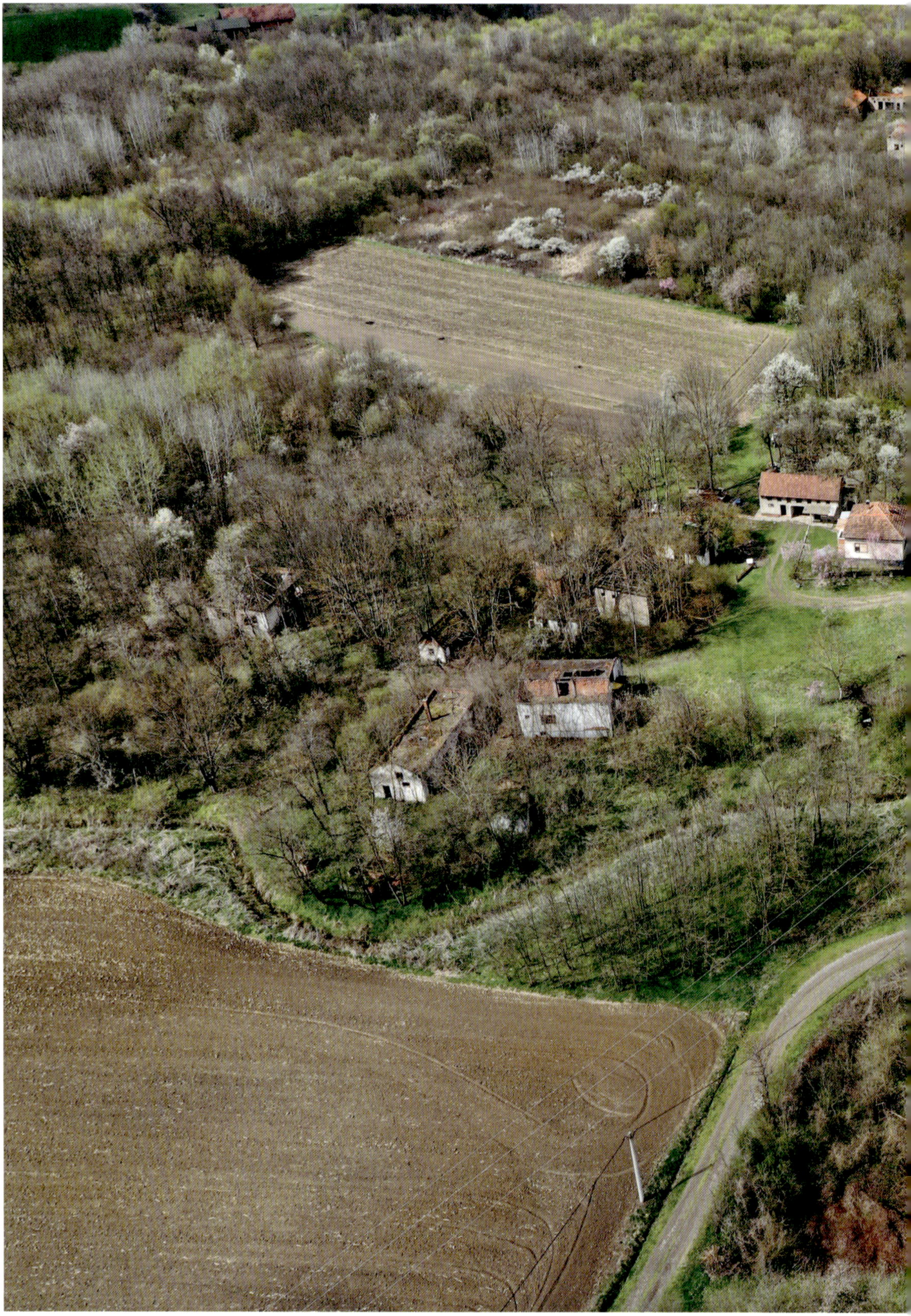

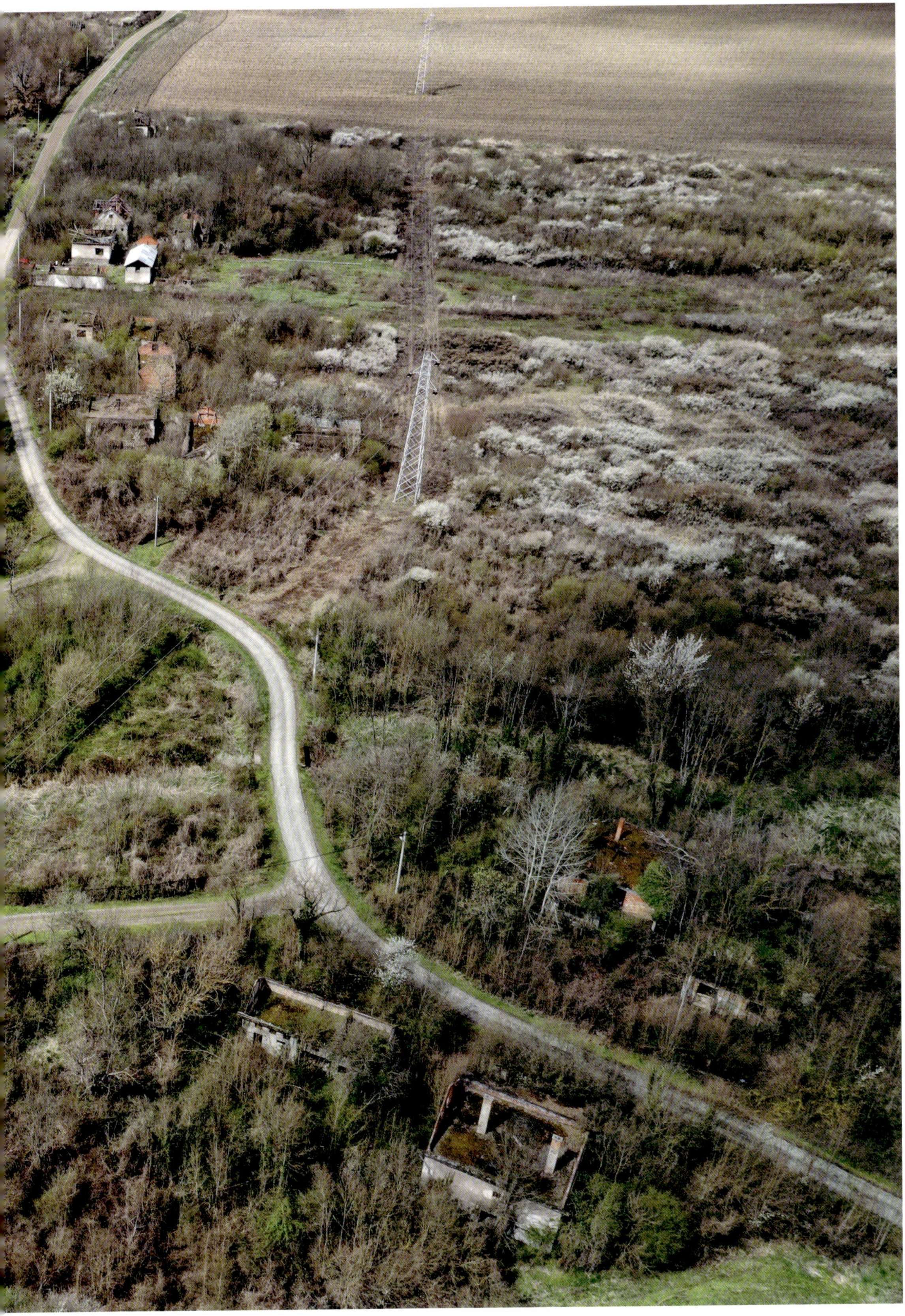

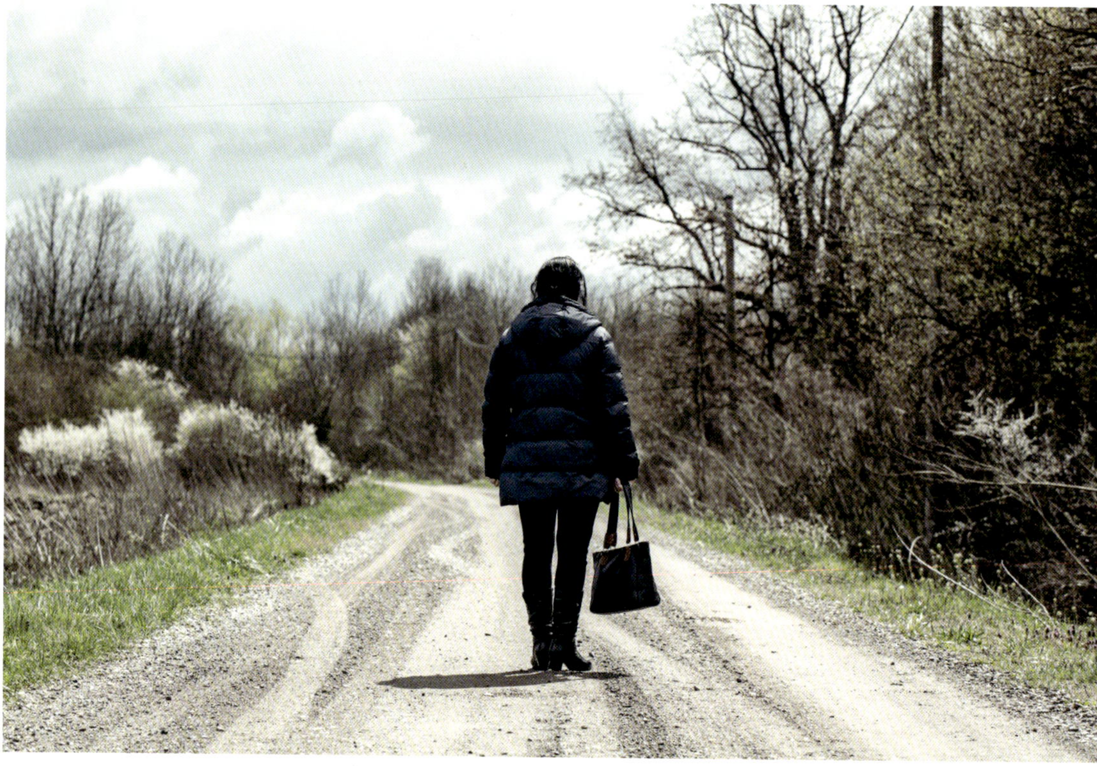

MILICA FROM MODRICA

'What happened? It happened in Odžak in 1992, what happened... The war happened... We were arrested in 1992. On the 8th of May. Children, women and all men, maybe up to 1,350, up to 1,300 citizens, something like that, as far as I know. Women, children and men.

The men were taken to the school in Odžak and to the factory in Strolit...stayed there, and they took us back to Novi Grad to our houses because they said they couldn't feed us...that's what they said. But they took us women and children back to our houses so they could do what they did.

They started mass rapes, mass shootings, mass beatings, all kinds of torture, all kinds of insults...where I was abused, raped, insulted...with my three minor children—seven years, five years, and nine months. My husband had already been murdered by that time.

Mainly us women and the children, maybe 300, they put us in houses so they knew where we were so they could come and get us more easily. And if anyone ran away or hid or disappeared, they said they would kill us. So we couldn't move away from those houses, so we were at their disposal to get us out whenever they wanted...which they did.

We went to the military police and asked for help because the HVO military were taking us away to be abused. The HVO soldiers were always on the move, with their vehicles, on foot. They took us with them. Even the children, girls, old women of seventy years... Children were raped...ten years old...seventeen... fifteen. Yes, they told us not to tell anyone who they were because we knew them, they were all our neighbours. We couldn't even tell the police who raped us, who abused us, tortured us, insulted us. No one dared to say who they were.

In my group, four women were kidnapped, if I'm not mistaken. Usually they took four to five women. They took us by vehicle or van. After the rapes, they threw us out, they kicked us, they shot after us...we ran...we crawled...so we returned to our homes unconscious, naked, barefoot, beaten, bloodied. Yes...that's what they wanted, and that's what they did. They took all our documents and it was practically house arrest. No, as I said, there were ten to fifteen women, children, mothers with children...and they came that night and they threw us out with guns and they took my sister from another house. And they took me and two other women. They picked and chose what was for them, and the rest they took back to the houses.

Once they took me, and on that one occasion five men raped me—later I fainted, and I didn't know how many there were... because when they took us there was a whole battalion of military, a whole yard, because that was their checkpoint. Yes, they were my neighbours.

Why did they do that? They only did it because we were Serbs. I didn't see a single reason they had for anything else.

Normal... Their life is normal and we were humiliated and are a nobody and nothing, that's how it is.

They act as if nothing happened, and if they are sentenced tomorrow, the sentences are too lenient. Two years, three, four or five, those are not sentences, that's not for our...whoever did it, these punishments are nothing.

Many women were afraid to tell their husbands. Many divorced and had problems when their husbands came out of the camp and were exchanged and so on. Fear...I am not afraid. I am not afraid. I can't wait for the trial so I can face it. And to tell them everything they did to me. And I hope it will be a proper trial and that the perpetrators will be punished severely for the crime they committed against me and against everyone else.

Shouldn't I talk?'

Overleaf

Republika Srpska - Novigrad

Private House

M[73 74] (Serbian Bosnian) testified that they separated her from her sister and took her with another woman to a house where there were already many drunk Croatian soldiers. M was first beaten by six Croatian soldiers and then raped, during which she lost consciousness. M reports in her statement that she regained consciousness around 4:30am when she and the other woman were thrown out of the house by Croatian soldiers. They fled on foot. The next day, M reported the case to the International Red Cross, who took her to the health centre in Odžak. However, she was denied medical attention there. M was brought back to the house where her children and other women were detained. She remained there until she was taken to the prisoner exchange by HVO soldiers in July 1992.

45°04'40.0"N 18°19'04.7"E

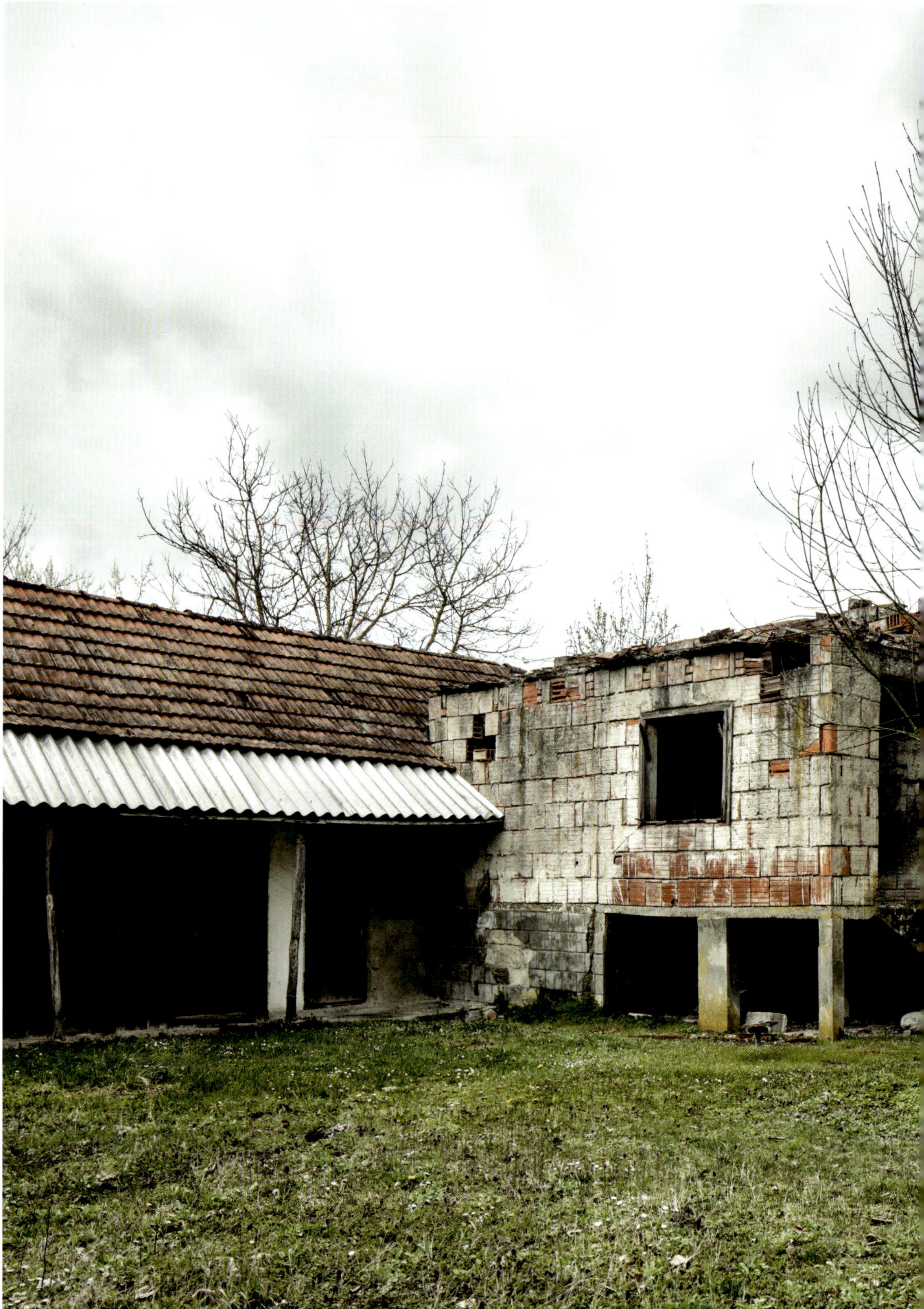

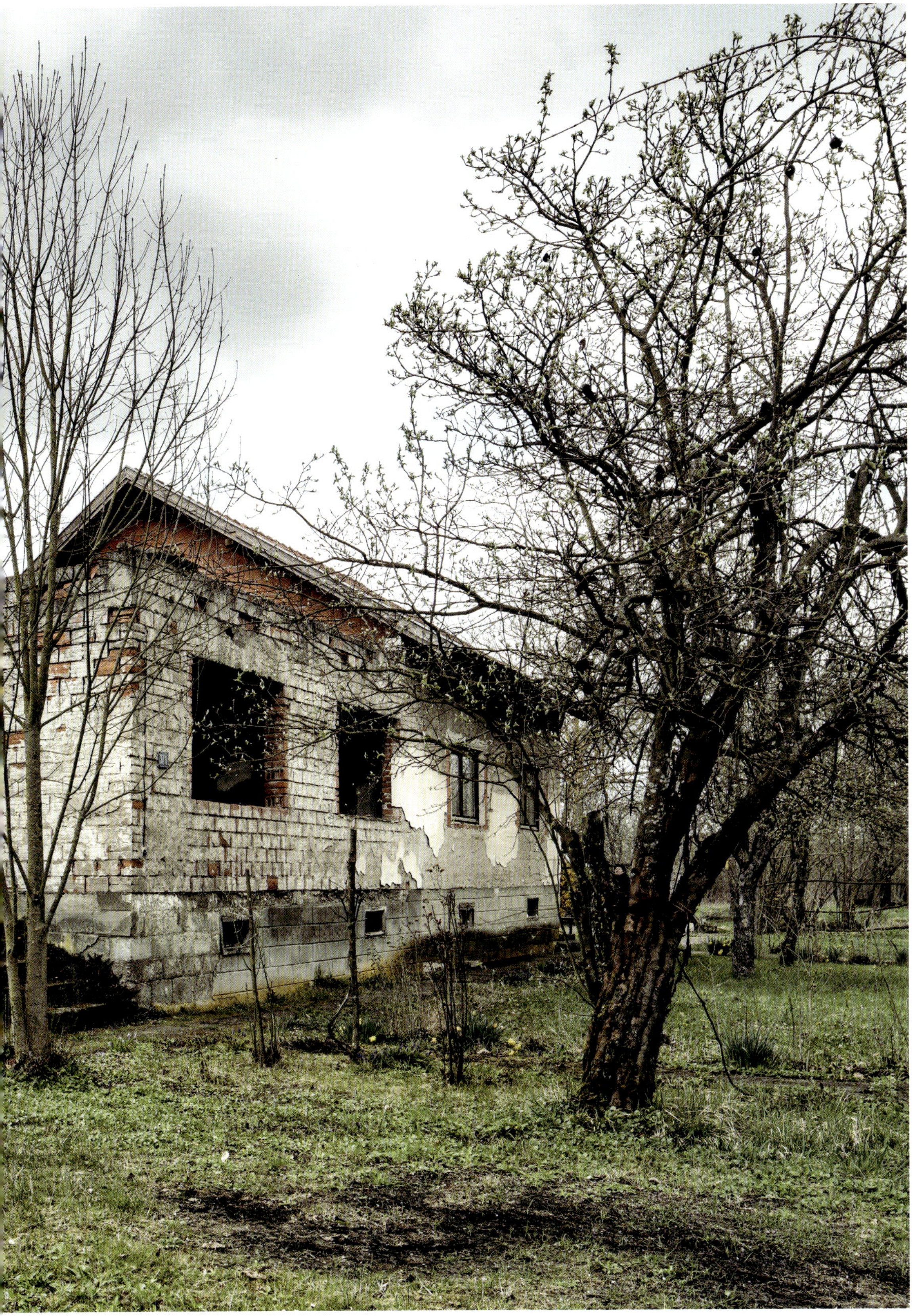

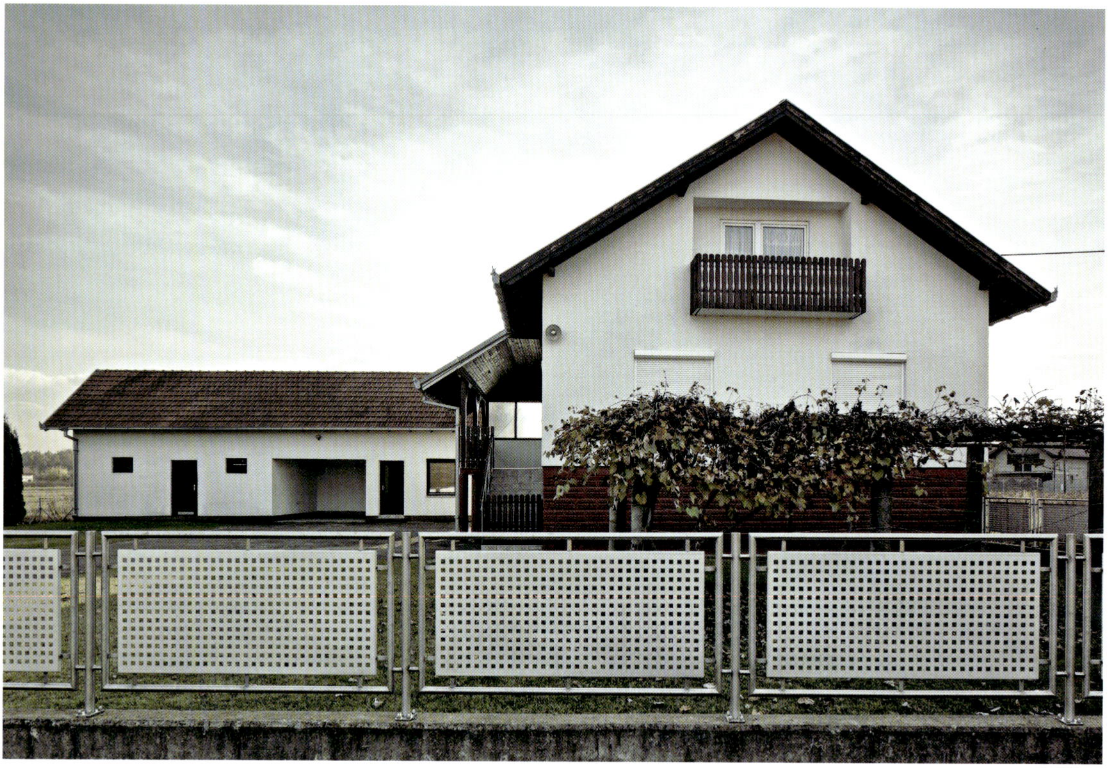

Left
Republika Srpska
Odžak, Posavska Mahala

In the summer of 1992, members of the 102nd Odzaci Brigade of the Croatian Defense Council (HVO), who formed a unit within the brigade known as the 'Fire Horses,' committed mass rapes of girls and women of Serbian descent.[75] The Bosnian Serb village of Novi Grad in the municipality of Odžak was occupied by HVO soldiers after weeks of resistance. In this context, on 8 May 1992, M, together with her family and other residents of Novi Grad, surrendered to the HVO for the prisoner exchange.[76] This was fatal for M and some women from this group. M, her sister L and two other women were singled out and taken at gunpoint to a Croatian base at Posavska Mahala. There they were taken over by ten Croatian soldiers, also members of the 'Fire Horses' group, and distributed to different houses.

45°03'42.0"N 18°18'57.0"E

Overleaf
Bosanski Brod
Polet Stadium

The Polet Stadium in Bosanski Brod served as a prison in the early days of the war (from early May to mid-September 1992). The military police of the Croatian Defense Council were in charge of control. The detainees were civilians, mostly Serbs. Men and women were housed in separate rooms.[77] Indira Kameric Vrbanjac was the leader of the women's camp in this stadium. Before she held this position, she already brought women to soldiers at the front and thus 'managed' their sexual care as a 'reward.' The leader of the women's camp was characterised by cruelty.[78] An undercover testimony to what happened at the stadium was given by a woman in 1994. At the stadium, she was taken to a room full of women. Soon after, a man she knew, DČ from Novo Selo in Croatian uniform, 'grabbed by hair and very roughly led me into a room, hit me and threatened to butcher me.' Over the course of that night, eleven soldiers raped her. The witness was transferred several times: to Slavonski Brod to the Bardak camp, from there to Županja and then to the primary school in Orašje, where she was raped again and then transferred to a camp in Donja Mahala, also near Orašje.[79] In the camp, she witnessed the suffering of Desanka Blagojević from Tešanj, who was raped by HVO soldiers and later forced to sit on a burning stove. A Bosniak woman who worked in the health centre at Slavonski Brod before the war was also charged in 1992 with links to Serbs, arrested and transferred to Bosanski Brod.[80] In fact, at that time, Croatian HVO and the Bosnian Army fought together against Serbian units of the Republic of Srpska. This testimony shows that there was no security for women in terms of clear boundaries and how to perceive the enemy.

45°08'36.0"N 18°00'33.0"E

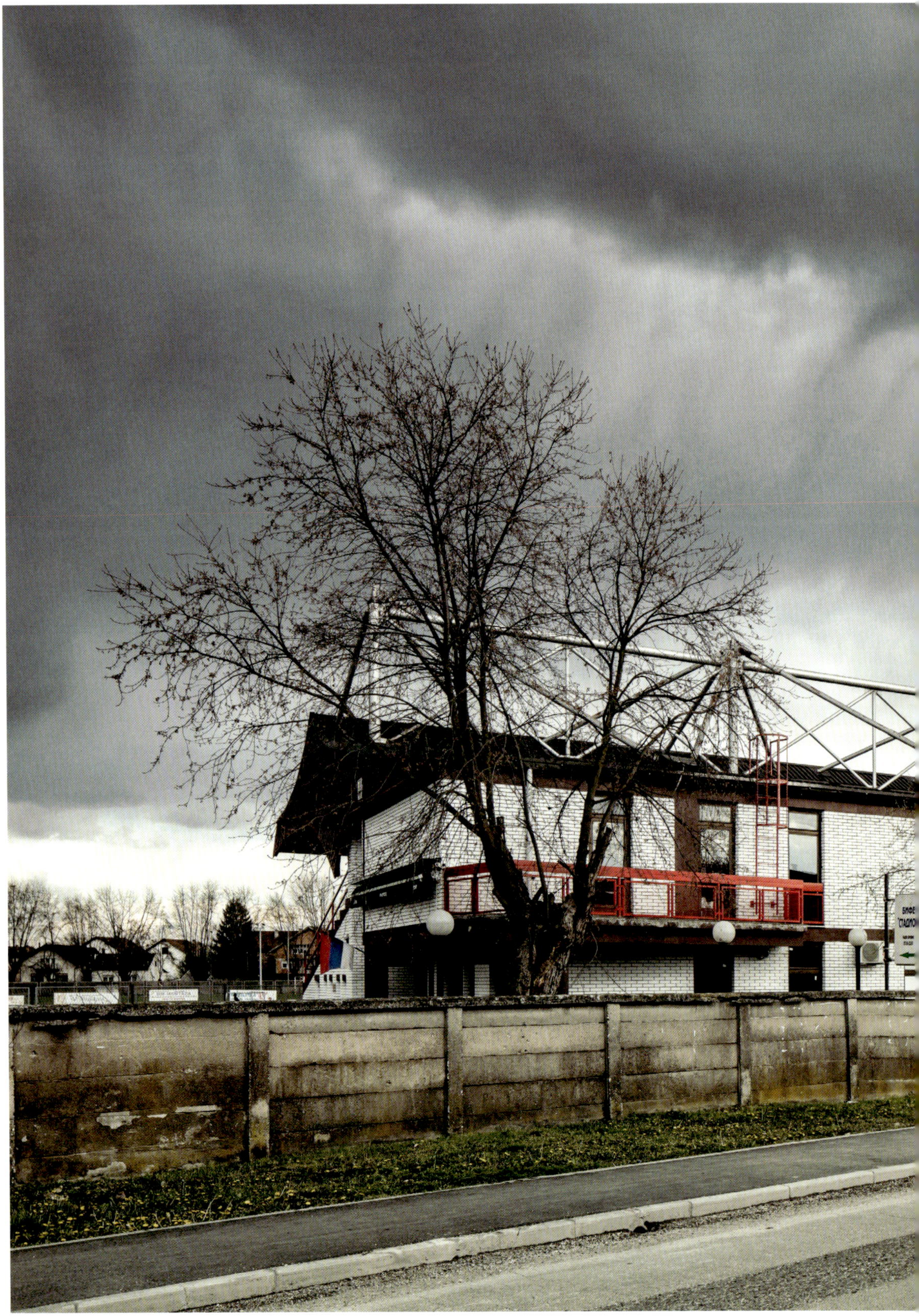

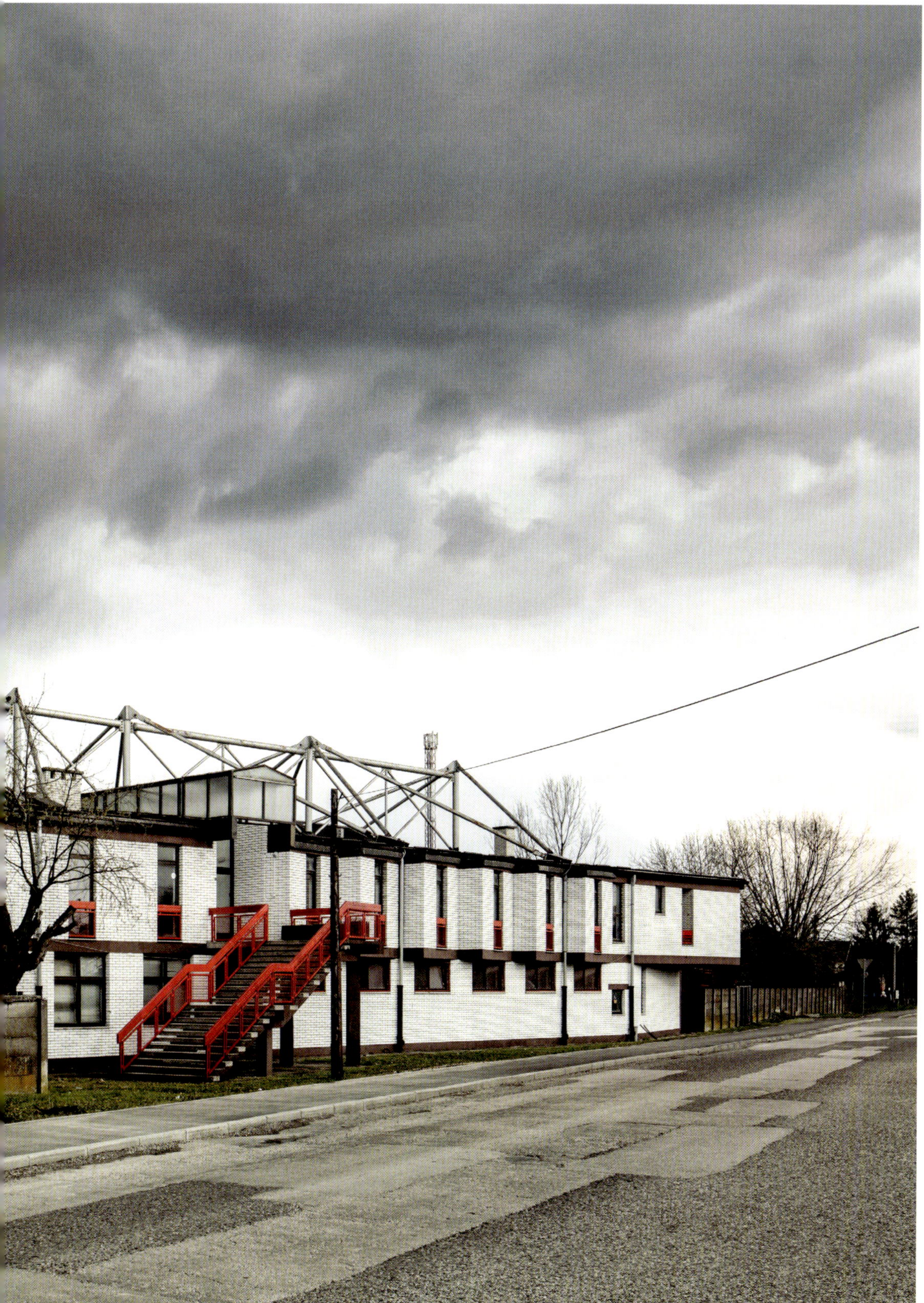

Opposite
Doboj
Headquarter JNA (Yugoslav People's Army House)

In May 1992, Doboj was controlled by Bosnian Serb forces and the Serb Democratic Party took over the city's government. This was followed by mass disarmament and mass arrests of all Bosniaks and Croats, and war crimes aimed at ethnic cleansing. Many of the non-Serbs were detained at various locations in the city and held in inhumane conditions including physical abuse, torture and forced labour. There were several camps where rapes also took place. In 2018, the Bosnia and Herzegovina court sentenced Slobodan Karagic, the commander of the Red Beret special unit operating in the Doboj security service centre, to twelve years in prison for war crimes against civilians. According to the verdict, Karagic was found guilty of, among other things, the rape of two women who were then minors in the summer of 1992. Witness K-1 stated that she was fifteen years old and attended the school 'Sutjeska.' She was taken from her home to the camp on 13 July 1992, where she was released about fifteen days later. She said that one day she visited a certain Zelenkovic from whom she needed help. On the way back from the camp to her home, a jeep stopped and the driver asked her to ride with him on the pretext that she should make certain statements. Then he took her to the JNA headquarters in Doboj. The witness states that at that moment she did not know that this man was the accused Karagic. He took her to one of the offices, which she assumed was his office. He got some blankets from the closet and started unbuttoning his pants, to which she told him she was only fifteen, but he replied that he would do it at all costs and asked, 'Do you know who I am?' She had to undress and lie down, the accused raped her on the ground. After the rape, after leaving the office, she heard someone call him 'Karagic.' She later learned his full name from the media.[81]

44°43'49.1"N 18°05'05.0"E

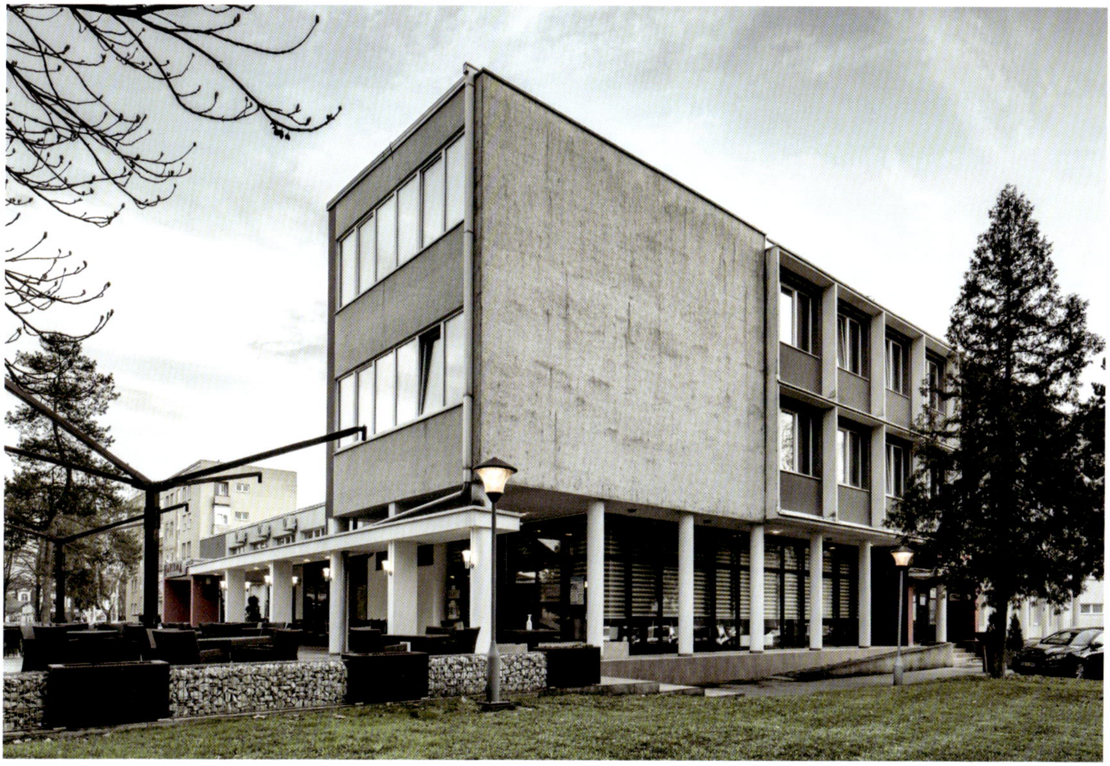

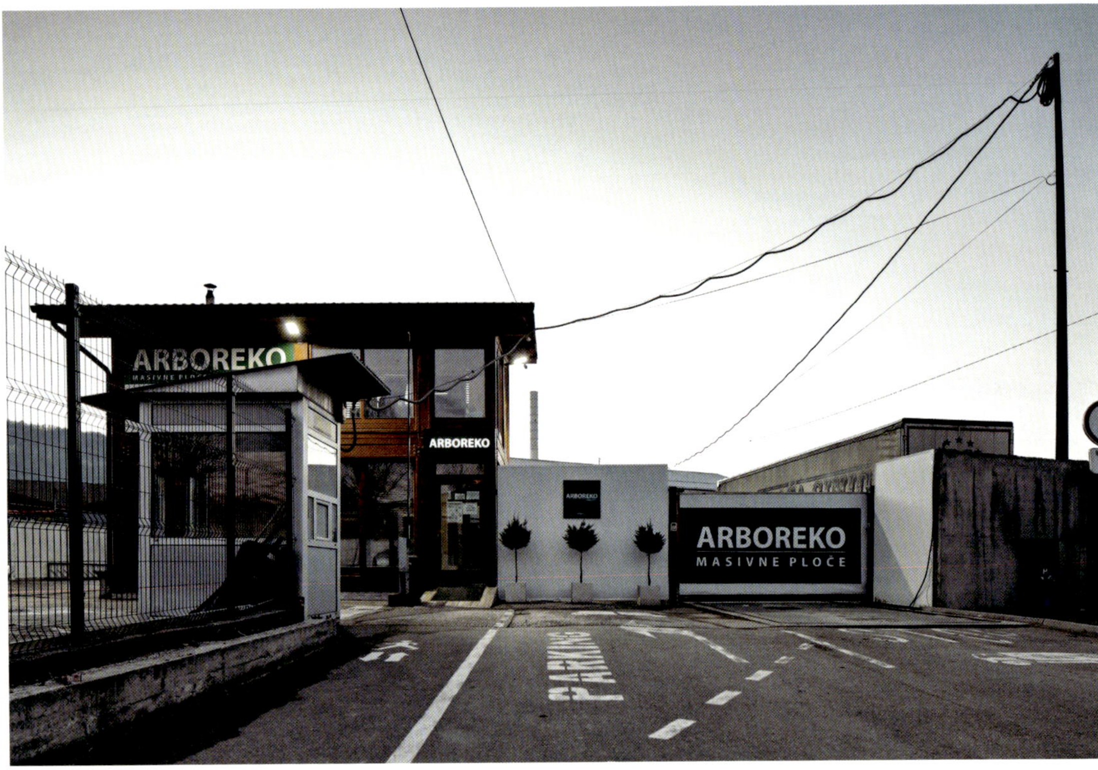

Kotor Varoš

Sawmill Vrbanja

From 11 June 1992 until the end of August 1992, the Serbian authorities used certain premises of the Vrbanja Drvna industry—the sawmill factory in Kotor Varoš as a detention facility. Bosniaks and Bosnian Croats were held at the sawmill. In August 1992 there were about 1,000 detained civilians—women, children and the elderly.[82] Through 14-16 August 1992, Muslim and Croatian women and girls were victims of a mass rape in the sawmill. In addition to the guards, units of the 1st Light Kotor Varos Brigade and the 22nd Brigade of the RS Army and members of the special unit of the Interior Ministry of the Banja Luka Security Centre (Red Berets) came to the camp. Members of these units took women and girls into offices and other premises inside the factory, or took them to apartments outside the factory, where they were repeatedly raped by groups of soldiers and police officers.[83] Witness LR: 'We were first housed in a factory restaurant where they brought new prisoners during the day, women and children from the villages of Hanifici, Cirkino Brdo and other villages. Nobody abused us in the camp that night, but then they took us to a hall and started taking women and girls out and raping them. Among the Chetniks who raped women, I recognised Milanko Tovilovic from Maslovar, who later raped my husband's cousin.'

44°37'20.0"N 17°22'12.8"E

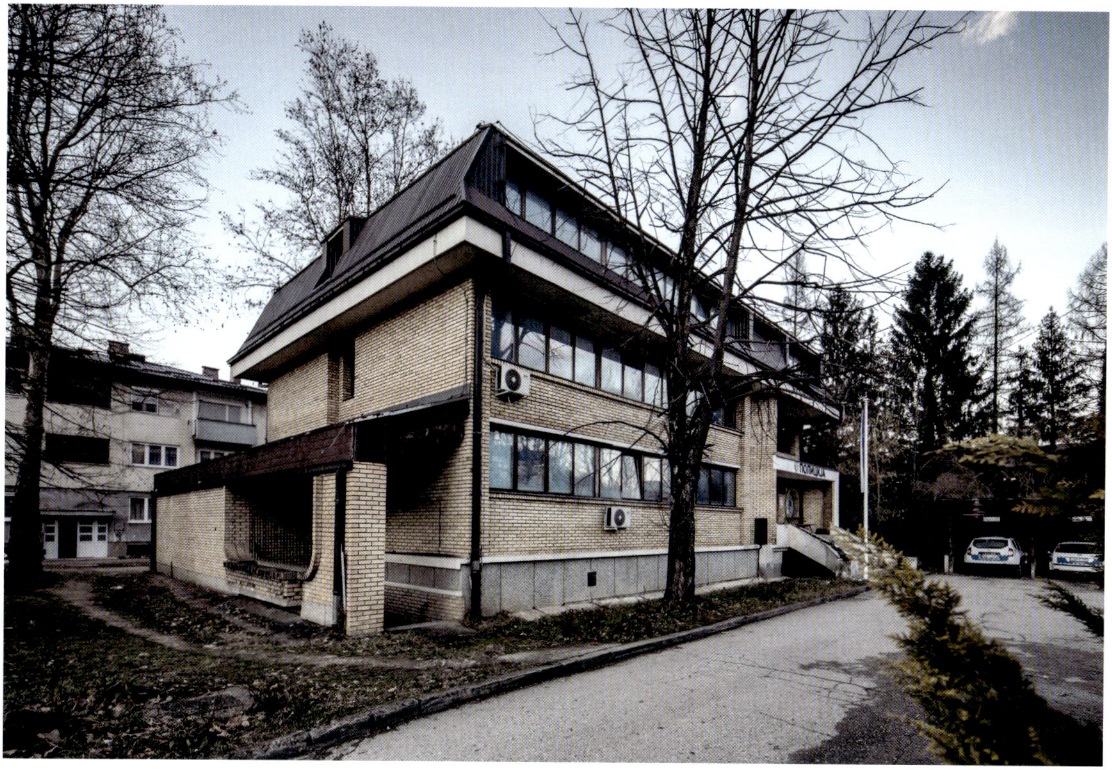

Kotor Varoš
Police Station

The police station was controlled by special units of the Banja Luka police and the Kotor Varos police. The detainees—100 mostly able-bodied men, Muslim and Croatian civilians, also women—were housed from 11 June 1992 until the end of 1992 in the premises that had previously been used for pre-trial detention by the police station and in the offices. Members of the Red Berets sexually abused the detainees and forced them to rape each other. A young man (HS from Kotor Varos) was raped several times, the witness KD was taken to the police station on 11 June 1992 and severely abused and raped that same day. Members of the Red Berets, together with members of the Kotor Varoš police force, beat her with baseball bats and police batons in the corridor of the police station in front of the detention room and in Zdravko Pejic's office, and then raped her.[84]

44°37'06.3"N 17°22'15.4"E

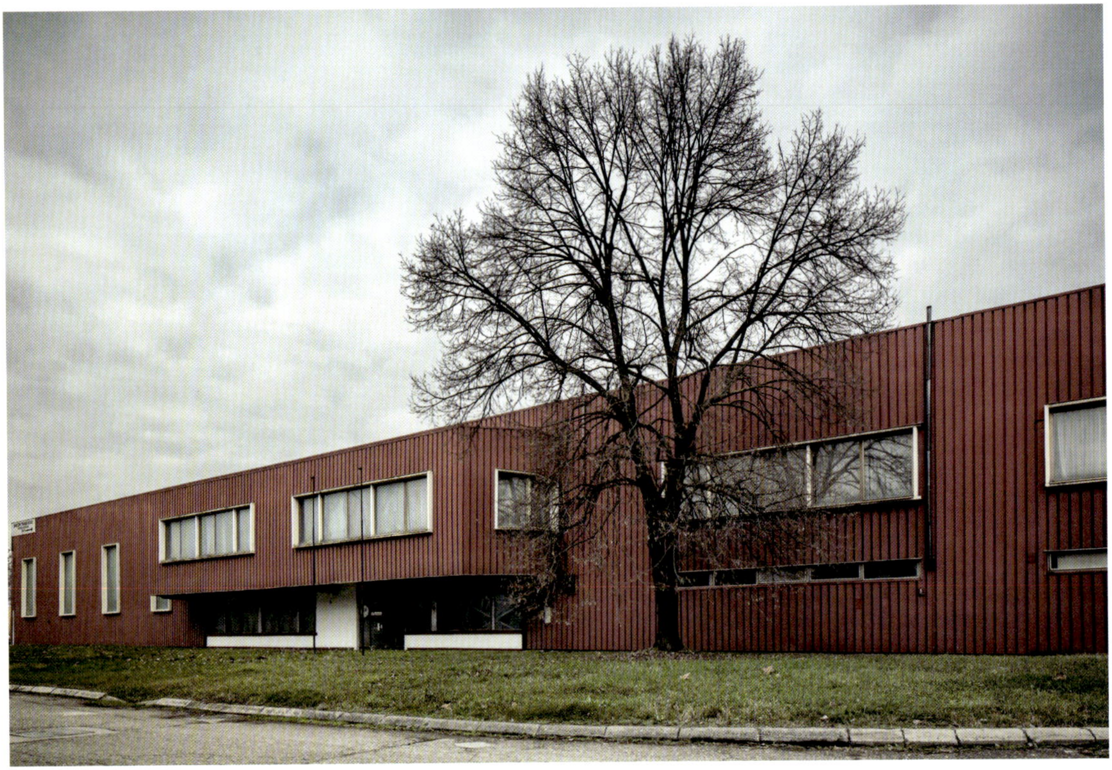

Left
Prijedor
Detention Camp, Pottery Factory

On 24 May 1992, the pre-war Keraterm ceramics factory was converted into a camp where prisoners of Muslim and Croatian origin were imprisoned mainly on ethnic grounds. The Keraterm camp was established by the civil authorities of the Municipality of Prijedor. Members of the Serbian Army and police in charge of the camp, as well as other employees of the Serbian Crisis Management Team, participated in the killing, physical and psychological torture, shootings and sexual torture and ill-treatment of the prisoners. Around 4,000 prisoners of military age between sixteen and sixty were held in the Keraterm camp. Among them were some Albanians and a Bosnian Serb accused of disloyalty as a Serb. About eighty-five percent of all prisoners were Bosniaks, fifteen percent Bosnian Croats. According to the testimonies of former camp inmates, the people here were held captive in four warehouses of the former factory. Keraterm was a predominantly male camp, but there were also women imprisoned, even mothers with children. Bosniak women were brought to this camp, raped and then transferred to the Omarska camp. A woman said that in an office in Keraterm she was raped all night by Nedeljko Timarac and then alternately by other men. Then she was taken outside and told to sit on a rock. At one point, a guard walked by and kicked her. In June or July 1992, other guards at Keraterm camp raped a female inmate on a table in a dark room until she passed out. She regained consciousness the next morning and found herself lying in a pool of blood.[85]

44°58'37.0"N 16°43'45.3"E

Overleaf
Trnopolje
Aerial view

44°56'12.18"N 16°48'25.98"E

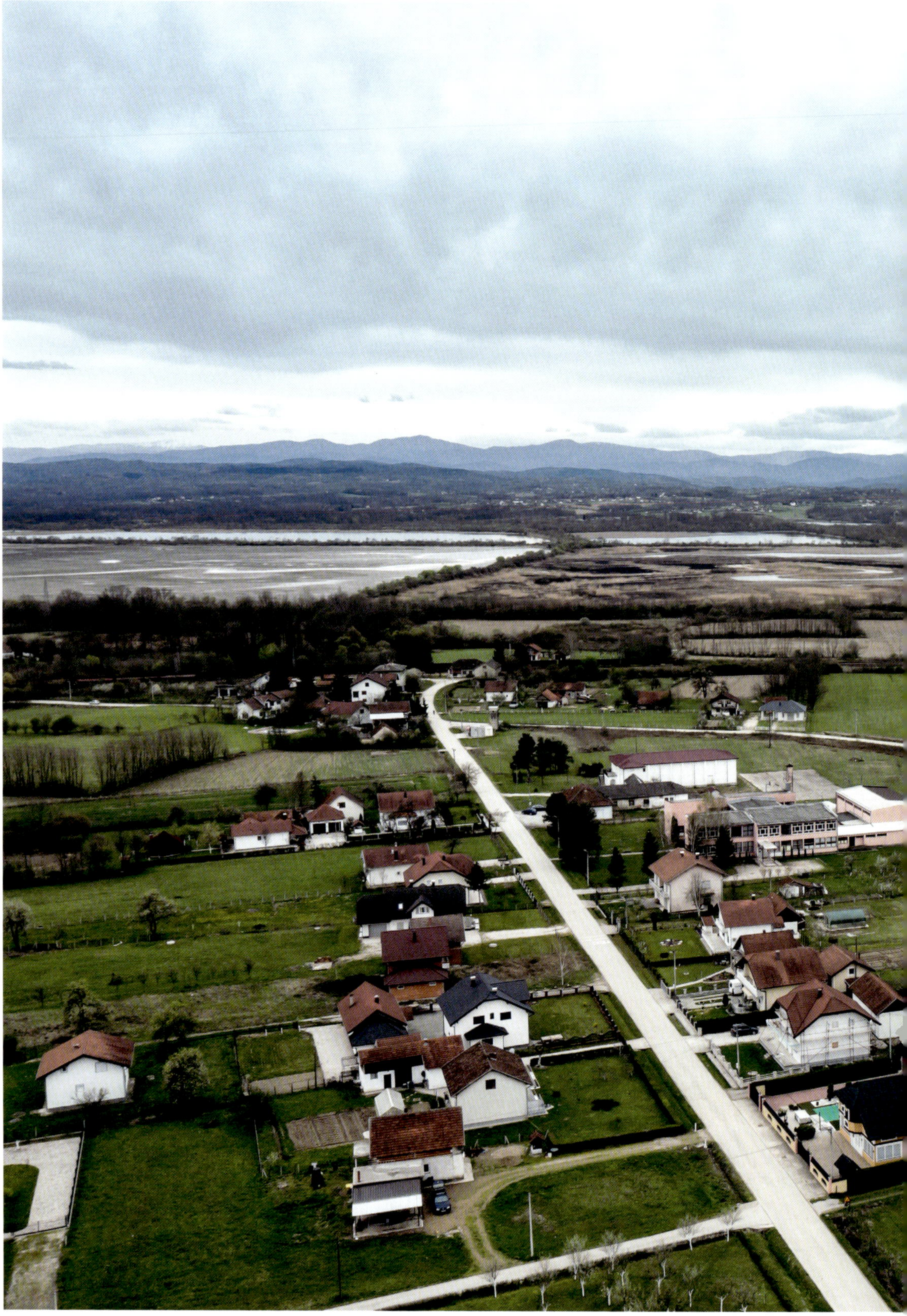

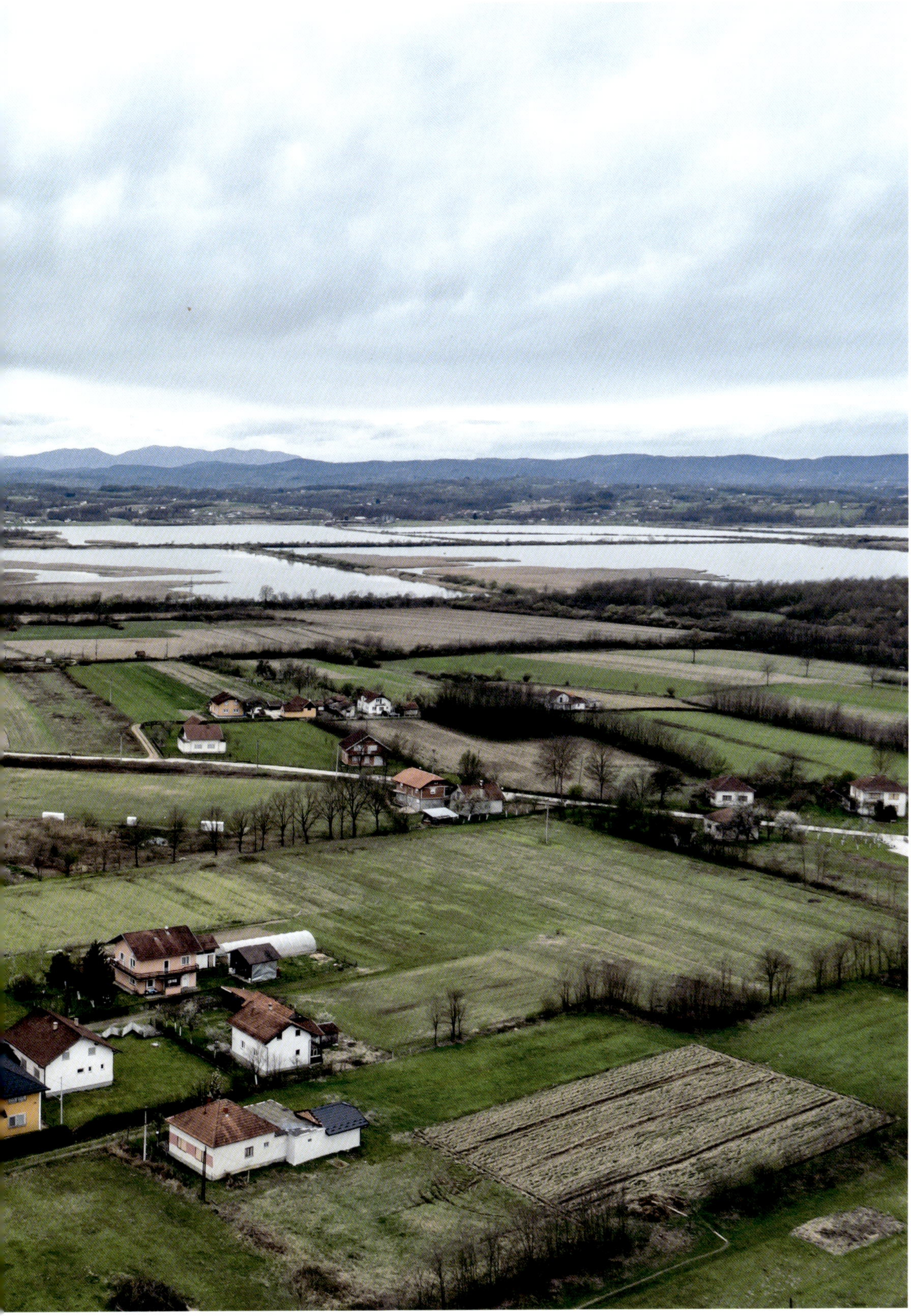

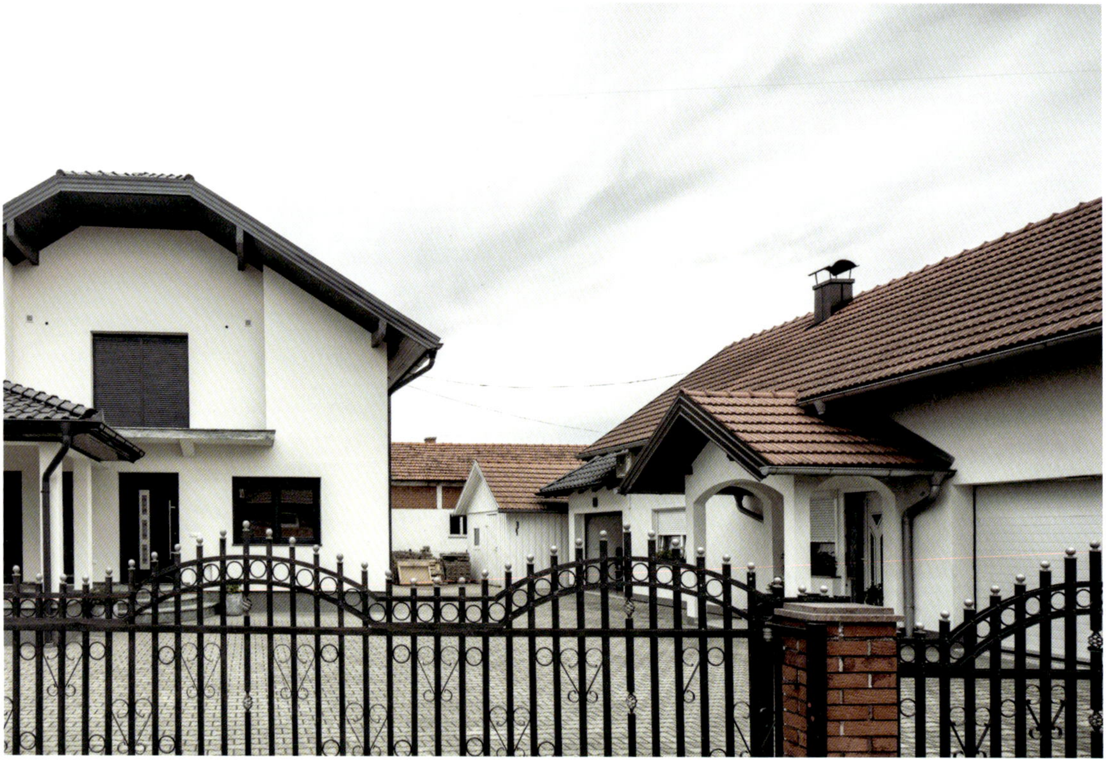

Left
Trnopolje
Private House

The headquarters of the Trnopolje camp was located in the smaller house in the middle of the picture. The commander of the Trnopolje camp was Slobodan Kuruzović. Many women were raped in this house. Some of these witnesses testified at the ICTY in The Hague that they were held there for a long time to 'entertain' the commander of the camp—Kuruzović.[86]

44°56'04.8"N 16°48'19.0"E

Overleaf
Trnopolje
Rebuilt Private House

This house in Trnopolje was near the camp. Several displaced persons (women and children) were accommodated in this house. They tried to survive there. The rape of a woman from this group was documented. She was registered as a witness with Izvor/NGO in Prijedor. She came from Kozaruša, from where she and her family had been expelled. Her house had been set on fire. She was looking for a place to stay, and she ended up here. The house was eventually rebuilt on it's old foundation.

44°56'08.4N 16°48'19.9E

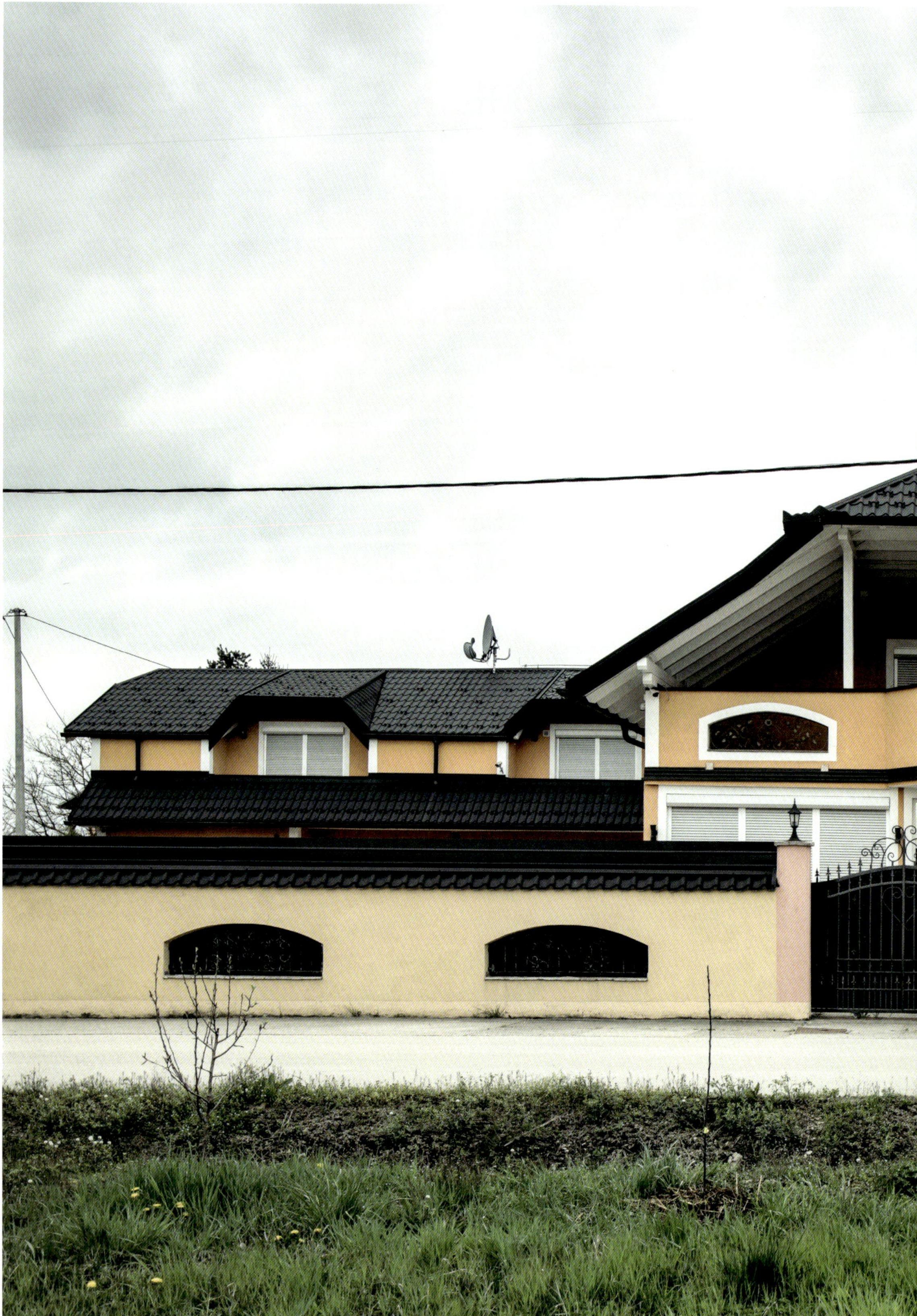

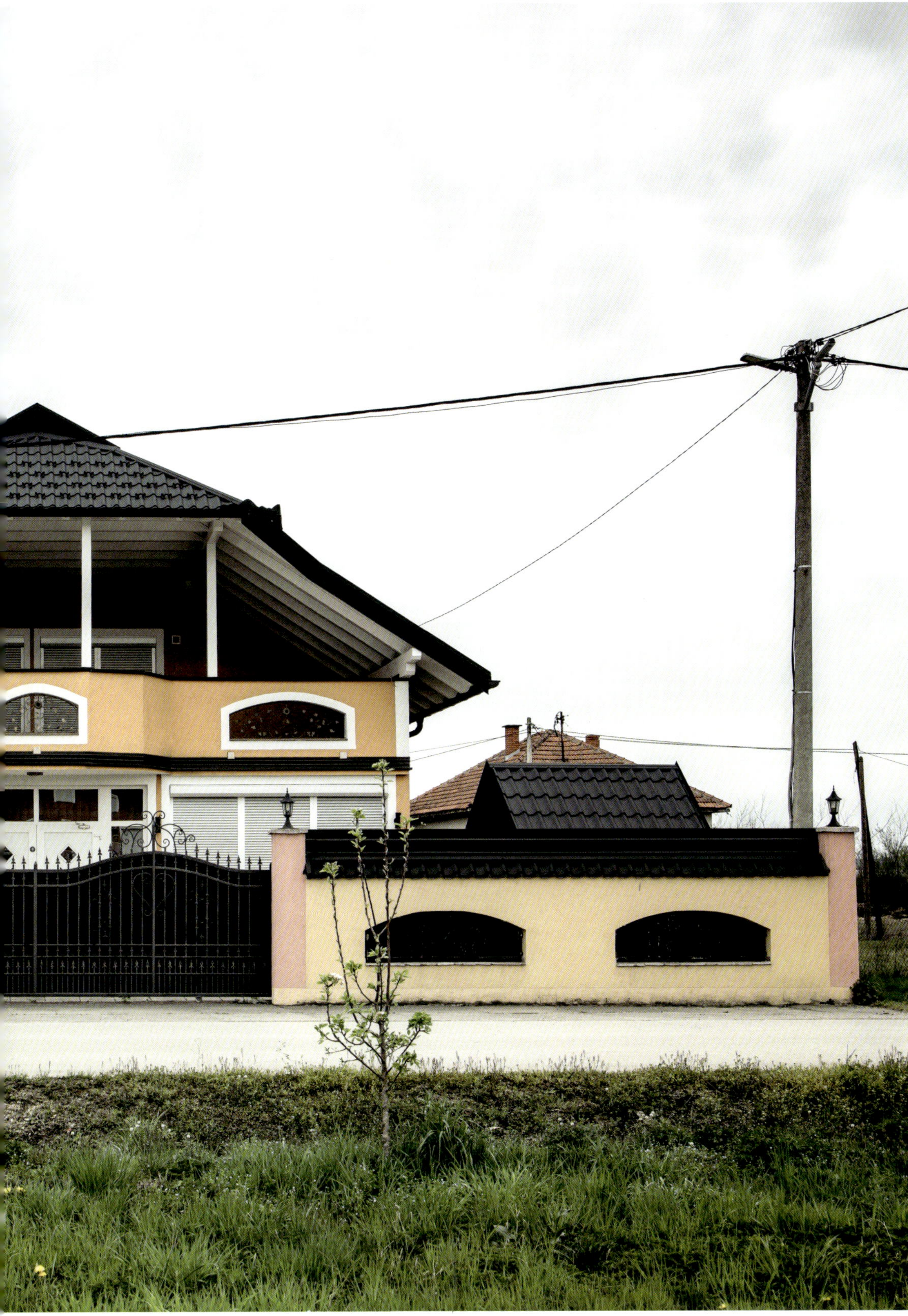

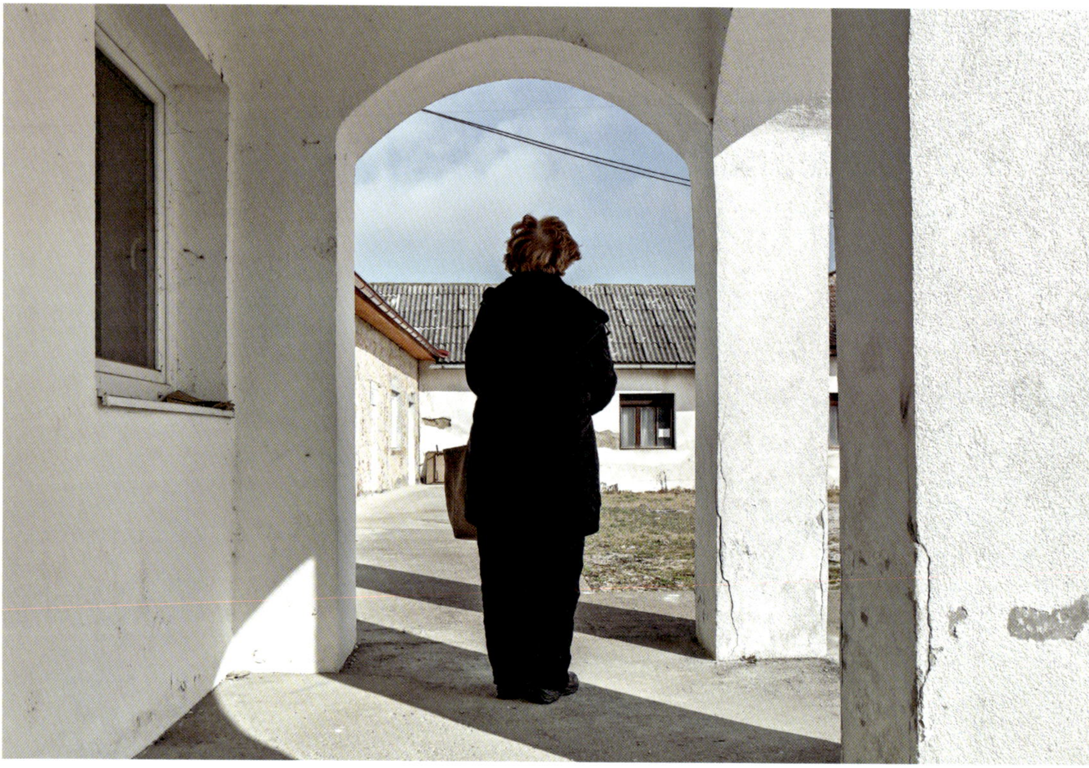

NUSRETA FROM PRIJEDOR

'Yes, unfortunately in 1992 I was unlucky enough to be taken to one of the Prijedor camps, Omarska. I was the first woman from Prijedor in the camp. During my two-month imprisonment, the number of women in the camp increased to thirty-seven out of a total of around 3,500 prisoners.

Everything worked according to plan and program, it didn't happen by accident, it didn't happen overnight. Most of those who worked there were from the police. The Crisis Management Committee (CMC) took over the role of civil authority in Prijedor during this period and developed the camp structure in the premises of the former camp, with administration, shift foremen, guards, etc. Today the premises are not open to the public. They were converted into offices where employees of today's Acelor Mittal company work. Every year on 6 August we visit the Omarska camp, but we could never go to these rooms to leave flowers for the five murdered women.

We women were accommodated in two rooms above the restaurant. From there we did our daily chores around the restaurant, mainly physical labour: distributing food to the prisoners in the camp, washing dishes, scrubbing, cleaning...whatever the guards ordered us to do. Then after this work, which lasted from morning to night, we went to our dormitories. There really wasn't any sleep...sexual abuse and rape mostly happened at night.

During the day, these premises were used for interrogations of prisoners in the camp. Investigators interrogated detainees all day and beat some to death. So the floor and walls were covered in blood. We had to clean them to be able to stay there overnight. We often found people's clothes covered in blood, torture devices used during interrogations. And we could hear it all in the restaurant, people were screaming, crying and crying... So, like I said, we had to clean the rooms first so we could spend the night on that floor. On this floor, where we lived, there were all sorts of rooms, including a room for nighttime sexual abuse. Most of the time they came during the night, either the guards or other men from the camp staff. They took women out of the rooms...and weren't really picky. The thirty-seven women were all ages, from young women, university students to women who had already retired. The women didn't talk to each other about what happened to them that night... There was silence. It was fear that blocked us. We were afraid that there would be listening devices. We didn't tell each other about it.

It was particularly bad when I heard others coming back... This helplessness was a terrible feeling because you can see everything but you couldn't change anything. You could only run the risk of being finally executed. Me, for example, I set myself a task...' (Nusreta memorised everything very specifically during the time in the camp so that she could later testify against the perpetrators in court).

'There were moments when you thought you could not survive. Then you wished for an option of death, the quickest, being killed by a bullet or dying naturally. The situation changed hourly and you never knew what the new day tomorrow would bring. Then you would hope maybe someone survives this and one day will talk about it so everyone knows what happened in Omarska. Five women did not survive Omarska, they were executed and found in mass graves after the war. Their story will never be heard.

There's trauma and fear—fear of how family members will change their attitudes when they find out about it...we're from that type of environment. So many thought silence might be best for them... It doesn't mean they won't speak up after all this time. Before, it was normal not to speak, so they kept quiet.

When you find yourself in such a horrible environment every day, where you see the blood every morning and start the day counting the dead, a clear view through the large windows of the restaurant of the White House, the camp's torture centre and the lawn in front of it—it shapes the overall atmosphere.

Later, several of us women gave information and spoke to investigators from the Tribunal (The Hague, ICTY). We gave information so they could get a more complete picture. That helped, and the work of The Hague tribunal began with the opening of files on the Omarska camp.

One day, on the 3rd or 5th of August, some women were transferred to another camp in Trnopolje. At that time, Radovan Karadžić was President of the Republic of Srpska. He was at the peace negotiations in London. CNN and ITN, Penny Marshall from the International Red Cross, Ed Vulliamy, then reporters from *The Guardian* in Great Britain, insisted on coming to the Omarska camp because there were rumours that there was a camp near Prijedor where people were horribly tortured and women were raped. Karadzic said it was a lie, it wasn't true. They got permission and got into the camp...these were those legendary pictures of live skeletons that you can allegedly see behind the wire fence. The camp administration and the CMC in Prijedor knew about the impending visit of the journalists, so we women were transferred to another camp in Trnopolje. So we were hidden from the public since Karadzic had declared that there were no women in Omarska. He had given the journalists permission in London, but did not expect that they would take the next possible flight and be on the ground via Belgrade that same evening. The videos are from 5 August 1992. It helped in a way...even though a number of prisoners had already been transferred to Trnopolje and some to Manjaca. Only a part remained in the camp and were filmed there when the International Red Cross came to Omarska with TV crews.

I don't know exactly how many later spoke about it or testified in court, some died growing old and ill. But the number of witnesses was enough to prove that Omarska was classified as one of the most brutal camps in ex-Yugoslavia. There was a paragraph in the verdict on the sexual abuse of women. However, there was no separate charge of rape in the Omarska trial.

The leaders of the Omarska camp who were accused, I don't know exactly, fourteen or eighteen men, many, the largest number, not only the accused but also the convicts came from Prijedor. I don't like using dates or numbers, I'm always very careful with that...but it's no problem to find out on the internet how many were convicted in Prijedor. Some of the accused accepted guilt before the tribunal and court of Bosnia and Herzegovina, mostly they denied...they usually deny. Many are now out of prison... Some of them have been released after serving two-thirds of their sentences. These are the rules. One of the guards responsible got twenty years in prison. The punishment...that's what really puts the witnesses off, especially if you're a victim witness, since the length of the sentence doesn't reflect the seriousness of the crime being committed. But for me it is important that he was convicted. At one point this will be extremely important. I usually say it's very hard to go back and live where you've experienced all these horrible things.

Neither politicians of the Republic of Srpska nor ordinary citizens or intellectuals have distanced themselves from or condemned the crimes. After the perpetrators return to their old surroundings after only serving two-thirds of their sentence, they are still considered heroes. Many there believe they have been falsely accused and deny the authority of the ITCY in The Hague. Most of the perpetrators released from prison get jobs immediately, many of the convicts were still on their old payroll, they received the salary of the companies in which they worked until the trial. They mostly have the support of the local community. But women don't. Of course. Those are the paradoxes, absurd, terrible, but unfortunately that's the way it is. There are many women who have chosen not to return, they don't even want to come visit. I returned to Prijedor in 2002, ten years after the camp. In the beginning it was terrible. I also thought that I couldn't stand it here for long, but over time I got used to it. I'm not afraid. I was a refugee in Croatia in Zagreb and believed that the war would soon be over. Before I finally returned, I came to visit to secure my property like everyone else going through all those bureaucratic offices. My neighbours saw me coming, but once they realised that I really wanted to live here, hardly anyone greeted me anymore. You probably don't believe it. Once someone wrote Omarska next to my door. Big letters. Luckily I didn't have any major problems. However, the situation is different now. I got used to living here. It wasn't comfortable at first, I really thought I couldn't do it. You meet people who worked in the camp, interrogators, none of whom have been summoned to a trial yet...you meet them on the street... people you know what they did during the war...who killed, stole, raped. But as time goes by... I've been twelve years now in Prijedor. Serbs are the vast majority today, we Bosniaks are a minority. The people mostly live in the villages in this area to which they have returned.

Yes, I know of a case that was in front of the White House. What happened in Omarska during the day: they forced a respectable man from Prijedor to rape a woman in front of the White House. Both did not survive. He was found in one of the mass graves, as was she. It was horrific that day when they forced Mehmedalija Sarajlic to rape one of the female inmates, Hajra Hadzic, in front of the White House. I haven't seen any other cases, but they probably happened. If I was a judge, a responsible judge, I would try to be objective, to stick to the legislation.' (Nusreta worked as a judge until the war). 'On the other hand, as an affected woman, you have an internal struggle to be objective...at work, especially when you're a judge, you have to keep those emotions out. Unfortunately, there is no death sentence in The Hague. There is a life sentence, but as far as I know no one has ever gotten it. I would still try to be a professional no matter how I feel and what I think about it now.'

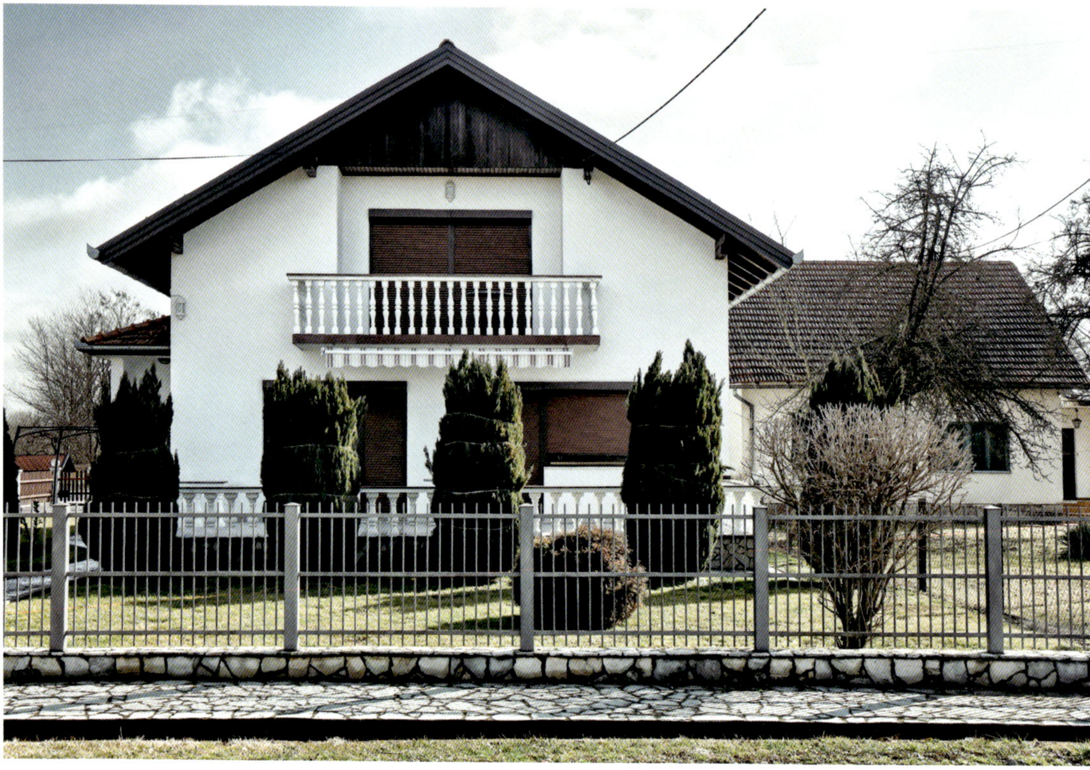

Left
Trnopolje
Private House

This house opposite the above-mentioned cultural centre and the former camp has been renovated again, but is mostly empty. Like many of its kind in Trnopolje, it is inhabited only in summer. In quite a number of these houses women were raped.[87]

44°56'04.0"N 16°48'19.0"E

Overleaf
Prijedor
Cultural Centre

The Trnopolje camp was established by the civil authorities of the Municipality of Prijedor and guarded by Bosnian Serb soldiers from Prijedor. Slobodan Kuruzovic headed the camp. Trnopolje was essentially a transit camp whose main purpose was the forced relocation of the Bosnian Muslim population, especially women, children and the elderly. Due to its transitional character, the number of detainees fluctuated greatly. Between May and October 1992, numerous rapes occurred here. Not all perpetrators were camp workers. Some were allowed to visit the camp from the outside. Soldiers took girls aged sixteen and seventeen from the camp and raped them on a truck on the way to Kozarac. In one case, a thirteen-year-old Bosnian Muslim girl was raped. A rape victim was told by a member of the camp staff that it was war and nothing could be done about these things. In August 1992, Slobodan Kuruzovic not only allowed women to be taken out of the camp to be raped, but he himself arranged for the detention of a Bosnian Muslim woman in the house where he had his office. The first night he entered her room with a gun and a knife. He undressed and told the woman he wanted to see 'how Muslim women fuck.' She replied, 'You better kill me.' When the woman started screaming, Kuruzovic said, 'You scream in vain. There is no one here who can help you.' He started to rape her and when she kept screaming he warned her: 'You had better keep quiet. Did you see all those soldiers standing outside? They will all take turns with you.' He left saying 'See you tomorrow.' The woman was bleeding, spent the whole night crying and wanted to kill herself. Kuruzovic raped this woman almost every night for about a month. He stabbed her shoulder and leg twice with his knife because she was resisting the rape.[88] [89] [90]

44°56'02.4"N 16°48'16.8"E

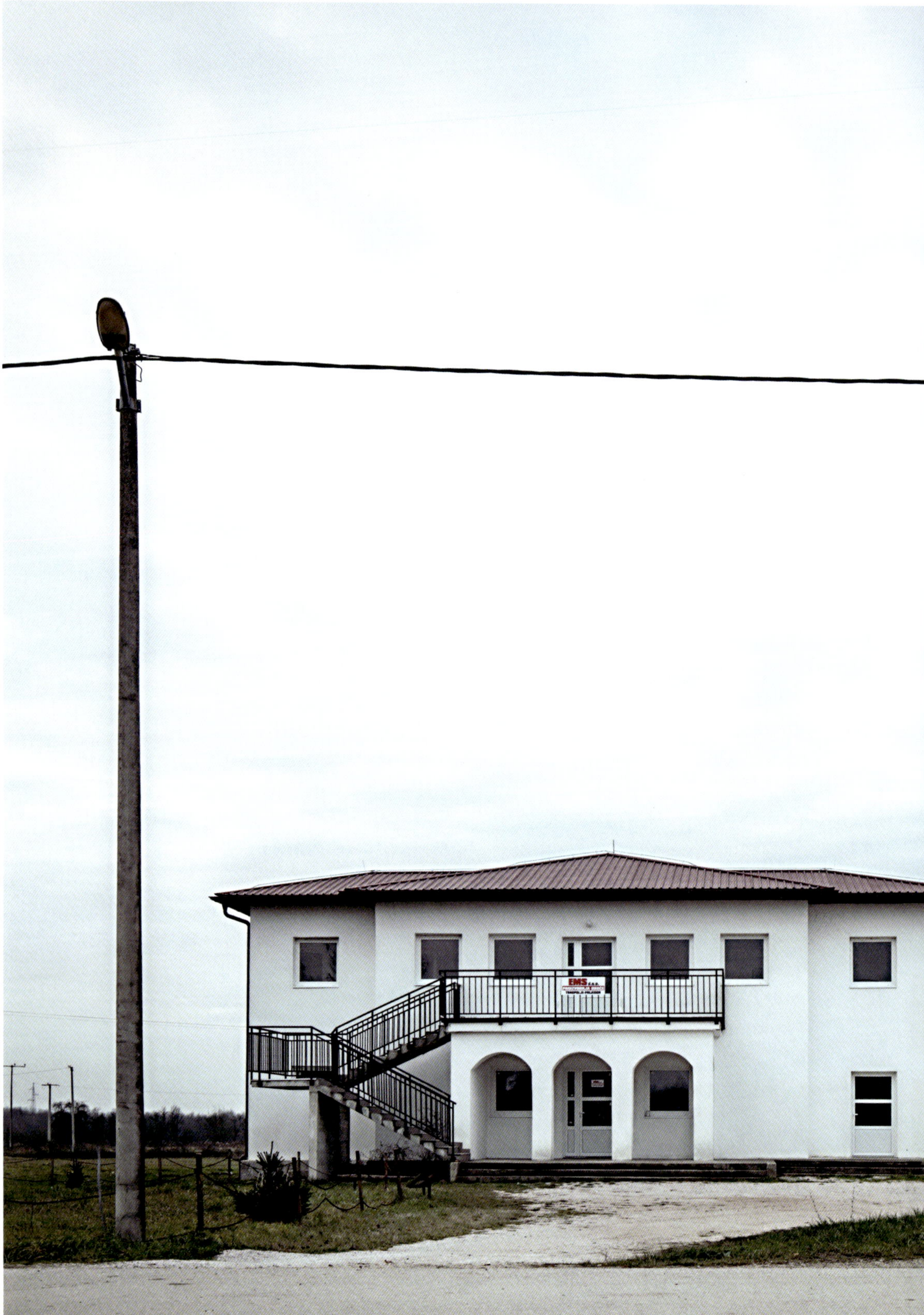
EMS

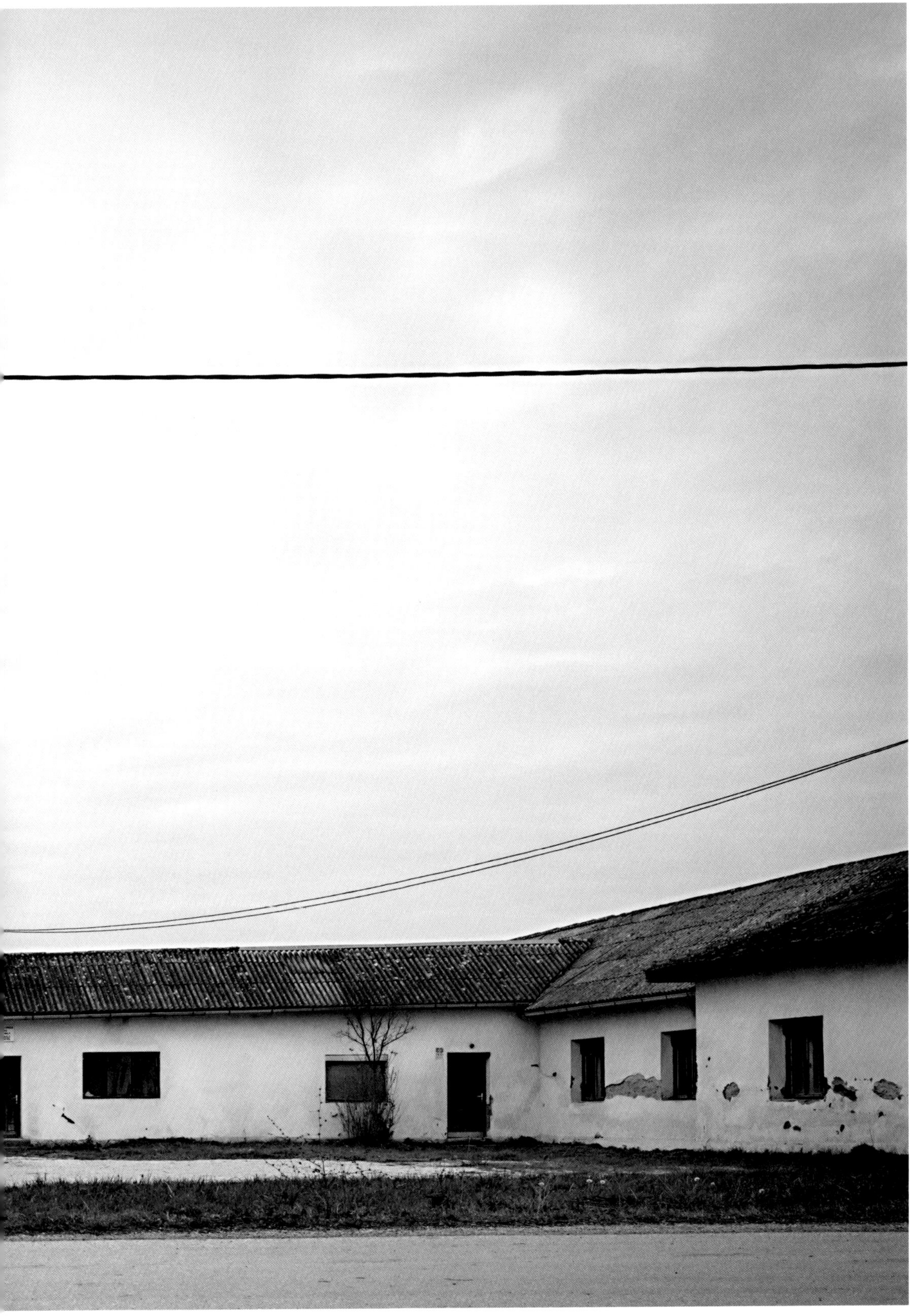

Opposite and overleaf
Omarska
Omarska Camp: White House and Administration Building with Canteen

From 25 May to 21 August 1992, the Omarska 'death camp' was one of the most notorious of the 677 camps in the Bosnian war. It was located on the site of an ironworks in a mining town in northern Bosnia and Herzegovina near Prijedor. Prisoners were mostly men. It is proven that thirty-seven women were detained, who were repeatedly raped and abused by several soldiers, investigators and also the commander of the station, e.g. in the bathroom of this building. The building where the rapes took place can be seen through the window. In addition to sexual services, the women also had to do housework (cooking, cleaning and washing, etc.). At night they were then taken out of the shared bedroom for 'special duties.' At all times the screams of the tortured could be heard from the White House. Thirty-two of the women were later released, but five women were killed: Mugbila Besirevic (economist), Edna Dautovic (student), Hajra Hodic (student), Velida Mahmuljin (teacher) and Sadeta Medunjanin (professor).[91]
—Witness: Nusreta Sivac

44°52'11.7"N 16°52'56.6"E

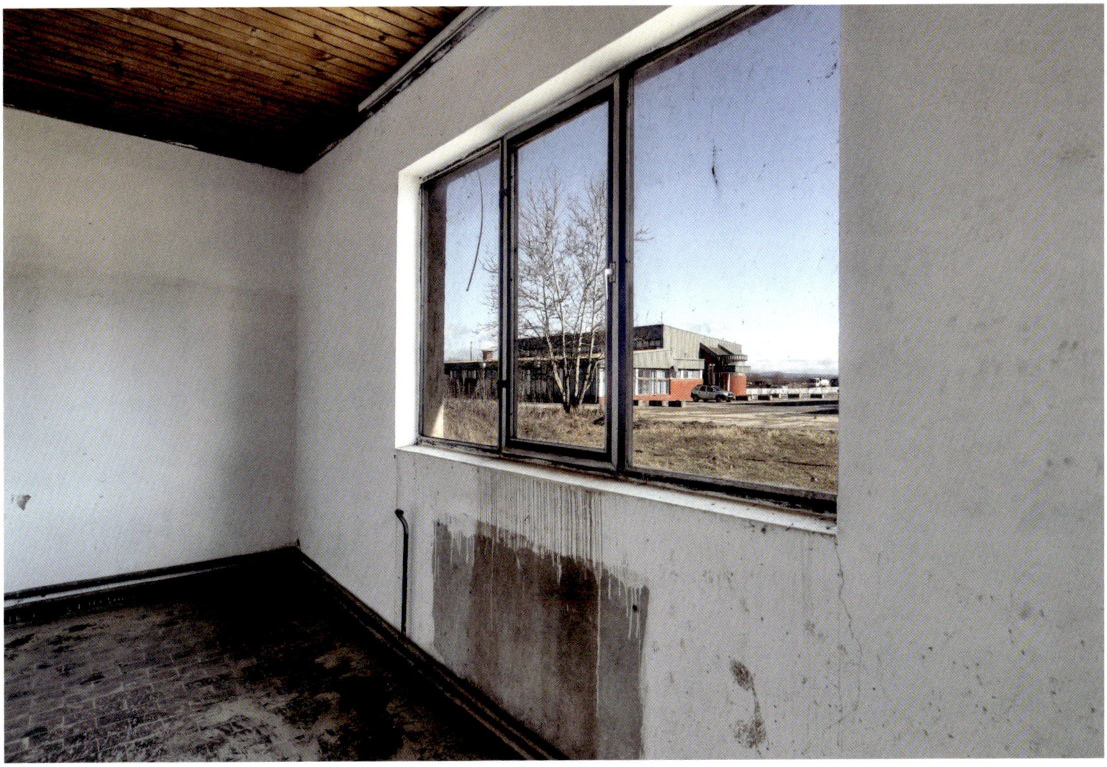

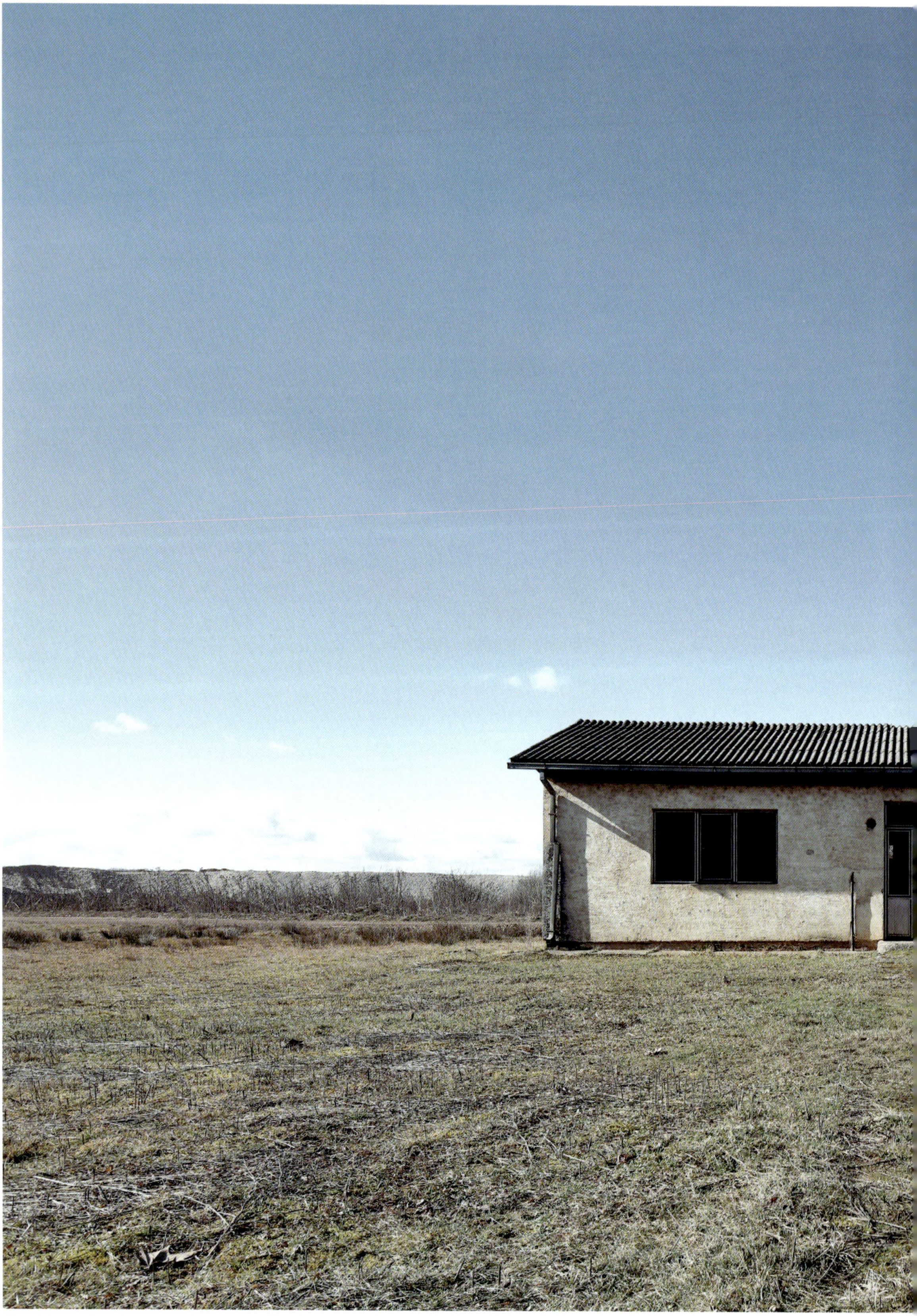

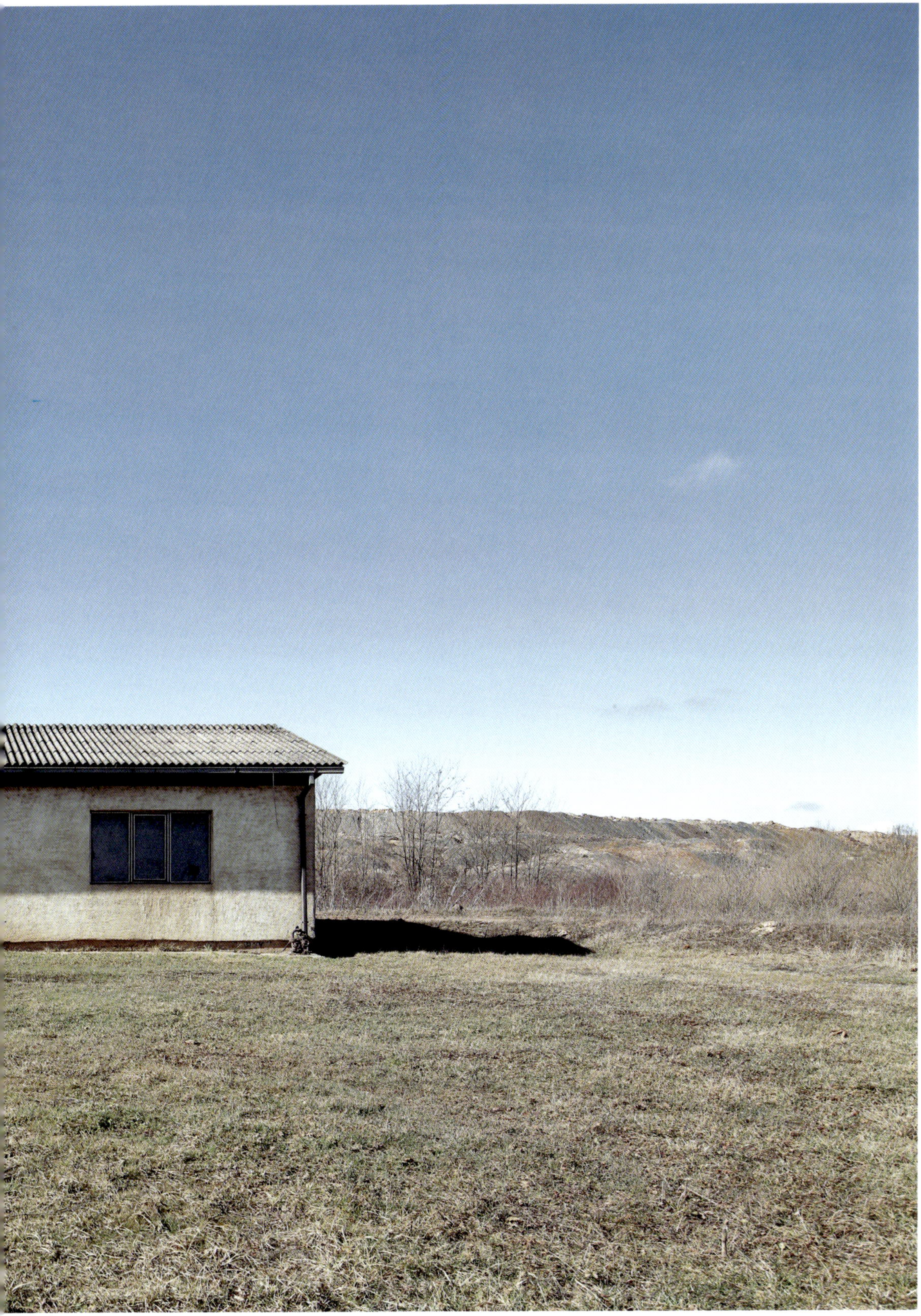

SILENT WITNESSES OR VICTIMS FALLEN SILENT?

DR. BRANKA ANTIC-STAUBER

Time has always been measured with the help of clocks, seasons, birthdays. But we in BiH are now doing something different. Our timing is different. There is the time before and after the war. Time flies like the wind. I find it difficult to catch her. But one thing I know for sure: time flies. I associate wartime with loss, expulsion, death, poverty, trauma...human shame and suffering. I left the country for a couple of months and had completely new experiences. My future was not planned, my future simply arose from the circumstances of my life.

I first encountered the stories and experiences of women from Prijedor during my temporary stay in Dortmund, Germany. I worked as a doctor for Caritas and the local social welfare office. My job was to accompany the displaced people and provide assistance. I encountered a whole community of Kozarac survivors whose stories are etched into my memory. I remember a petite young woman with two small children. Amina was her first name. I can't remember her family name anymore. She looked at me with her big green eyes full of desperation. In a low voice she told about the events in Kozaraz and the surrounding area. She reported on traumatised families in her neighbourhood, with fear, uncertainty and despair. Our conversation was recorded in a refugee facility, far away from her homeland.

I I haven't heard from her or her family since returning to Bosnia and Herzegovina. I often think of her and ask myself, 'how is...today?' During my stay in Dortmund I became acquainted with the members of the Dortmund women's organisation Vive Žene e.V., who were already active in Tuzla, in a reception centre, providing care for women and children. In the hurricane of war Vive Žene founded Dortmund e.V. a centre for the reception of women and children had left their homes as a result of the war and who had found themselves on the street with nothing but a plastic bag in their hands. Everything that was left of her life fit into this bag. Fathers, husbands, brothers were missing...

I returned and started working at Vive Žene e.V. in Tuzla relatively quickly. Working with Gabi, Cornelia, Margit and Elke meant a lot to me. Our work essentially consisted of offering help and support to the refugees on site, in schools, sports halls, football stadiums, private accommodation and everywhere else. Everywhere there was misery, suffering, sadness and an indescribable heaviness.

The wounds still haven't healed. Parents' unresolved traumatic experiences are passed on to the next generation. A confusingly long chain reaction that is reflected in the next generation in new, multi-layered and complex problems of everyday life. The task we set ourselves as part of our work was to locate the adult and young women who survived the sexual abuse and rape. We knew one thing: they are among us, but invisible because of the cultural conditions, the shame and the imminent stigmatisation. They would not identify themselves, let alone talk to us about their personal experiences.

After all, they believed that after they had lived through the flight, the loss of close family members, the loss of the family home, the fear of death they have lived through, sexual abuse was not worth mentioning again. It was as if the surviving women had taken a vow of silence about the rapes. As a kind of self-protection from the experience. It was their experience and belongs only and exclusively to them. Silence was her best friend, protecting her from the painful memory of lost husbands, brothers, fathers and friends. But this friend also protected them from the public shame and stigma that raped and sexually abused women faced during the war. The traditional and cultural character of gender relations within Bosnian-Herzegovinian society and the many taboos surrounding sexual assault do not allow the traumatic experiences of the raped women to be processed. A lack of understanding about what has been experienced ultimately leads to more silence.

A lot of energy and work has gone into creating a collective awareness of this. In cooperation with like-minded institutions and facilities, we have succeeded in shaping the legal framework in such a way that the victims of sexual abuse are recognised as victims of war and have at least a right to material support and some form of compensation. By achieving these goals, we managed to break the silence. The stories entrusted to us could hardly be surpassed in terms of brutality and cruelty. We asked ourselves, 'how it is possible for a man to do something like this to a woman?'

The silence that surrounded the victims had other causes. The women feared the perpetrators, who often lived in the same community, free and unpunished. They feared being judged and cast out by their closest social circle—their own family—because of the lack of understanding for what they had experienced.

They feared that if they revealed their own story, their own children would bear the stamp of being 'unclean.' Being condemned by one's own family, rejected by society, being stigmatised and labeled were the greatest barriers that had to be overcome in order to break through the eternal silence.

The cultural conditions of our society do not allow a dialogue about such divisive topics. The problem of sexual abuse and rape is multifaceted and complex. It starts in the family and continues seamlessly through the state institutions. When we talk about sexual abuse today, we do so freely and confidently. We have indeed been able to move something. The victims of sexual crimes were able to overcome their silence and reveal their experiences. They have reopened their wounds and it is now our collective responsibility to heal them nearly thirty years later.

It is the task of professionals, state institutions and families, with full commitment to the victims, as best they can and within the scope of their possibilities, to take this burden, if not in its entirety, then at least for the most part, and thus to bear the consequences to mitigate traumatic experiences.

The women want justice. They want the perpetrators to be convicted for their crimes. This is the only possible way for them to get rid of the accusation, the suspicion that their own 'sexualised behaviour' has somehow contributed to provoking the sexual crimes. For the women, the distribution of the perpetrators meant shedding forever the supposed 'partial guilt' that weighed on their shoulders. The accusation, the suspicion of partial guilt, meant that a collective dispute—and criminal prosecution—of the perpetrators was never taken up, since the victim status could never be recognised if partial guilt existed. The culture of collective silence served as invisible protection for the perpetrators, because where there are officially no victims, there can be no crime and therefore no perpetrators. The discouragement of the surviving victims resulted from the fact that the perpetrators were cleared of rape charges in court due to a lack of evidence, which often led to the victim's withdrawal not only from the criminal proceedings, but also from the laboriously installed help and therapy systems.

The acquittal of the perpetrators due to a lack of evidence drives the victims through a deep valley of traumatisation. Failing to hold the perpetrators accountable and revealing the truth to the public in the right narrative, hoping to rid oneself of partial guilt once and for all, is another harrowing experience—an experience had in the bright public spotlight. The echo of the voices in their heads, 'But she wanted that herself,' 'It's her own fault,' tear open the not-yet-healed wounds like pointed arrows. Criminal proceedings involving perpetrators who already knew the victims before the crime, former neighbours and work colleagues, are particularly serious. In a way, the acquittal legitimises the crime and once again encourages and sends the message that sexual crimes and rapes are merely misdemeanors. This trivialisation of such crimes, ensures they will be repeated in the future—without consequence.

Therefore, together with the survivors of sexual crimes, the international community as well as some enlightened parts of the civil society of Bosnia and Herzegovina, we strive to promote the strategy of transitional justice in order to create new conditions of justice for future generations.

The strategy of transitional justice is based on three extrajudicial pillars and primarily reflects the mechanisms of civil society. These are:

- Establishing the facts and telling the truth
- Reparations, memorials and rehabilitation
- Institutional and procedural reforms

After coming to terms with the trauma of the recent past, the memorials at the crime scenes now represent an important segment of rehabilitation. It is the wish of the victims to be able to return to these places without fear, to confront the truth face to face again and again and thus to set in motion the painful process of coming to terms with oneself—knowing full well that this will lead to re-traumitisation through what has been experienced and can lead to the deterioration of one's own well-being. It is the recurring images of the criminal act that play out again and again before the eyes of the victims, like in a film, and trigger the re-traumitisation.

The initiatives and appeals to those responsible for politics to actively expand the second pillar are equally strong in all three entities of the country, but often remain unheard and without adequate support. The women's victim associations and their representatives find it shameful that after almost thirty years, at the places of rape, torture and killing, despite all efforts and appeals, there is not a single memorial for the crimes against women. Some of the political dignitaries are even slowing down the process of transitional justice with their polemical attitude, claiming that such memorials would only make the reconciliation of the divided ethnic groups more difficult. As far as we know, there is only a single and very modest memorial plaque intended to commemorate the crimes of sexual violence. One of the women victim's we work with, brought us to the house where she was born and where she was later raped along with other women from the same place.

This is what she had written on the heart-shaped marble tablet:

Liplje death camp
In this place, on 25 May 1992, many lives of raped mothers and sisters were extinguished by the hands of the Chetniks

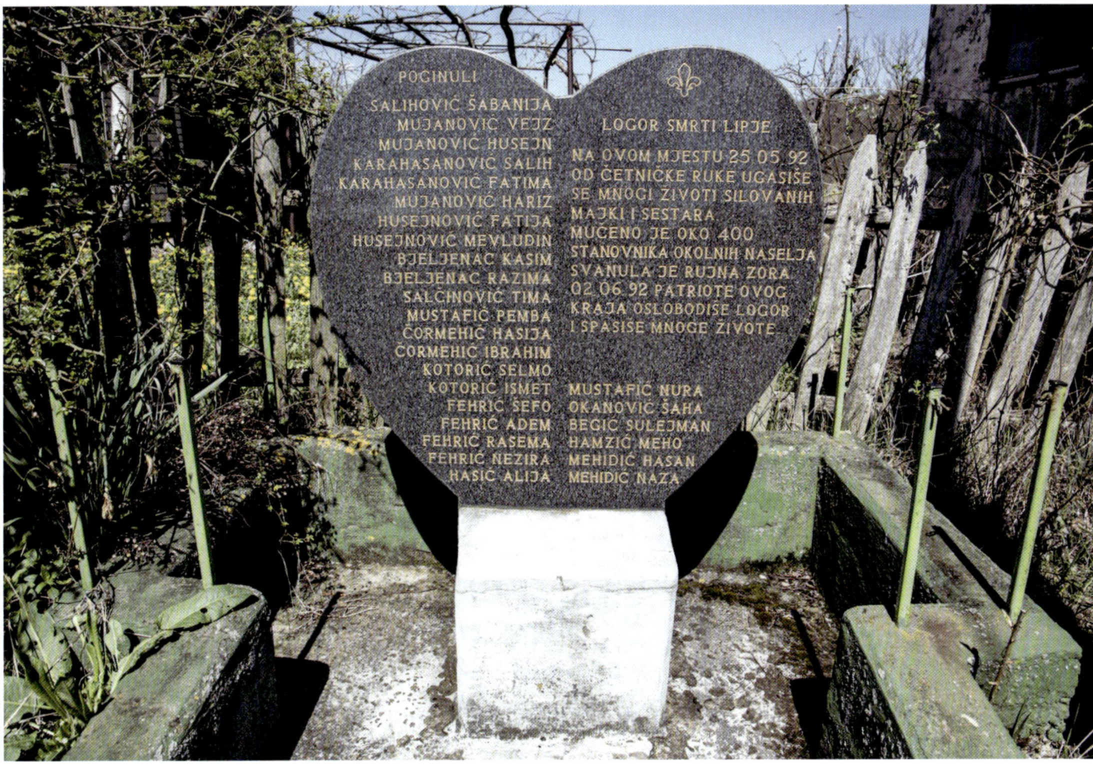
POGINULI
SALIHOVIĆ ŠABANIJA
MUJANOVIĆ VEJZ
MUJANOVIĆ HUSEJN
KARAHASANOVIĆ SALIH
KARAHASANOVIĆ FATIMA
MUJANOVIĆ HARIZ
HUSEJNOVIĆ FATIJA
HUSEJNOVIĆ MEVLUDIN
BJELJENAC KASIM
BJELJENAC RAZIMA
SALČINOVIĆ TIMA
MUSTAFIĆ PEMBA
ČORMEHIĆ HASIJA
ČORMEHIĆ IBRAHIM
KOTORIĆ SELMO
KOTORIĆ ISMET
FEHRIĆ ŠEFO
FEHRIĆ ADEM
FEHRIĆ RASEMA
FEHRIĆ NEZIRA
HASIĆ ALIJA
LOGOR SMRTI LIPJE
NA OVOM MJESTU 25.05.92
OD ČETNIČKE RUKE UGASIŠE
SE MNOGI ŽIVOTI SILOVANIH
MAJKI I SESTARA
MUČENO JE OKO 400
STANOVNIKA OKOLNIH NASELJA
SVANULA JE RUJNA ZORA
02.06.92 PATRIOTE OVOG
KRAJA OSLOBODIŠE LOGOR
I SPASIŠE MNOGE ŽIVOTE
MUSTAFIĆ NURA
OKANOVIĆ ŠAHA
BEGIĆ SULEJMAN
HAMZIĆ MEHO
MEHIDIĆ HASAN
MEHIDIĆ NAZA

AFTERWORD

CORNELIA
SUHAN

A war is not over when the weapons are silent. The Bosnian War (1992-1995) has left deep psychological wounds in the survivors through its immeasurable cruelty. Since the beginning of the war in the former Yugoslavia, women were raped on all sides. By far the largest number concerned, Muslim women, at least 25,000 of whom were systematically raped by Bosnian Serbs, both young and old. The aim of these brutal acts was, among other things, the ethnic expulsion of Muslim Bosnians from areas of today's Republika Srpska. But the systematic rapes were not only a weapon of war as a brutal means of ethnic cleansing, they were also a war against women themselves. The aim was to destroy the women of an ethnic population group or a culture and thus deprive them of their livelihood in their homeland.

To this day, the three state-bearing population groups, i.e. Bosniak, Serb and Croat inhabitants, live in conflict with each other. The system of government, often described as 'the most complicated in the world' and based on the internationally agreed Dayton Agreement, is not functional. Nationalism and hate speech dominate political debates. This is also evident in the handling of war crimes. To date, there is no comprehensive empirical and comparative study on the extent, prevalence, different dynamics and motives of sexual violence as well as on the different groups of perpetrators and victims. This is despite the fact that the high level of this violence triggered a worldwide wave of outrage in the 1990s, resulting in thousands of studies on sexual war violence across history and across countless other theatres of war. To this day, despite numerous trials for war rape, many women have not received justice because perpetrators are acquitted or the recording of trials is obstructed. To this day, the issue of sexual war violence in the successor republics is a pawn in ideological battles along ethnic lines. There is hardly a place to pause, to mourn, to want to understand and to commemorate the victims, regardless of ethnicity. The political discourse is characterised by blame; the finger is always pointing at the others. And among women, the great silence has long since resumed. After all, the Bosnian government was the first in the world to award a war victim's pension to women who were raped during the war—even if only since 2006. Bosniak women were the first to benefit from this. Serbian Bosnian women have only had the right to receive a war victim's pension since 2018.

In August 1993, I went to Bosnia for the first time, my camera in my backpack, which was to remain in the background; because this time, it was not about a photo reportage, but about setting up a therapy centre for raped women and their children in Tuzla (BiH). Several women from Dortmund founded the association Vive Žene e.V. ('Women Live!') in 1994, built up two partner organisations with Bosnian women and still work together with Snaga Žene ('Strength of Women') in Tuzla on a project basis. I have been going to Bosnia year after year since 1993; I only missed one year when I gave birth to my daughter in May 1995. That year Srebrenica fell and I watched the capture of the UN protected zone by Radko Mladic's units on television, my two-month-old baby in my arms. The images of the children, women and men who fled to Potočari have never left my mind.

The horror of the subsequent mass murder of Muslim men later slowly spread like an octopus through my consciousness. The whole extent of the war rapes in Bosnia and Herzegovina also penetrated me with ever new aspects; I learned in Bosnia to adapt to this slow and steady process of making these crimes visible. To this day, women are also slow to perforate the public discourse.

Some of the women I photographed also told their stories in front of other cameras, hoping to be seen and to get their due. They also spoke for all those who had chosen to remain silent. All of them, despite numerous supportive projects, were always alone with their fate. Their aloneness, their not being seen and their bravery drove me when I photographed the first crime scenes in autumn 2018. I kept driving past buildings where the crimes had been committed during my stays in Bosnia. They are scattered all over the national territory somewhere completely innocuous on a country road, on a village street, on the grounds of a factory, the grounds of an agricultural cooperative, in a residential area in the city or on school grounds. There was a short note from Dr. Branka Antic Stauber, doctor and chairperson of our partner organisation in Tuzla, while we were driving to a project site such as: 'HT was raped here and ML...there.'

Abandoned, these buildings lay there; nothing indicated the crimes committed there anymore, dead walls of houses stared at me. And whenever I put the camera on the tripod to capture the greatest possible detail with the high-resolution camera, I looked around uncertainly, afraid of having to give an account of what I was doing. I feared being caught illegally documenting the sites of war crimes. And indeed, in several places, e.g. in Foča in front of the newly renovated 'Partisan Hall' sports hall, I had to explain to the local police authorities why I was photographing that particular building. I often described my actions as harmless and banal and so they let me go. It became more difficult to take photos on factory premises, because even with a photo permit I was not allowed to take photos of the administration building in Omarska, for example, where the women were interned and raped in 1992. Only the well known White House—

the interrogation and torture centre of the camp at that time—was allowed to be photographed. Two security officers continuously monitored me while I was taking pictures, and I asked myself, 'Who is supposed to be protected here?'

With the programme manager of Snaga Žene in Tuzla, Daniela Micevic, I researched the crime scenes more systematically from 2019 onwards in order to document war crimes in different regions throughout the national territory. We tried to take different aspects into account as examples; in doing so, I was shocked to see how many school buildings were involved. They seemed to be particularly well suited for the logistics of wartime rape. Nowhere did I discover plaques on the buildings commemorating the crimes or paying tribute to the survivors and women murdered in the context of war rape. All this stayed with me, because for me the buildings seemed to maintain a connection to the former events of the war like silent witnesses, whether renovated, abandoned, reoccupied or revived in their original function. I noticed how some houses still stood abandoned after the war; to me they seemed like the 'untouchables,' while in others all traces had been removed. Families had moved back in who had fled to Germany, where they had survived the war period. One of these returned owners told me in fluent German that there had been a military hospital in her house during the war. The history of this house, which we researched, revealed that Croatian women had been raped here by Bosnian Army soldiers during the war. I imagined how I would feel in my house if it had such a war history behind it.

Particularly in the Republika Srpska areas, many private houses lie renovated and seemingly abandoned; the Bosniak families probably only return in the summer during the holidays. And then there are the many schools and hotels, almost all of which have been restored to their original function. Who still thinks of the terrible scenes that took place in the hotel rooms of the SPA Hotel in Visegrad? To this day, Bosnian women's organisations, together with their international partners, are fighting to ensure that these legendary places of terror and suffering are duly remembered. But how can one relax in a hotel where rape was systematically committed during the war? And what about the schoolchildren in the classrooms where their grandmothers may have been raped? How can that be?

Many of the buildings seemed so banal, so infinitely innocuous. As I photographed, the sound of the research and documentation provided a different ambience in my consciousness, contrasting with the material present. The times of war and the documented present overlapped in the click of the camera.

I kept asking myself, 'How can I use a visual medium to tell about an event that is no longer visible?' Making the buildings the content of the photographic narrative seemed to me to open new windows, to tell the stories of wartime events again and differently without exposing those affected to the public again. Some of the buildings could become places of remembrance where the crimes committed against Bosnian women could be commemorated together in the future.

My wish is that people can open up to the subject—that it will be possible for them to look in a different way, to expose themselves to the images, the information, the effects, without getting into the details of the horrors and humiliations. Façade techniques serve to conceal, we need healing and work about enlightening memory.

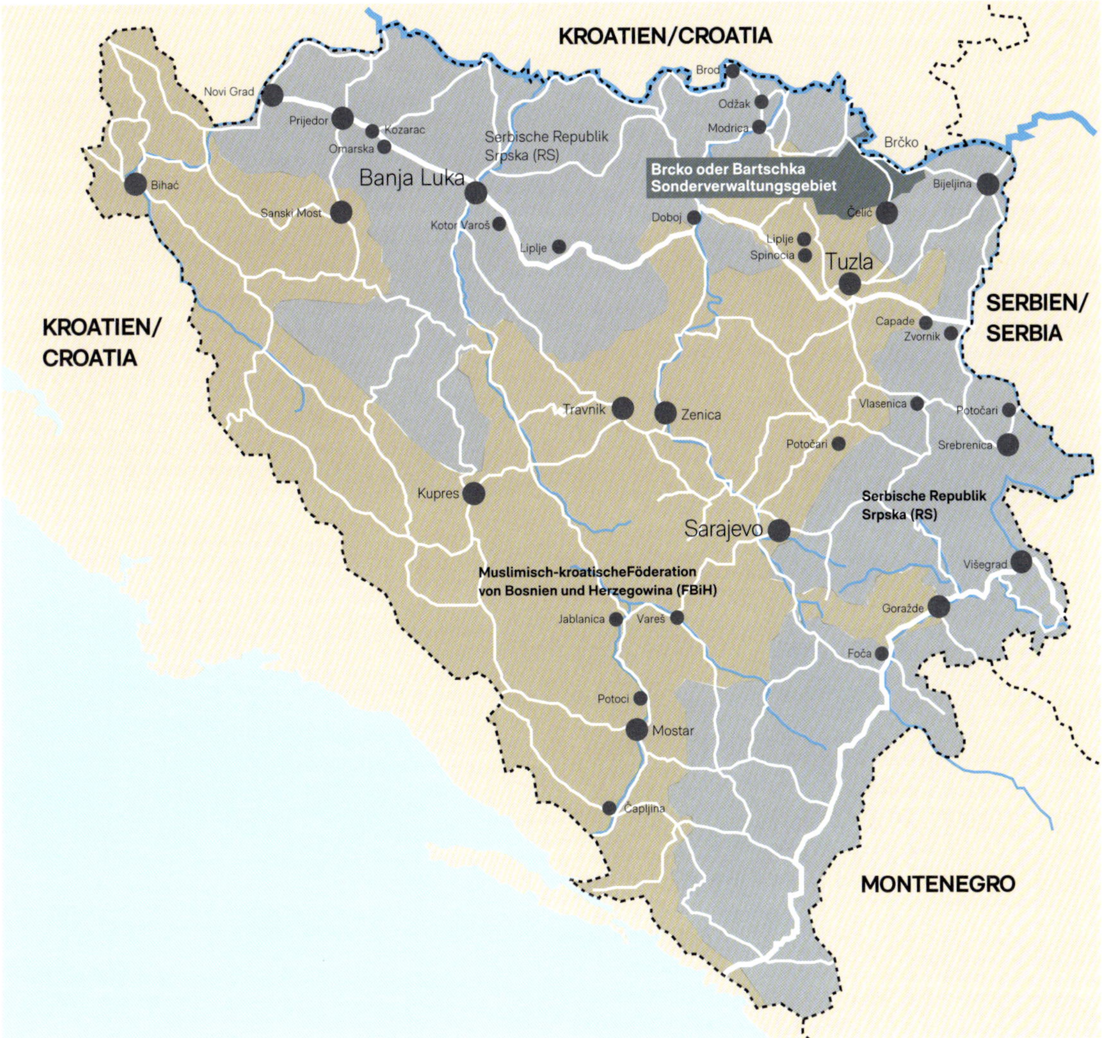
KROATIEN/CROATIA
Brod
Novi Grad
Odžak
Prijedor
Kozarac
Modrica
Omarska
Serbische Republik
Srpska (RS)
Brčko
Brcko oder Bartschka
Sonderverwaltungsgebiet
Banja Luka
Bihać
Bijeljina
Sanski Most
Čelić
Kotor Varoš
Doboj
Liplje
Liplje
Spinocia
Tuzla
KROATIEN/
CROATIA
SERBIEN/
SERBIA
Capade
Zvornik
Travnik
Zenica
Vlasenica
Potočari
Potočari
Srebrenica
Kupres
Serbische Republik
Srpska (RS)
Sarajevo
Višegrad
Muslimisch-kroatischeFöderation
von Bosnien und Herzegowina (FBiH)
Goražde
Jablanica
Vareš
Foča
Potoci
Mostar
Čapljina
MONTENEGRO

REFERENCES FOR 'LIVE ON, THINK ON' (PAGES 5-8)

Hannah Arendt (1970): On Violence. A Harvest Book. NY, London.

Pascale R. Bos (2008): Feminist interpretation of sexual violence in war. Berlin 1945, Yugoslavia 1992-1993. In: Insa Eschebach and Regina Mühlhäuser, War and Gender. Sexual violence in war and forced sex labor in Nazi war camps. Materials from the Brandenburg Memorials Foundation, Volume 3.

Metropol Verlag Berlin. pages 103-123.

Susan Brownmiller (1994): 'Making Female Bodies the Battlefield', in: Alexandra Stiglmayer (ed.) Mass Rape: The War against Women in Bosnia-Herzegovina, pages 180–182. London: University of Nebraska Press.

Albana Gërxhi, Women a(t) Battlefield, https://www.researchgate.net/publication/322098172_Women_at_Battlefield

Matthias Hirsch (2010): On the psychoanalysis of the house. In: Free Association. Journal for the unconscious in organisation and culture, Psychosocial Publishing, 13th year, issue 1+2/ 2010

Maria B. Olujic (1998): Embodiment of Terror: Gendered Violence in Peacetime and Wartime in Croatia and Bosnia-Herzegovina, Medical Anthropology Quarterly, vol. 12, no. 1, 1998, pages 31–50. JSTOR, http://www.jstor.org/stable/649476. Accessed July 20, 2022.

Alexandra Stiglmayer (1993) (ed.): Mass rape. War against women. KORE. Freiburg i.B.

Harald Welzer (2005/202, 9th edition): Perpetrator. How normal people become mass murderers. Fischer Verlag, Frankfurt a.M.

NOTES

1 Statement of Associations of victims of aggression 1992-1995; Statement from Prosecution Office BiH; http://www.justice-report.com/bh/sadr%C5%BEaj-%C4%8Dlanci/vojnik-%C5%A1ekova%C4%8Dkegardeuhap% C5%A1en-zbog-silovanja; BIRN, Bosnian War Rape Survivors' Still Afraid to Speak Out', 02/26/2021; https://detektor.ba/2021/02/26/zrtva-ratnog-silovanjapustite-zrtve-da-govore-kadbudu-spremne/?lang=en

2 Source: Witness S documentation, women's organisation, Snaga Žene, Tuzla

3 Source: Witness A documentation, women's organisation, Snaga Žene, Tuzla

4 Source: Witness ED documentation, women's organisation, Snaga Žene Tuzla

5 Source: Statement from Witness M, April 2021, women's organisation, Snaga Žene, Tuzla

6 Source: Witness R from Vlasenica, documentation, women's organisation, Snaga Žene, Tuzla

7 Source: Personal statement from Witness F and case documentation, women's organisation, Snaga Žene, Tuzla

8 ICTY, Momcilo Krajšnik Case (IT-00-39), Judgement, page 131; ICTY, Dragan Nikolic case (IT-94-2-S), Judgement, page 21; Indictment para 46; Ibid, Judgement pages 21-22; Indictment para 20 & 21; The Court of Bosnia and Herzegovina, Predrag Bastah et al Case (X-KR-05/122), Judgement, page 4

9 The author's own source at a photo shoot on site, 22 October 2018

10 https://www.oslobodjenje.ba/vijesti/bih/kroz-logor-batkovic-je-proslovise-od-4-000-ljudi-a-bijenoje-najmanje-80-zarobljenika-356394 http://institut genocid.unsa.ba/userfiles/file/genocid_kljuc_187-408.pdf, page 339

11 Ibid, pages 10 and 11

12 https://www.scribd.com/doc/17282194/Ispovest-ratnih-zatochenika-istradalnika-na-podruchju-Tuzle; page 1

13 CDTP, Mapping detention camps 1992-1995 in BiH, Tuzla County Prison - https://drive.google.com/file/d/0B-LooexrvXilVVlyblhMOXJ6eHc/view?resourcekey=0-rh0z35La_eTvWdkPln60Tw

14 Source: Witness Ž, women's organisation, Snaga Žene, Tuzla

15 Source: Witness documentation, women's organisation, Snaga Žene, Tuzla. Information provided by Dr. Branka Antic-Stauber, April 2021.

16 Tuathail, Gearóid; Toal, Gerard; Dahlman, Carl T. (16 February 2011). Bosnia Remade: Ethnic Cleansing and Its Reversal; page 116.

17 https://balkaninsight.com/2020/07/20/how-bosnian-villagers-liberated-a-wartime-detention-camp/

18 https://tip.ba/2020/08/16/dragan-bursac-tijelo-silovane-djevojcice-pita-zasto/

19 https://web.archive.org/web/20150513073127/http://www.zzi.at/files/subasic_molila_sam.pdf

20 Tuathail, Gearóid; Toal, Gerard; Dahlman, Carl T. (16 February 2011). Bosnia Remade: Ethnic Cleansing and Its Reversal; page 116.

21 The Court of Bosnia and Herzegovina, Veselin Vlahovic Case (S1 1 K 00465913 Kr), Judgement, pages: 8,9,10,13,27,28

22 The dissolution of the JNA (Yugoslav People's Army) occurred simultaneously with the dissolution of the state of Yugoslavia. While the army was initially used as a buffer between the individual ethnic groups and was intended to guarantee the unity of Yugoslavia, over the course of 1992 it came increasingly under Serbia's control.

23 Semizovac is a village in the municipality of Vogošca near Sarajevo, Sarajevo Canton, Federation of BiH. It consists of several business complexes located at the infamous Semizovac intersection.

24 The Court of Bosnia and Herzegovina, Dragan Damjanovic Case (X-KRŽ-05/51), Judgement, page 13

25 https://onms.nenasilje.org/2019/pansion-kod-sonje-i-bunker-iza-pansiona-vogosca/

26 Association of ex-detainees Ilidža, Statement of F.S. and Association of exdetainees of Ilidža. Mapping detention camps 1992-1995 in BiH, Auto-kamp Lužani, Ilidža; https://drive.google.com/file/d/0B-LooexrvXilZWs3bEZPMThlcVU/view?resourcekey=0-5agQL3oZTuM2K0hKCUZHeQ

27 ICTY, Momcilo Karajšnik Case (IT-00-39-T), Judgement, page 209

28 CDTP, Mapping Detention Camps 1992-1995 in BiH, https://drive.google.com/file/d/0B-LooexrvXilQVg5c2J0RjNjWnc/view?resourcekey=0-tl54qJziWEr9UjUgSE3x6Q

29 HULDR (Croatian Association of Ex-detainees of Homeland War), Od tvorca logora do radosti poricanja, page 304; Balkan Transitional Justice, 1 November 2013

30 List from Gorana Mlinarevic, trial monitoring of war crimes cases at the BiH court

31 The Court of Bosnia and Herzegovina, Nihad Bojadžic Case (S1 1 K 008494 17 Kžk), Appellate Judgement, page 51

32 HULDR, http://www.hrlog.ba/logori-za-hrvate-u bih/24-jablanicalogori-za-hrvate.html

33 https://detektor.ba/2013/11/07/raped-under-threat-ofmurder/?long=en; The Court of Bosnia and Herzegovina, Nihad Bojadžic Case (S1 1 K 008494 17 Kžk), Appellate Judgement, page 57; See source: Balkan Transitional Justice, 1 November 2013

34 http://gfbv-voices.org

35 ICTY, Kunarac et al Case (IT-96-23 and 23/1), Judgement, pages 190 and 291

36 Ibid, page 26

37 Ibid, pages 1, 65 and 74

38 Ibid, pages 22 and 32

39 Cantonal Court in Sarajevo, Rajak Novo Case (K-53/04), Judgement, page 4

40 BIRN BH, Investigation: Višegrad rape victims say their cries go unheard, https://detektor.ba/2006/10/20/investigation-visegrad-rape-victimssaytheir-cries-go-unherd/?lang=en

41 https://fočanskidani.wordpress.com/2017/04/25/foča-slucaj-gradakampa-za-silovanje-koristenog-kao-oruzje-rata-foto/ and ICTY, Dragan Gagovic, Gojko Jankovic, Janko Janjic, Radomir Kovac, Zoran Vukovic, Dragan Zelenovic, Dragoljub Kunarac, Radovan Stankovic Case (IT-96-23-I), Indictment, page 13

42 ICTY, Dragan Gagovic, Gojko Jankovic, Janko Janjic, Radomir Kovac, Zoran Vukovic, Dragan Zelenovic, Dragoljub Kunarac, Radovan Stankovic Case (IT-96-23-I), Indictment, page 15

43 ICTY, Outreach program: Bridging the gap between ICTY and local communities in BiH, Series of Conference, Foča, 09/10/2004, Conference transcript, Peter Mitford-Burgess, investigator, Prosecution Office, ICTY , page 6; ICTY, Kunarac et al Case (IT-96-23 and 23/1), Judgement, pages 29 and 294; ICTY, Outreach program: Bridging the gap between ICTY and local communities in BiH, Series of Conference, Foča, 09/10/2004, Conference transcript, Peter Mitford-Burgess, investigator, Prosecution Office, ICTY, page 6

44 BIRN BH, A Month In The Hands of Milan Lukic, https://detektor. ba/2009/11/06/a-month-in-the-hands-of-milan-lukic/?lang=en

45 'Visegrad rape victims say their cries go unheard.' Balkan Investigative Reporting Network. 20 October 2006 (https://web.archive.org/web/20090618031047/http://www.bim.ba/en/32/10/1312)

46 https://www.kathmanduandbeyond.com/motel-emos-miljevina-bosniaherzegovina/ Final Report Of The United Nations Commission Of Experts Established Pursuant To Security Council Resolution 780 (1992), Annex Ix - Rape And Sexual Assault, page 28; The Court of Bosnia and Herzegovina, Nedo Samardžic Case (X-KRŽ-05/49), Judgement, page 4, The court of Bosnia and Herzegovina, Radovan Stankovic Case (X-KRŽ-05/70), Judgement, page 4

47 The Court of Bosnia and Herzegovina, Nedo Samardžic Case (X-KRŽ-05/49), Judgement, pages 2, 6, 10, 11, 16, 23 & 30; ICTY, Kunarac et al Case (IT-96-23 and 23/1), Case data, page 2

48 Ibid, Judgement, page 297, The Court of Bosnia and Herzegovina, Nedo Samardžic Case (X-KRŽ-05/49), Judgement, page 17 c

49 ICTY, Kunarac et al. Case (IT-96-23-T & IT-96-23/1-T), Judgement page 313

50 ICTY, Outreach Program, Bridging the Gap between ICTY and Local Communities - Foča Conference Proceedings, page 6

51 ICTY, Kunarac et al. Case (IT-96-23-T & IT-96-23/1-T), Judgement page 313

52 ICTY, Jankovic et al. Indictment (IT-96-23/2), https://www.icty.org/x/ cases/stankovic/ind/en/foc-1ai991007e.htm

53 ICTY, Outreach Program, Bridging the Gap between ICTY and Local Communities - Foča Conference Proceedings, page 6; ICTY, Zelenovic Case (IT-96-23/2), Indictment, page 5-6

54 See NZZ of 21 February 2001 (review of the Judgements in the Celebici case) https://www.icty.org/en/press/sentencing-judgement-celebici-case

55 The New York Times 3 May 1996.; ICTY, Mucic et al. Case (IT-96-21-T), Judgement, pages 324 – 334 https://www.icty.org/x/file/Outreach/view_from_hague/jit_celebici_en.pdf Courting Democracy in Bosnia and Herzegovina. Cambridge University Press. ISBN 978-0-52176-380-6. 'Prosecutor v. Delalic, Mucic, Delic and Landzo (Celebici case), Case no. IT-96-21, Judgement of 16 November 1998,' pg 60, 61; https://www.icty.org/en/features/crimes-sexual-violence/landmark-cases

56 ICTY, Outreach program: Bridging the gap between ICTY and local communities in BiH, Series of Conference, Foča, 09/10/2004, Conference transcript, page 8; ICTY, Zelenovic Case (IT-96-23/2), Case data, page 10; ICTY, Kunarac et al Case (IT-96-23 and 23/1), Judgement, page 20

57 Ibid, page 21

58 Ibid, page 297

59 The Court of Bosnia and Herzegovina, Jankovic Gojko Case (X-KR-06/161), Judgement, page 53

60 Private source: statement from a former prisoner

61 Transverzala zla, Svjedocsnstva bjelopoljskih hrvata, Oci moje kceri (Transversal of Evil, Testimonies of Croats of Bijelo Polje, My Daughter's Eyes), pages 194-195

62 Case Information Sheet JELISIC (IT-95-10) ICTY (https://www.icty.org/x/cases/jelisic/cis/en/cis_jelisic.pdf)

63 ICTY, Momcilo Krajšnik Case (IT-00-39), Judgement, page 125 ICTY, Momcilo Krajšnik Case (IT-00-39), Judgement, page 125; http://institut-genocid. unsa.ba/userfiles/file/Muratovic%20-%20Brcko%20I%20DIO.pdf

64 The Court of Bosnia and Herzegovina, Albina Terzic Case (S1 1K 005 665 11 Krl), Judgement, pages 33 and 39

65 Ibid, page 4

66 Mapping Detention Camps 1992-1995 in BiH, Livinica, Odžak https://drive.google.com/file/d/0B-LooexrvXilMC1OeDN4ckxqODA/view?resourcekey=0-pYB-6d_T5MQkGj289 imSqA: Court of Bosnia and Herzegovina, Albina Terzic Case (S1 1K 00566511 Krl), Judgement, page 4

67 The Hrvatsko vijece obrane, HVO for short, was the Croat army in Bosnia-Herzegovina during the Bosnian War. The HVO operated primarily in the territory of the Croatian Republic of Herceg-Bosna, an internationally unrecognised de facto state.

68 The Court of Bosnia and Herzegovina, Jozo Áojic Case (S1 1 K 017362 17 Krž), Judgement, page 7; The Court of Bosnia and Herzegovina, Jozo Áojic Case (S1 1 K 017362 17 Krž), Judgement, page 7; The Court of Bosnia and Herzegovina, Jozo Áojic Case (S1 1 K 017362 17 Krž), Judgement, page 3; https://detektor.ba/2017/10/06/analiza-jozo-dojic-dva-tri-sata-kaovjecnost/

69 https://www.slobodanpraljak.com/knjige/knjiga_logori.pdf, page 141

70 CDTP, Mapping detention camps 1992-1995 in BiH, 4th Elementary School Mostar - https://drive.google.com/file/d/0B-LooexrvXilQlBFbGFaT- 3VrM2M/view?resourcekey=0-FvT8tAXfE6vHPePi6ZSZTA

71 Odžak is a city in the northeast of Bosnia and Herzegovina and the administrative seat of the large municipality of the same name. It is located in the Posavina Canton in the Federation of Bosnia and Herzegovina, 10 kilometres from the Croatian border. Modrica is a city in the north of Bosnia and Herzegovina and the capital of the municipality of the same name with almost 28,000 inhabitants. It has been part of the Republika Srpska since the Bosnian War.

72 Private source: Witness M, women's organisation, Snaga Žene, Tuzla (communication from April 2021) Novigrad 45°04'37.5 N, 18°19'18.2E

73 Private source: Witness M, women's organisation, Snaga Žene, Tuzla (communication from April 2021) Novigrad 45°04'37.5 N, 18°19'18.2E

74 https://sveosrpskoj.com/komentari/vranjes-srpkinje-zrtve-i-ratnih-silovatelja-i-mucitelja-i-poratne-pravdebih/?script=lat

75 https://detektor.ba/2016/04/06/visestruka-silovanja-u-posavskojmahali/

76 CDTP, Mapping detention camps 1992-1995 in BiH, Bosanski Brod Polet Stadium - https://drive.google.com/file/d/0B-Looexrv XilQjQ4UVpQeFVj- Z1U/view?resourcekey=0-ZNOd3i1h90QiqxRMP9qBxA

77 https://detektor.ba/2011/02/07/bosnian-war%c2%92s-wickedwomen-get-off-lightly/?lang=en

78 Doboj District Prosecutor's Office, Dalibor Slabic Case (T 15 O KT 0000408 04), Indictment, page 2

79 https://www.portalnovosti.com/kako-su-harali-nasi-decki

80 https://warcrimesmap.balkaninsight.com/verdicts/slobodan-karagic/

81 ICTY, Stanišic i Župljanin case (IT-08-91-T), Judgement, pages 137 and 139; ICTY, Radoslav Brêanin case (IT-99-36-T), Judgement, page 287

82 ICTY, Momcilo Karjšnik case (IT-00-39-T), Judgement page 173; ICTY, Stanišic i Župljanin case (IT-08-91-T), Judgement, page 138; ICTY, Radoslav Brêanin case (IT-99-36-T), Judgement, page 269

83 Source: Liaison Office to the ICTY, Kotr Varoš, SJB ICTY, Stanišic i Župljanin case (IT-08-91-T), Judgement, page 126 and CDTP, Mapping Detention Camps 1992-1995 in BiH, Policijska stanica Kotor Varoš https:// drive.google.com/file/d/0B-LooexrvXilTlZyUF9jOVdhaWc/view?resourcekey=0-htRwd6_BkE-UvuEHfcomA

84 ICTY, Radoslav Brêanin Case (IT-99-36-T), Judgement, page 285; ICTY, Drljaca and Kovacevic Case (IT-96-24); indictment; ICTY, Radoslav Brêanin Case (IT-99-36-T), Judgement, page 285; ICTY, Drljaca and Kovacevic Case (IT-96-24); indictment; ICTY, Sikirica et al Case (IT-95-8-S), Judgement, page 30; ICTY, Radoslav Brêanin Case (IT-99-36-T), Judgement, page 195

85 Source: Seida Karabasic, Izvor Prijedor

86 Source: Seida Karabasic, Izvor Prijedor

87 ICTY, Radoslav Brêanin Case (IT-99-36-T), Judgement, page 286

88 Ibid, page 196

89 Ibid, page 195

90 ICTY, Milomir Stakic case (IT-97-24-T), Judgement, page 71

91 ICTY Milomir Stakić Judgement, Case IT-97-24-A (www.icty.org/x/cases/stakic/acjug/en/sta-aj060322e.pdf)

Acknowledgments
I would like to thank everyone who contributed to the success of this project:

—to the women in Bosnia and Herzegovina who trusted me and shared their experiences during the war and gave me extensive information about war crimes sites;

—to all employees of our partner organisation Snaga Žene in Tuzla for their trust and many years of successful cooperation. Especially with Dr. Branka Antic-Stauber, for her support, contacts and extensive information she has gained through years of working with the women concerned; Daniela Micevic, who tirelessly researched the sites of former war crimes on the Internet with her old computer, and Sanela Zahirovic, who translated all the interviews with the women and then tirelessly transcribed them.

—to all people, organisations and institutions that have made our work in Bosnia and Herzegovina possible through financial support over many years

—to Verena Bruchhagen for the exchange of content and her tireless encouragement and help in editing the captions and interviews;

—to Gerd Schmedes for layout and design;

—to Deni Halilovic and the SAB. Ruhr in Bochum for the sensitive translation of Bosnian texts into German and for the financial support of the book project;

—to Gabriela Mischkowski for her support and sharing her knowledge from the Foča process;

—to Nadine Barth for her support in finding a suitable publisher;

—to Harry Lausch and Lucca Suhan for the encouraging conversations when nothing went right and the patient proofreading

—In Dortmund I would like to expressly thank my friends and fellow campaigners in our organisation Vive Žene e.V. Margrit Spindeler († 1 April 2013), Gabi Krämer, Agnes Bernzen, Smiljana Hesse, Elke Materne and Sabine Fründt; For more than twenty-five years we have developed and implemented projects to support traumatised girls and women in Bosnia and Herzegovina.

In loving memory of Helga and Margrit ('Mäggie')

First published in 2023 by
GOST Books, London

info@gostbooks.com
gostbooks.com

Silent Witness

Edited and designed by GOST:
Rossella Castello, Katie Clifford,
Gemma Gerhard, Justine Hucker,
Allon Kaye, Eleanor Macnair,
Claudia Paladini, Ana Rocha

Printed in Italy by EBS

British Library cataloguing-in-publication data. A catalogue record of this book is available from the British Library.

Isbn 978-1-915423-21-4